CLIFFS

Scholastic Aptitude Test*

PREPARATION GUIDE

by

Jerry Bobrow, Ph.D.

and

William A. Covino, Ph.D.

Contributing Authors
Bernard V. Zandy, M.S.
Bill Bobrow, M.A.

Consultants
Merritt L. Weisinger, J.D.
David A. Kay, M.S.

*SAT and Scholastic Aptitude Test are registered trademarks of the College Entrance Examination Board. This book has been prepared by Cliffs Notes, Inc., which bears sole responsibility for its content.

Cliffs Notes
INCORPORATED
LINCOLN, NEBRASKA   68501

ACKNOWLEDGMENTS

I would like to thank the following people for their invaluable assistance in typing, proofreading, and editing the manuscript; my wife, Susan Bobrow; my coordinating assistant, Joy Mondragon, and my typist, Sally Reilly. I also wish to thank Harry Kaste of Cliffs Notes for his vigilant final editing and uncompromising attention to every detail of the production process.

We would like to thank the following authors and companies for letting us use excerpts from their materials.

Donald Jay Grout, *A Short History of Opera,* second edition, Copyright © 1965, Columbia University Press, New York and London. Used by permission.

Robert D. Chapman and John C. Brandt, *The Comet Book,* Jones and Bartlett Publishers, Inc., Boston 1984.

Howard S. Abramson, *National Geographic: America's Lens on the World,* New England Publishing Associates, Inc., Chester, CT.

CONTENTS

Preface vii

Study Guide Checklist.. ix

PART I: INTRODUCTION

COMMON FORMAT OF A RECENT SAT EXAM....................................... 2

GENERAL DESCRIPTION 3

QUESTIONS COMMONLY ASKED ABOUT THE SAT................................ 3

TAKING THE SAT: TWO SUCCESSFUL OVERALL APPROACHES.............. 5

PART II: ANALYSIS OF EXAM AREAS

INTRODUCTION TO VERBAL ABILITY... 9
    **Ability Tested • Basic Skills Necessary • Directions
    • Analysis • Suggested Approach with Samples**
Antonyms.. 9
Analogies.. 11
Sentence Completion 16
Reading Comprehension.. 18
Common Prefixes, Suffixes, and Roots 24

INTRODUCTION TO MATHEMATICAL ABILITY 26
    **Ability Tested • Basic Skills Necessary • Directions
    • Analysis • Data That May Be Used as Reference •
    Suggested Approach with Sample Problems**
Mathematical Ability 26
Quantitative Comparison.. 32
Important Terminology, Formulas, and General Mathematical
Information That You Should Be Familiar With 37
    Common Math Terms That You Should Be Familiar With.......... 37
    Math Formulas That You Should Be Familiar With 38
    Important Equivalents That Can Save You Time......................... 38

Measures 39
Words and Phrases That Can Be Helpful in Solving Problems 40
    Addition • Subtraction • Multiplication • Division ..
Geometry Terms and Basic Information 41
    Angles • Lines • Polygons • Circles

INTRODUCTION TO THE TEST OF STANDARD WRITTEN ENGLISH 43
    Ability Tested • Basic Skills Necessary • Usage •
    Directions • Analysis • Sentence Correction • Direc-
    tions • Analysis • Suggested Approach with Samples
Summary 47

PART III: PRACTICE-REVIEW-ANALYZE-PRACTICE
Two Full-Length Practice Tests

PRACTICE TEST NO. 1 51
Answer Sheet for SAT and TSWE Practice Test No. 1 53
Section I: Verbal Ability 57
    Antonyms 57
    Sentence Completion 59
    Reading Comprehension 60
    Sentence Completion 63
    Analogies 64
Section II: Mathematical Ability 66
    Quantitative Comparison 68
Section III: Test of Standard Written English 73
    Usage 73
    Sentence Correction 76
    Usage 80
Section IV: Verbal Ability 82
    Antonyms 82
    Sentence Completion 83
    Analogies 84
    Reading Comprehension 85
Section V: Mathematical Ability 92
Section VI: Mathematical Ability 97
    Quantitative Comparison 98
Answer Key for Practice Test No. 1 103
How to Score Your Exam 105
Analyzing Your Test Results 105
Practice Test No. 1: Verbal Ability Analysis Sheet 106
Practice Test No. 1: Mathematical Ability Analysis Sheet 107
Practice Test No. 1: Test of Standard Written English Analysis
    Sheet 108

Analysis: Tally Sheet for Problems Missed 109

COMPLETE ANSWERS AND EXPLANATIONS FOR PRACTICE TEST NO. 1   111
Section I: Verbal Ability.. 113
   Antonyms 113
   Sentence Completion 114
   Reading Comprehension.. 114
   Sentence Completion 115
   Analogies... 116
Section II: Mathematical Ability 117
   Quantitative Comparison... 118
Section III: Test of Standard Written English................................... 126
   Usage.. 126
   Sentence Correction.. 127
   Usage.. 128
Section IV: Verbal Ability.. 130
   Antonyms 130
   Sentence Completion 130
   Analogies... 131
   Reading Comprehension.. 132
Section V: Mathematical Ability 134
Section VI: Mathematical Ability 140
   Quantitative Comparison... 141

PRACTICE TEST NO. 2 149
Answer Sheet for SAT and TSWE Practice Test No. 2 151
Section I: Verbal Ability.. 155
   Antonyms 155
   Sentence Completion 157
   Reading Comprehension.. 157
   Sentence Completion 161
   Analogies... 162
Section II: Mathematical Ability 164
Section III: Test of Standard Written English................................... 169
   Usage.. 169
   Sentence Correction.. 171
   Usage.. 176
Section IV: Verbal Ability.. 179
   Antonyms 179
   Sentence Completion 180
   Analogies... 181
   Reading Comprehension.. 183
Section V: Mathematical Ability 189
   Quantitative Comparison... 190

Section VI: Verbal Ability 195
    Antonyms 195
    Sentence Completion 196
    Analogies 197
    Reading Comprehension 198
Answer Key for Practice Test No. 2 205
How to Score Your Exam 207
Analyzing Your Test Results 207
    Practice Test No. 2: Verbal Ability Analysis Sheet 208
    Practice Test No. 2: Mathematical Ability Analysis Sheet 209
    Practice Test No. 2: Test of Standard Written
        English Analysis Sheet 210
    Analysis: Tally Sheet for Problems Missed 211

COMPLETE ANSWERS AND EXPLANATIONS FOR PRACTICE TEST NO. 2 213
Section I: Verbal Ability 215
    Antonyms 215
    Sentence Completion 216
    Reading Comprehension 216
    Sentence Completion 217
    Analogies 217
Section II: Mathematical Ability 219
Section III: Test of Standard Written English 227
    Usage 227
    Sentence Correction 228
    Usage 229
Section IV: Verbal Ability 231
    Antonyms 231
    Sentence Completion 231
    Analogies 232
    Reading Comprehension 233
Section V: Mathematical Ability 235
    Quantitative Comparison 236
Section VI: Verbal Ability 243
    Antonyms 243
    Sentence Completion 243
    Analogies 244
    Reading Comprehension 245

Final Preparation: "The Final Touches" 247

PREFACE

YOUR SAT SCORE CAN MAKE THE DIFFERENCE! And because of this, we know that your study time is most valuable. You need the most comprehensive test preparation guide that you can realistically complete in a reasonable time. It must be short, direct, precise, compact, easy to use, and thorough, giving you all of the information that you would need to do your best on the SAT. In keeping with the fine tradition of Cliffs Notes, this guide was developed by leading experts in the field of test preparation specifically to meet these standards. The testing strategies, techniques, and materials have been researched, tested, and evaluated, and are presently used at SAT test preparation programs at many leading colleges and universities. This book emphasizes the BOBROW TEST PREPARATION SERVICES approach, which focuses on the six major areas that should be considered when preparing for the SAT:

1. Ability Tested
2. Basic Skills Necessary
3. Understanding Directions
4. Analysis of Directions
5. Suggested Approaches with Samples
6. Practice-Review-Analyze-Practice

These major areas include important mathematical terminology, formulas, and a helpful list of prefixes, suffixes, and roots, followed by two complete practice exams with answers and in-depth explanations.

This guide was written to give you the edge in doing your best by giving you maximum benefit in a reasonable amount of time and is meant to augment, not substitute for, formal or informal learning throughout junior high and high school. If you follow the Study Guide Checklist in this book, and study regularly, you will get the best test preparation possible.

STUDY GUIDE CHECKLIST

_____ 1. Read the SAT Information Bulletin.

_____ 2. Become familiar with the Test Format, page 2.

_____ 3. Familiarize yourself with the answers to Questions Commonly Asked about the SAT, page 3.

_____ 4. Learn the techniques of Two Successful Overall Approaches, page 5.

_____ 5. Carefully read Part II, Analysis of Exam Areas, beginning on page 9.

_____ 6. Review lists of Common Prefixes, Suffixes, and Roots, page 24.

_____ 7. Review math Terminology, Formulas, and General Information, page 37.

_____ 8. Strictly observing time allotments, take Practice Test No. 1, section-by-section, beginning on page 57.

_____ 9. Check your answers and compute your score, page 103.

_____ 10. Analyze your Practice Test No. 1 results, page 105.

_____ 11. Fill out the Tally Sheet for Problems Missed to pinpoint your mistakes, page 109.

_____ 12. While referring to each item of Practice Test No. 1, study ALL the Answers and Explanations that begin on page 113.

_____ 13. Review as necessary Basic Skills, Terminology, Formulas, and General Information given in Part II of this book.

_____ 14. Strictly observing time allotments, take Practice Test No. 2, section-by-section, beginning on page 155.

_____ 15. Check your answers and compute your score, page 205.

_____ 16. Analyze your Practice Test No. 2 results, page 207.

_____ 17. Fill out the Tally Sheet for Problems Missed to pinpoint your mistakes, page 211.

_____ 18. While referring to each item of Practice Test No. 2, study ALL the Answers and Explanations that begin on page 215.

_____ 19. Again, selectively review as needed Basic Skills, Terminology, Formulas, and General Information given in Part II of this book.

_____ 20. CAREFULLY READ "FINAL PREPARATION" on page 247.

Part I: Introduction

COMMON FORMAT OF A RECENT SAT EXAM

Section I	Verbal Ability	45 Questions
30 Minutes	Antonyms	15 Questions
	Sentence Completion	5 Questions
	Reading Comprehension (2 long passages)	10 Questions
	Sentence Completion	5 Questions
	Analogies	10 Questions
Section II	**Math Ability**	**25 Questions**
30 Minutes	Math Ability	25 Questions
Section III	**Test of Standard Written English**	**50 Questions**
30 Minutes	Grammar and Usage	25 Questions
	Sentence Correction	15 Questions
	Grammar and Usage	10 Questions
Section IV	**Verbal Ability**	**40 Questions**
30 Minutes	Antonyms	10 Questions
	Sentence Completion	5 Questions
	Analogies	10 Questions
	Reading Comprehension (4 passages)	15 Questions
Section V	**Math Ability**	**35 Questions**
30 Minutes	Math Ability	7 Questions
	Quantitative Comparison	20 Questions
	Math Ability	8 Questions
Section VI	**Math Ability or Verbal Ability**	**25 or 35 Questions**
30 Minutes		40 or 45 Questions
Total Testing Time 180 Minutes = 3 hours		Approximately 215–235 Questions

Note: The order in which the sections appear and the number of questions may vary, as there are many different forms of the SAT. Only two of the verbal sections (85 verbal questions) and two of the math sections (60 math questions) actually count toward your SAT score.

GENERAL DESCRIPTION

The SAT is used along with your high school record and other information to assess your competence for college work. The test lasts 2½ hours and consists entirely of multiple-choice questions.

The verbal section tests your reading comprehension and the breadth of your vocabulary. The math section presents problems in arithmetic, algebra, and geometry.

The Test of Standard Written English (TSWE) is a 30-minute supplement to the SAT. It tests your ability to recognize Standard Written English. The TSWE score is used differently by different colleges; some use it to decide what level of Freshman English you should enroll in.

QUESTIONS COMMONLY ASKED ABOUT THE SAT

Q: WHO ADMINISTERS THE SAT?
A: The SAT is part of the entire Admissions Testing Program (ATP), which is administered by the College Entrance Examination Board in conjunction with Educational Testing Service of Princeton, New Jersey.

Q: IS THERE A DIFFERENCE BETWEEN THIS APTITUDE TEST AND THE ACHIEVEMENT TEST?
A: Yes. The Scholastic Aptitude Test measures the general intellectual abilities you have developed over your lifetime. Achievement Tests, another component of the ATP, indicate your proficiency in specific subject areas.

Q: CAN I TAKE THE SAT MORE THAN ONCE?
A: Yes. But be aware that ATP score reporting is cumulative. That is, your score report will include scores from up to five previous test dates. It is not uncommon for students to take the test more than once.

Q: WHAT MATERIALS MAY I BRING TO THE SAT?
A: Bring your registration form, positive identification, a watch, three or four sharpened Number 2 pencils, and a good eraser. You may not bring scratch paper, calculators, or books. You may do your figuring in the margins of the test booklet or in the space provided.

Q: IF NECESSARY, MAY I CANCEL MY SCORE?
A: Yes. You may cancel your score on the day of the test by telling the test center supervisor, or you may write or telegraph a cancellation to College Board ATP. Your score report will record your cancellation, along with any completed test scores.

Q: SHOULD I GUESS ON THE SAT?
A: If you can eliminate one or more of the multiple-choice answers to a question, it is to your advantage to guess. Eliminating one or more answers increases your chance of choosing the right answer. To discourage wild guessing, a fraction of a point is subtracted for every wrong answer, but no points are subtracted if you leave the answer blank.

Q: HOW SHOULD I PREPARE FOR THE SAT?
A: Understanding and practicing test-taking strategies will help a great deal, especially on the verbal section. Subject-matter review is particularly useful for the math section. Both subject matter and strategies are fully covered in this book.

Q: WHAT SUBJECTS ARE COVERED BY THE ACHIEVEMENT TESTS?
A: There are Achievement Tests in the following areas: English composition, Literature, Mathematics Level I, Mathematics Level II, American History and Social Studies, European History and World Cultures, Biology, Chemistry, Physics, French, German, Hebrew, Latin, Russian, and Spanish. You may take up to three Achievement Tests on one test date.

Q: WHEN IS THE SAT ADMINISTERED?
A: The SAT is administered nationwide six times during the school year, in November, December, January, March, May, and June. A special October administration is given in limited locations.

Q: WHERE IS THE SAT ADMINISTERED?
A: Your local college testing or placement office will have information about local administrations; ask for the *Student Bulletin*. The SAT is administered at hundreds of schools in and out of the United States.

Q: HOW AND WHEN SHOULD I REGISTER?
A: A registration packet, complete with return envelope, is attached to the *Student Bulletin.* Mailing in these forms, plus the appropriate fees, completes the registration process. You should register about six weeks prior to the exam date.

Q: IS WALK-IN REGISTRATION PROVIDED?
A: Yes, on a limited basis. If you are unable to meet regular registration deadlines, you may attempt to register on the day of the test. (An additional fee is required.) You will only be admitted if space remains after preregistered students have been seated.

Q: CAN I GET MORE INFORMATION?
A: Yes. If you require information which is not available in this book, write or call one of these College Board Regional Offices.

Middle States:	65 East Elizabeth Ave., Bethlehem, PA, 18018. (215) 691-5906
Midwest:	990 Grove St., Evanston, IL, 60201. (312) 869-1840
New England:	470 Totten Pond Road, Waltham, MA, 02154. (617) 890-9150
South:	Suite 200, 17 Executive Park Dr., N.E., Atlanta, GA, 30329. (404) 636-9465
Southwest:	Suite 119, 3810 Medical Parkway, Austin, TX, 78756. (512) 454-7791
West:	800 Welch Road, Palo Alto, CA, 94304. (415) 654-1200
	Suite 23, 2142 South High St., Denver, CO, 80210. (303) 777-4434

TAKING THE SAT: TWO SUCCESSFUL OVERALL APPROACHES

I. The "Plus-Minus" System

Many who take the SAT don't get their best possible score because they spend too much time on difficult questions, leaving insufficient time to answer the easy questions. Don't let this happen to you. Since every question within each section is worth the same amount, use the following system, *marking on your answer sheet:*

1. Answer easy questions immediately.
2. Place a "+" next to any problem that seems solvable but is too time-consuming.
3. Place a "−" next to any problem that seems impossible. Act quickly; don't waste time deciding whether a problem is a "+" or a "−".

After working all the problems you can do immediately, go back and work your "+" problems. If you finish them, try your "−" problems (sometimes when you come back to a problem that seemed impossible you will suddenly realize how to solve it).

Your answer sheet should look something like this after you finish working your easy questions:

1. Ⓐ ● Ⓒ Ⓓ Ⓔ
+2. Ⓐ Ⓑ Ⓒ Ⓓ Ⓔ
3. Ⓐ Ⓑ ● Ⓓ Ⓔ
−4. Ⓐ Ⓑ Ⓒ Ⓓ Ⓔ
+5. Ⓐ Ⓑ Ⓒ Ⓓ Ⓔ

Make sure to erase your "+" and "−" marks before your time is up. The scoring machine may count extraneous marks as wrong answers.

II. The Elimination Strategy

Take advantage of being allowed to mark in your testing booklet. As you eliminate an answer choice from consideration, *make sure to mark it out in your question booklet* as follows:

(A̶)
? (B)
(C̶)
(D̶)
? (E)

Notice that some choices are marked with question marks, signifying that they may be possible answers. This technique will help you avoid reconsidering those choices you have already eliminated and will help you narrow down your possible answers.

These marks in your testing booklet do not need to be erased.

PART II: Analysis of Exam Areas

This section is designed to introduce you to each SAT area by carefully reviewing the—

1. Ability Tested
2. Basic Skills Necessary
3. Directions
4. Analysis of Directions
5. Suggested Approach with Sample Problems

This section emphasizes important test-taking techniques and strategies and how to apply them to a variety of problem types. It also includes valuable terminology, formulas, basic math information, and a compact list of prefixes, suffixes, and roots to assist you in the verbal section.

INTRODUCTION TO VERBAL ABILITY

The Verbal Ability sections of the SAT consist of four types of questions: antonyms and analogies (which combined give a vocabulary subscore), and sentence completion and reading comprehension (which combined give a reading subscore). Each section is 30 minutes long and contains 40 to 45 questions. The total of two Verbal Ability sections yields a scaled Verbal Ability score from 200 to 800, with an average scaled score of about 430.

Traditionally, the questions within each of the antonym, analogy, and sentence completion sections are arranged in slight gradation of difficulty from easier to more demanding questions. Basically, the first few questions are the easiest, the middle few are of average difficulty, and the last few are difficult. There is no such pattern for the reading comprehension questions or passages.

ANTONYMS

Ability Tested

The Antonym section tests your vocabulary—your ability to understand meanings of words and to distinguish between fine shades of meaning.

Basic Skills Necessary

This section requires a strong twelfth-grade-level vocabulary. Knowing the meanings of prefixes, suffixes, and roots will also be helpful in deriving word meanings. Reviewing antonym questions from previous SATs can be helpful in understanding the levels of difficulty and types of words commonly used. But don't bother memorizing lists of words from previous SATs, as they are not supposed to be reused.

Directions

Each word in CAPITAL LETTERS is followed by five words or phrases. The correct choice is the word or phrase whose meaning is most nearly *opposite* to the meaning of the word in capitals. You may be required to distinguish fine shades of meaning. Look at all choices before marking your answer.

Analysis

1. Although the correct answer may not be a "perfect opposite," it will be the "best opposite" from among the five choices presented.

2. Consider all the choices. In most cases, *three* of the five choices can be quickly eliminated as not at all opposite to the original word.

Suggested Approach with Samples

1. Use "word parts." Sometimes the prefix, root, or suffix of the original word may help you determine its opposite. *Example:*

PRESENTIMENT
(A) maturity
(B) connection
(C) tardiness
(D) regulation
(E) afterthought

Here we have two clues to help us with the original word. First, the prefix: *pre* usually means *before*. And the root is from the Latin *sentire*, which means to *feel* or to *sense*. So the best opposite of a *before-feeling* would be (E) *afterthought.*

2. Use "connotations." You may be able to detect whether the original word is "positive" or "negative" in meaning. If the original word is "negative," the correct choice will likely be "positive." *Example:*

HIDEOUS
(A) bizarre
(B) dreadful
(C) sympathetic
(D) obvious
(E) beautiful

Hideous is a strongly negative word. Only *sympathetic* and *beautiful* are positive in connotation. Of the two, *beautiful* is the best opposite, as a meaning of *hideous* is *ugly*. By using "positive-negative connotations" in this question, you easily limit your possibilities to two.

3. "Degrees of opposite." Consider this example:

PARCHED
(A) wet
(B) crazy
(C) high
(D) certain
(E) saturated

Occasionally, you may be confronted with two choices, both of which appear to be opposites. In such a case, you must determine the degree or extent of the original word and match it with the same degree or extent of its opposite. Note that *parched* does not simply mean *dry*. *Parched* means *extremely dry*. So its best opposite from among the choices is *saturated*, which means *thoroughly wet*. A scale of these words might look like this:

PARCHED   DRY   WET SATURATED
———— 2 ———— 1 ———— 0 ———— 1 ———— 2 ————

A similar scale of temperature might look like this:

FRIGID   COLD   COOL   WARM   HOT   SCORCHING
—3———2———1——0——1———2———————3——

Notice how *frigid* is the best opposite of *scorching*, while *warm* is the best opposite of *cool*.

4. Try it in a sentence. Sometimes using the original word in a sentence can help you discover its meaning. *Example:*

CATASTROPHIC
(A) certain   (D) happy
(B) accidental   (E) manageable
(C) disastrous

Sentence: "The catastrophic results of the storm were death and devastation." Since a catastrophic experience is negative, the correct choice is positive, choice (D).

ANALOGIES

Ability Tested

The Analogy section tests your ability to understand logical relationships between pairs of words.

Basic Skills Necessary

The basic skills necessary for this section are a strong twelfth-grade vocabulary and the ability to distinguish relationships between words and ideas.

Directions

You are given a pair of CAPITALIZED words or phrases. Select the lettered pair that *best* expresses a relationship most similar to that of the original CAPITALIZED pair.

Analysis

It is important that you focus on understanding the *relationship* between the original pair, because this is really what you are trying to parallel.

Notice that you are to select the BEST answer or most similar relationship; therefore, the correct answer may not be directly parallel. The use of the word "best" also implies that there may be more than one good answer.

Suggested Approach with Samples

1. To help determine the relationship between the original pair, construct a sentence explaining how the two words are related. *Example:*

SONNET : LITERATURE ::

(A) rhythm : poetry   (D) research : biology
(B) football : sport   (E) acting : actor
(C) dancing : ballet

In this case, you might say to yourself, "A *sonnet* is a type of *literature*," and therefore recognize that the relationship here is between specific and general. Now doing the same with the answer choices, you will find that the correct answer is (B), since *football* is a type of *sport*.

This sentence can be expressed as "A is to B in the same way as C is to D." *For example:*

ANONYMOUS : NAME ::

(A) careful : measurement   (D) large : body
(B) quick : importance   (E) hue : color
(C) formless : shape

Your sentence should go something like this: "*Anonymous* is the lack of a *name* in the same way as . . ." The correct answer is (C) because it correctly completes the sentence: "*Anonymous* is the lack of a *name* in the same way as *formless* is the lack of *shape*.

2. Analogies may require a more precise relationship. *For example:*

HEART : HUMAN

(A) tail : dog   (D) brick : wall
(B) hand : child   (E) engine : car
(C) kitchen : house

While *heart* is part of a *human*, a more precise relationship is that the heart is the *essential*, *life-giving* part of a human. Therefore, while every answer here satisfies the part-whole relationship, (E) is the best answer, since *engine* is the *essential*, *life-giving* part of the *car*.

3. The order of the correct pair will be in the same sequence as the original pair. *For example:*

HOMEOWNER : SMOKE ALARM ::

(A) snake : hiss   (D) sailor : lighthouse
(B) air raid : siren   (E) crossing : bell
(C) car horn : driver

Here a *homeowner* is warned by a *smoke alarm* in the same way as (D) a *sailor* is warned by a *lighthouse*. Choice (C) is incorrect because the order is reversed.

4. Occasionally, you will need to consider not only the *primary* relationship between the original words, but also a *secondary* relationship as well. *Example:*

VANDALIZE : PROPERTY

(A) judge : murderer   (D) slander : reputation
(B) criticize : creativity   (E) courage : villainy
(C) incinerate : combustibles

"To *vandalize* is to destroy *property*." This sentence tells us that the original relationship is between an *action* and its *object:* property is the object of vandalism. Beyond this primary relationship, there are secondary relationships to consider: first, notice that *destruction* is the object of vandalism; second, notice that it is *unlawful* destruction. Scanning the choices, you see that to judge *can* destroy (condemn to death) a murderer; to criticize *can* destroy (by discouraging) creativity; and courage *can* (under certain conditions) destroy villainy. But in none of these choices—(A), (B), or (E)—is the relationship between the terms *typically* or *necessarily* one of destruction. In choice (C), to *incinerate necessarily* destroys *combustibles* (flammable objects); and in choice (D), *slander typically* destroys *reputation*. So both of these are possible choices. However, only one of them refers to a typically *unlawful* act as well, choice (D). Thus, taking the secondary relationships of the original pair fully into account, you should conclude that (D) is the best choice.

5. Understand that the second pair of words does not have to be from the same category, class, or type as the first pair of words. For example, if PUPPY : DOG is the original pair, the correct choice could be SAPLING : TREE, since in both pairs the first word is a youthful version of the second word. It is not important that the first pair are animals and the second pair are plants. What is essential is the *relationship*.

A Little Extra on Analogies

The more practice you have working analogy problems, the more quickly you'll recognize some of the common relationships. Some relationships are given below. There are many other possibilities as well.

CLASSIFICATIONS: sorts, kinds, general to specific, specific to general, thing to quality or characteristic, opposites, degree, etc.

A broad category is compared to a narrower category

RODENT : SQUIRREL : : fish : flounder
(broad   (narrower   (broad   (narrower
category)   category)   category)   category)

A person is compared to a characteristic
GIANT : BIGNESS :: baby : helplessness
(person) (character-   (person) (character-
          istic)   istic)

The general is compared to the specific
PERSON : BOY :: vehicle : bus
(general) (specific) (general) (specific)

A word is compared to a synonym of itself
VACUOUS : EMPTY :: seemly : fit
(word)   (synonym)   (word)   (synonym)

A word is compared to an antonym of itself
SLAVE : FREEMAN :: desolate : joyous
(word)   (antonym)   (word)   (antonym)

A word is compared to a definition of itself
ASSEVERATE : AFFIRM :: segregate : separate
(word)   (definition) (word)   (definition)

A male is compared to a female
COLT : FILLY :: buck : doe
(male) (female) (male) (female)

A family relationship is compared to a similar family relationship
FATHER : SON :: uncle : nephew
(family relationship)   (family relationship)

A virtue is compared to a failing
FORTITUDE : COWARDICE :: honesty : dishonesty
(virtue)   (failing)   (virtue)   (failing)

An element is compared to a greater degree
WIND : TORNADO :: water : flood
(element) (extreme)   (element) (extreme)

A lesser degree is compared to a greater degree
HAPPY : ECSTATIC :: warm : hot
(lesser)   (greater)   (lesser) (greater)

The plural is compared to the singular
WE : I :: they : he
(plural) (singular) (plural) (singular)

STRUCTURALS: part to whole, whole to part, part to part, etc.

A part is compared to a whole
LEG : BODY :: wheel : car
(part) (whole)   (part)   (whole)

A whole is compared to a part
TABLE : LEGS :: building : foundations
(whole) (part)   (whole)   (part)

OPERATIONALS: time sequence, operations, stages, phases, beginning to ending, before to after, etc.

One element of time is compared to another element of time
DAY : NIGHT :: sunrise : sunset
(time   (time   (time   (time
element)   element)   element)   element)

A time sequence relationship is expressed
START : FINISH :: birth   : death
(beginning)   (ending)   (beginning)   (ending)

A complete operation is compared to a stage
FOOTBALL GAME : QUARTER :: baseball game : inning
(operation)   (stage)   (operation)   (stage)

OVERLAPPING: Many analogies will overlap into more than one of the above basic types and will have to be analyzed by their purpose, use, cause-effect relationship, etc.

A user is compared to his tool
FARMER : HOE :: dentist : drill
(user)   (tool)   (user)   (tool)

A creator is compared to a creation
ARTIST : PICTURE :: poet   : poem
(creator)   (creation)   (creator)   (creation)

A cause is compared to its effect
CLOUD : RAIN :: sun   : heat
(cause)   (effect)   (cause)   (effect)

A person is compared to his profession
TEACHER : EDUCATION :: doctor : medicine
(person)   (profession)   (person)   (profession)

An instrument is compared to a function it performs
CAMERA : PHOTOGRAPHY :: yardstick : measurement
(instrument)   (function)   (instrument)   (function)

A symbol is compared to an institution
FLAG : GOVERNMENT :: cross   : Christianity
(symbol)   (institution)   (symbol)   (institution)

A reward is compared to an action
MEDAL : BRAVERY :: trophy : championship
(reward)   (action)   (reward)   (action)

An object is compared to an obstacle that hinders it
AIRPLANE : FOG   :: car   : rut
(object)   (obstacle)   (object)   (obstacle)

Something is compared to a need that it satisfies
WATER : THIRST :: food : hunger
(thing)   (need)   (thing)   (need)

Something is compared to its natural medium

SHIP : WATER :: airplane : air
(thing)   (natural   (thing)   (natural
           medium)   medium)

Something is compared to something else that can operate it

DOOR : KEY :: safe : combination

An object is compared to the material of which it is made

COAT : WOOL :: dress : cotton
(object)   (material)   (object)   (material)

SENTENCE COMPLETION

Ability Tested

This section tests your ability to complete sentences with a word or words that retain the meaning of the sentence, and are structurally and stylistically correct.

Basic Skills Necessary

Good reading comprehension skills help in this section, as does a good twelfth-grade vocabulary.

Directions

Each blank in the following sentences indicates that something has been omitted. Considering the lettered words beneath the sentence, choose the word or set of words that best fits the whole sentence.

Analysis

Note that you must choose the *best* word or words. In cases where several choices *might* fit, prefer the one that fits the meaning of the sentence most precisely. If the sentence contains two blanks, remember that *both* of the words corresponding to your choice must fit.

Suggested Approach With Samples

After reading the sentence and *before* looking at the answer choices, think of words that you would insert and look for synonyms to them. *Example:*

Money _____ to a political campaign should be used for political purposes and nothing else.

How would you fill in the blank? Maybe with the word *given* or *donated*?

Now look at the choices and find a synonym for *given* or *donated:*

(A) used	**(C)** contributed	**(E)** channeled
(B) forwarded	**(D)** spent	

The best choice is (C), *contributed;* it is the nearest synonym to *given* or *donated* and makes good sense in the sentence.

2. Look for signal words. Some signal words are "however," "although," "on the other hand," and "but." *Example:*

Most candidates spend _____ they can raise on their campaigns, but others wind up on election day with a _____ .

(A) so . . . bankroll	**(D)** every cent . . . deficit
(B) time . . . vacation	**(E)** nothing . . . war chest
(C) everything . . . surplus	

But signals that the first half of the sentence *contrasts* with the second half. The fact that most candidates spend *everything* (and end up with nothing) contrasts with those who end up with a *surplus.* (C) is the correct answer.

3. Watch for contrasts between positive and negative words. Look for words like "not," "never," and "no." *Example:*

A virtuous person will not shout _____ in public; he will respect the _____ of other people.

The first blank is obviously a negative word, something a good person would *not* do; the second blank is a positive word, something that a good person *would* do. *Here are the choices:*

(A) obscenities . . . feelings	**(D)** blessings . . . cynicism
(B) loudly . . . comfort	**(E)** insults . . . threat
(C) anywhere . . . presence	

(B) is neutral-positive; (C) is neutral-neutral; (D) is positive-negative; (E) is negative-negative. Only (A) offers a negative-positive pair of words; (A) is the best choice.

4. Sometimes it is more efficient to work from the second blank first. *Example:*

The merger will eliminate _____ and provide more _____ cross-training of staff.

(A) profit . . . and more	**(D)** bosses . . . wasteful
(B) paperwork . . . or less	**(E)** competitors . . . aggressive
(C) duplication . . . effective	

The second blank is something that is "provided." Chances are that something provided is a positive word, and *effective* seems like a good choice. Reading choice (C) into the sentence, we find that it makes good sense and is stylistically or structurally correct.

5. What "sounds wrong" should be eliminated. *Example:*

High school students should not be _____ as being immature or naive.

(A) helped   (C) directed   (E) taught
(B) shoved   (D) categorized

The only word that sounds right with "as" is "categorized"; (D) is the best choice.

READING COMPREHENSION

Ability Tested

This section tests your ability to understand, interpret, and analyze reading passages on a variety of topics. Passages are generally 200 to 600 words long and are generally taken from each of the following categories

Narrative passages from novels, short stories, essays, and biographies
Argumentative passages presenting different points of view
Biological Science passages about botany, medicine, or zoology
Physical Science passages about chemistry, physics, or astronomy
Humanities passages about art, literature, music, folklore, or philosophy
Social Studies passages about history, government, economics, or sociology

The common types of questions are those that ask you

—about the *main idea, main point,* or *possible title* of the passage
—about *information* that is directly *stated* in the passage
—about *information* that is *implied, suggested,* or *can be inferred*
—to recognize *applications* of the author's *opinions* or *ideas*
—to evaluate how the author *develops* and *presents* the passage
—to recognize the *style* or *tone* of the passage

Basic Skills Necessary

Students who have read widely and know how to read and mark a passage actively and efficiently tend to do well on this section.

Directions

Questions follow each of the passages below. Using only the stated or implied information in each passage, answer the questions.

Analysis

1. Answer all the questions for one passage before moving on to the next one. If you don't know the answer, take an educated guess or skip it.
2. Use only the information given or implied in a passage. Do not consider outside information, even if it seems more accurate than the given information.

Suggested Approach With Sample Passages

1. Skim the questions first, marking words which give you a clue about what to look for when you read the passage.
2. Read the passage actively, marking main points and other items you feel are important such as conclusions, names, definitions, places, and/or numbers. Make only a few marks per paragraph. Remember, these marks are to help you understand the passage.

Short Passage

*By the time a child starts school, he has mastered the major part of the rules of his grammar. He has managed to accomplish this remarkable feat in such a short time by experimenting with and generalizing the rules all by himself. Each child, in effect, rediscovers language in the first few years of his life.

When it comes to vocabulary growth, it is a different story. Unlike grammar, the chief means through which vocabulary is learned is memorization. And some people have a hard time learning and remembering new words.

*—Indicates portions of the passage which refer directly to a question you've skimmed. Also marked are main points and key terms.

1. A child has mastered many rules of grammar by about the age of
   (A) 3   (B) 5   (C) 8   (D) 10   (E) 18

The first sentence of the passage contains several words from this question, so it is likely to contain the correct answer. *By the time a child starts school* tells us that the answer is 5. Before choosing (B), you should look at all the answers and cross out those which seem incorrect.

2. Although vocabulary growth involves memorization and grammar-learning doesn't, we may conclude that <u>both vocabulary and grammar make use of</u>

(A) memorization
(B) study skills
(C) words
(D) children
(E) teachers

The question asks you to simply use your common sense. (A) is incorrect; it contradicts both the passage and the question itself. (D) and (E) make no sense. (B) is a possibility, but (C) is better because grammar-learning in young children does not necessarily involve study skills, but does involve words.

3. The <u>last sentence</u> in the passage implies that

(A) some people have no trouble learning and remembering new words
(B) some people have a hard time remembering new words
(C) grammar does not involve remembering words
(D) old words are not often remembered
(E) learning and remembering are kinds of growth

Implies tells us that the answer is something suggested but not explicitly stated in the passage. (B) is explicitly stated in the passage, so it may be eliminated. But (B) implies the opposite: if *some* people have a hard time, then it must be true that *some* people don't. (A) is therefore the correct choice. (C), (D), and (E) are altogether apart from the meaning of the last sentence.

Long Passage

Woodrow Wilson is usually ranked among the country's great presidents in spite of his failures to win Senate approval of the League of Nations. Wilson had yearned for a political career all his life; he won his first office in 1910 when he was elected governor of New Jersey. Two years later he was elected president in one of the most rapid political rises in our history. For a while Wilson had practiced law but found it both boring and unprofitable; then he became a political scientist of great renown and finally president of Princeton University. He did an outstanding job at Princeton but lost out in a battle with Dean Andrew West for control of the graduate school. When he was asked by the Democratic boss of New Jersey, Jim Smith, to run for governor, Wilson readily accepted because his position at Princeton was becoming untenable.

Until 1910 Wilson seemed to be a conservative Democrat in the Grover Cleveland tradition. He had denounced Bryan in 1896 and had voted for the National Democratic candidate who supported gold. In fact, when the

Democratic machine first pushed Wilson's nomination in 1912, the young New Jersey progressives wanted no part of him. Wilson later assured them that he would champion the progressive cause, and so they decided to work for his election. It is easy to accuse Wilson of political expediency, but it is entirely possible that by 1912 he had changed his views as had countless other Americans. While governor of New Jersey, he carried out his election pledges by enacting an impressive list of reforms.

Wilson secured the Democratic nomination on the forty-sixth ballot after a fierce battle with Champ Clark of Missouri and Oscar W. Underwood of Alabama. Clark actually had a majority of votes but was unable to attract the necessary two-thirds. In the campaign, Wilson emerged as the middle-of-the-road candidate—between the conservative William H. Taft and the more radical Theodore Roosevelt. Wilson called his program the New Freedom, which he said was the restoration of free competition as it had existed before the growth of the trusts. In contrast, Theodore Roosevelt was advocating a New Nationalism, which seemed to call for massive federal intervention in the economic life of the nation. Wilson felt that the trusts should be destroyed, but he made a distinction between a trust and a legitimately successful big business. Theodore Roosevelt, on the other hand, accepted the trusts as inevitable but said that the government should regulate them by establishing a new regulatory agency. The former president also felt that a distinction should be made between the "good" trusts and the "bad" trusts.

Questions

1. The author's main purpose in writing this passage is to
   (A) argue that Wilson is one of the great U.S. presidents
   (B) survey the differences between Wilson, Taft, and Roosevelt
   (C) explain Wilson's concept of the New Freedom
   (D) discuss some major events of Wilson's career
   (E) suggest reasons that Wilson's presidency may have started World War I

2. The author implies which of the following about the New Jersey progressives?
   (A) They did not support Wilson after he was governor.
   (B) They were not conservative Democrats.
   (C) They were more interested in political expediency than in political causes or reforms.
   (D) Along with Wilson, they were supporters of Bryan in 1896.
   (E) They particularly admired Wilson's experience as president of Princeton University.

3. The passage supports which of the following conclusions about the progress of Wilson's political career?
   (A) Few politicians have progressed so rapidly toward the attainment of higher office.
   (B) Failures late in his career cause him to be regarded as a president who regressed instead of progressed.
   (C) Wilson encountered little opposition once he determined to seek the presidency.
   (D) The League of Nations marked the end of Wilson's reputation as a strong leader.
   (E) Wilson's political progress was aided by Champ Clark and Oscar Underwood.

4. In the statement "Wilson readily accepted because his position at Princeton was becoming untenable," the meaning of *untenable* is probably which of the following?
   (A) unlikely to last for ten years
   (B) filled with considerably less tension
   (C) difficult to maintain or continue
   (D) filled with achievements that would appeal to voters
   (E) something he did not have a tenacious desire to continue

5. According to the passage, which of the following was probably true about the presidential campaign of 1912?
   (A) Woodrow Wilson won the election by an overwhelming majority.
   (B) The inexperience of Theordore Roosevelt accounted for his radical position.
   (C) Wilson was unable to attract two-thirds of the votes but won anyway.
   (D) There were three nominated candidates for the presidency.
   (E) Wilson's New Freedom did not represent Democratic interests.

Answers and Explanations

1. (D) Choices (A) and (E) are irrelevant to the information in the passage, and choices (B) and (C) mention *secondary* purposes rather than the primary one.

2. (B) In the second paragraph, Wilson's decision to *champion the progressive cause* after 1912 is contrasted with his earlier career, when *he seemed to be a conservative Democrat*. Thus, we may conclude that the progressives, whom Wilson finally joined, were not conservative Democrats, as was Wilson earlier in his career. Choices (A) and (D) contradict

information in the paragraph, while choices (C) and (E) are not suggested by any information given in the passage.

3. (A) This choice is explicitly supported by the third sentence in paragraph one in which we are told that Wilson was *elected president in one of the most rapid political rises in our history.*

4. (C) On any reading comprehension test, it is best to be alert to the positive and negative connotations of words and phrases in each passage as well as in the questions themselves. In the case of *untenable,* the prefix *un-* suggests that the word has a negative connotation. The context in which the word occurs does so as well. Wilson *left* his position at Princeton; therefore, we may conclude that the position was somehow unappealing. Only two of the answer choices, (C) and (E), provide a negative definition. Although choice (E) may attract your attention because *tenacious* looks similar to *tenable,* the correct choice is (C), which is the conventional definition of *untenable.*

5. (D) Choices (A), (B), and (C) contain information that is not addressed in the passage. We may eliminate them as irrelevant. Choice (E) contradicts the fact that Wilson was a Democratic candidate. The discussion of Taft and Roosevelt as the candidates who finally ran against Wilson for the presidency supports choice (D).

COMMON PREFIXES, SUFFIXES, AND ROOTS

The following list should help you to arrive at definitions of unfamiliar words on the Verbal Section of the SAT. These prefixes, suffixes, and roots apply to thousands of words.

Prefixes

Prefix	Meaning	Example
1. pre-	before	precede
2. de-	away, from	deter
3. inter-	between	interstate
4. ob-	against	objection
5. in-	into	instruct
6. mono-	alone, one	monolith
7. epi-	upon	epilogue
8. mis-	wrong	mistake
9. sub-	under	submarine
10. trans-	across, beyond	transcend
11. over-	above	overbearing
12. ad-	to, toward	advance
13. non-	not	nonentity
14. com-	together, with	composite
15. re-	back, again	regress
16. ex-	out of	expel
17. in-	not	insufficient
18. pro-	forward	propel
19. anti-	against	antidote
20. omni-	all, everywhere	omniscient
21. equi-	equal, equally	equivalent
22. homo-	same, equal, like	homogenized
23. semi-	half, partly	semicircle
24. un-	not	unneeded
25. bi-	two	bicycle
26. poly-	many	polymorphous
27. retro-	backward	retrograde
28. mal-	bad	malfunction
29. hyper-	over, too much	hyperactive
30. hypo-	under, too little	hypodermic

Suffixes

Suffix	Meaning	Example
1. -able, -ible	able to	usable
2. -er, -or	one who does	competitor
3. -ism	the practice of	rationalism
4. -ist	one who is occupied with	feminist
5. -less	without, lacking	meaningless
6. -ship	the art or skill of	statesmanship
7. -fy	to make	dignify
8. -ness	the quality of	aggressiveness
9. -tude	the state of	rectitude
10. -logue	a particular kind of speaking or writing	prologue

Roots

Root	Meaning	Example
1. arch	to rule	monarch
2. belli	war, warlike	belligerent
3. bene	good	benevolent
4. chron	time	chronology
5. dic	to say	indicative
6. fac	to make, to do	artifact
7. graph	writing	telegraph
8. mort	to die	mortal
9. port	to carry	deport
10. vid, vis	to see	invisible

INTRODUCTION TO MATHEMATICAL ABILITY

The Mathematical Ability sections of the SAT consist of two basic types of questions; regular Math Ability multiple-choice questions, and Quantitative Comparison (comparisons). Some sections contain regular Math Ability multiple-choice questions only, while others contain about half Quantitative Comparison problems. Each section is 30 minutes in length and contains 25 to 35 questions. The total of two sections generates a scaled Mathematical Ability score that ranges from 200 to 800, with an average score of about 479.

The math sections are slightly graduated in difficulty. That is, the easiest questions are basically at the beginning and the more difficult ones at the end. If there are quantitative comparison questions in the sections, they also start with the easiest problems.

MATHEMATICAL ABILITY

Ability Tested

The Mathematical Ability section tests your ability to solve mathematical problems involving arithmetic, algebra, and geometry by using problem–solving insight, logic, and application of basic skills.

Basic Skills Necessary

The basic skills necessary to do well on this section include high school algebra and geometry—no formal trigonometry or calculus is necessary. Skills in arithmetic and basic algebra, along with some logical insight into problem-solving situations, are also necessary.

Directions

Solve each problem in this section by using the information given and your own mathematical calculations. Then select the *one* correct answer of the five choices given. Use the available space on the page for scratchwork.

Analysis

All scratchwork is to be done in the test booklet; get used to doing this because no scratch paper is allowed into the testing area.

You are looking for the *one* correct answer; therefore, although other answers may be close, there is never more than one right answer.

Make a special note of the data that may be used for reference *during* this section.

Data That May Be Used as Reference for This Section

The area formula for a circle of radius r is: $A = \pi r^2$
The circumference formula is: $C = 2\pi r$
A circle is composed of 360°.
A straight angle measures 180°.

Triangle: The sum of the angles of a triangle is 180°.
If angle ADB is a right angle, then

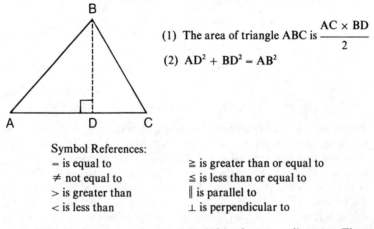

(1) The area of triangle ABC is $\dfrac{AC \times BD}{2}$

(2) $AD^2 + BD^2 = AB^2$

Symbol References:
= is equal to	≧ is greater than or equal to
≠ not equal to	≦ is less than or equal to
> is greater than	‖ is parallel to
< is less than	⊥ is perpendicular to

NOTE: Some problems may be accompanied by figures or diagrams. These figures are drawn as accurately as possible, EXCEPT when it is stated in a specific problem that the figure is not drawn to scale. The figures are meant to provide information useful in solving the problem or problems but are not meant to be measured.

All numbers used are real numbers.

Suggested Approach With Sample Problems

1. Take advantage of being allowed to mark on the test booklet by always underlining or circling what you are looking for. This will make you sure that you are answering the right question. *Sample:*

If $x + 6 = 9$, then $3x + 1 =$
(A) 3   (B) 9   (C) 10   (D) 34   (E) 46

You should first circle or underline $3x + 1$, because this is what you are solving for. Solving for x leaves $x = 3$ and then substituting into $3x + 1$ gives $3(3) + 1$, or 10. The most common mistake is to solve for x, which is 3, and mistakenly choose (A) as your answer. But remember, you are solving for $3x + 1$, not just x. You should also notice that most of the other choices would all be possible answers if you make common or simple mistakes. The correct answer is (C). *Make sure that you are answering the right question.*

2. Substituting numbers for variables can often be an aid to understanding a problem. Remember to substitute simple numbers, since *you* have to do the work. *Sample:*

If $x > 1$, which of the following decreases as x decreases?

$$\text{I. } x + x^2$$
$$\text{II. } 2x^2 - x$$
$$\text{III. } \frac{1}{x + 1}$$

(A) I   (B) II   (C) III   (D) I and II   (E) II and III

This problem is most easily solved by taking each situation and substituting simple numbers. However, in the first situation, (I), $x + x^2$, you should recognize that this expression will decrease as x decreases. Trying $x = 2$ gives $2 + (2)^2$, which equals 6. Now trying $x = 3$ gives $3 + (3)^2 = 12$. Notice that choices (B), (C), and (E) are already eliminated because they do not contain I. You should also realize that now you only need to try the values in II; since III is not paired with I as a possible choice, III cannot be one of the answers. Trying $x = 2$ in the expression $2x^2 - x$ gives $2(2)^2 - 2$, or $2(4) - 2$, which leaves 6. Now trying $x = 3$ gives $2(3)^2 - 3$, or $2(9) - 3, = 18 - 3 = 15$. This expression also decreases as x decreases. Therefore the correct answer is (D). Once again notice that III was not even attempted, because it was not one of the possible choices.

3. Sometimes you will immediately recognize the proper formula or method to solve a problem. If this is the situation, try a reasonable approach and then work from the answers. *Sample:*

Barney can mow the lawn in 5 hours and Fred can mow the lawn in 4 hours. How long will it take them to mow the lawn together?

(A) 5 hours   (C) 4 hours   (E) 1 hour
(B) 4½ hours   (D) 2⅖ hours

Suppose that you are unfamiliar with the type of equation for this problem. Try the "reasonable" method. Since Fred can mow the lawn in 4 hours by himself, he will take less than 4 hours if Barney helps him. Therefore choices (A), (B), and (C) are ridiculous. Taking this method a little further, suppose that Barney could also mow the lawn in 4 hours. Then together it would take

Barney and Fred 2 hours. But since Barney is a little slower than this, the total time should be a little more than 2 hours. The correct answer is (D), $2\frac{2}{9}$ hours.

Using the equation for this problem would give the following calculations:

$$\frac{1}{5} + \frac{1}{4} = \frac{1}{x}$$

In 1 hour, Barney could do $\frac{1}{5}$ of the job and in 1 hour Fred could do $\frac{1}{4}$ of the job; unknown $(1/x)$ is that part of the job they could do together in one hour. Now solving, you calculate as follows:

$$\frac{4}{20} + \frac{5}{20} = \frac{1}{x}$$

$$\frac{9}{20} = \frac{1}{x}$$

Cross multiplying gives $9x = 20$
Therefore, $x = \frac{20}{9}$, or $2\frac{2}{9}$.

4. "Pulling" information out of the word problem structure can often give you a better look at what you are working with and therefore you gain additional insight into the problem. *Sample:*

If a mixture is $\frac{3}{7}$ alcohol by volume and $\frac{4}{7}$ water by volume, what is the ratio of the volume of alcohol to the volume of water in this mixture?

(A) $\frac{3}{7}$ (B) $\frac{4}{7}$ (C) $\frac{3}{4}$ (D) $\frac{4}{3}$ (E) $\frac{7}{4}$

The first bit of information that should be pulled out should be what you are looking for: "ratio of the volume of alcohol to the volume of water." Rewrite it as A:W and then into its working form: A/W. Next, you should pull out the volumes of each; $A = \frac{3}{7}$ and $W = \frac{4}{7}$. Now the answer can be easily figured by inspection or substitution: using $(\frac{3}{7})/(\frac{4}{7})$ invert the bottom fraction and multiply to get $\frac{3}{7} \times \frac{7}{4} = \frac{3}{4}$. The ratio of the volume of alcohol to the volume of water is 3 to 4. The correct answer is (C). When pulling out information, actually write out the numbers and/or letters to the side of the problem, putting them into some helpful form and eliminating some of the wording.

5. Sketching diagrams or simple pictures can also be very helpful in problem solving because the diagram may tip off either a simple solution or a method for solving the problem. *Sample:*

What is the maximum number of pieces of birthday cake of size 4″ by 4″ that can be cut from a cake 20 inches by 20 inches?

(A) 5   (B) 10   (C) 16   (D) 20   (E) 25

Sketching the cake and marking in as follows makes this a fairly simple problem.

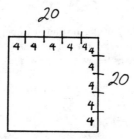

Notice that 5 pieces of cake will fit along each side, therefore $5 \times 5 = 25$. The correct answer is (E). Finding the total area of the cake and dividing it by the area of one of the 4 x 4 pieces would have also given you the correct answer, but beware of this method because it may not work if the pieces do not fit evenly into the original area.

6. Marking in diagrams as you read them can save you valuable time. Marking can also give you insight into how to solve a problem because you will have the complete picture clearly in front of you. *Sample:*

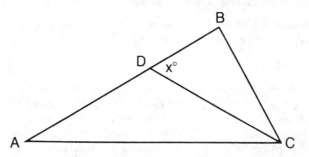

In the triangle, CD is an angle bisector, angle ACD is 30° and angle ABC is a right angle. Find the measurement of angle x in degrees.

(A) 80°   (B) 75°   (C) 60°   (D) 45°   (E) 30°

You should have read the problem and marked as follows:

In the triangle above, CD is an angle bisector (STOP AND MARK IN THE DRAWING), angle ACD is 30° (STOP AND MARK IN THE DRAWING), and angle

ABC is a right angle (STOP AND MARK IN THE DRAWING). Find the measurement of angle x in degrees (STOP AND MARK IN OR CIRCLE WHAT YOU ARE
LOOKING FOR IN THE DRAWING).

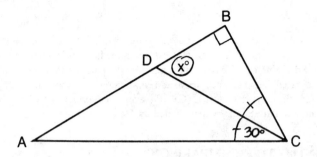

Now with the drawing marked in, it is evident that, since angle ACD is
30°, then angle BCD is also 30° because they are formed by an angle bisector
(divides an angle into two equal parts). Since angle ABC is 90° (right angle)
and BCD is 30°, then angle x is 60°, because there are 180° in a triangle,
180 − (90 + 30) = 60. The correct answer is (C). ALWAYS MARK IN
DIAGRAMS AS YOU READ THEIR DESCRIPTIONS AND INFORMATION ABOUT
THEM. THIS INCLUDES WHAT YOU ARE LOOKING FOR.

7. If it appears that extensive calculations are going to be necessary to
solve a problem, check to see how far apart the choices are, and then
approximate. The reason for checking the answers first is to give you a guide
for how freely you can approximate. *Sample:*

The value for (.889 × 55)/9.97 to the nearest tenth is

(A) 49.1   (C) 4.9   (E) .5
(B) 7.7   (D) 4.63

Before starting any computations, take a glance at the answers to see how far
apart they are. Notice that the only close answers are (C) and (D), except
(D) is not a possible choice, since it is to the nearest hundreth, not tenth.
Now making some quick approximations .889 = 1 and 9.97 = 10 leaves the
problem in this form

$$\frac{1 \times 55}{10} = \frac{55}{10} = 5.5$$

The closest answer is (C), therefore it is the correct answer. Notice that
choices (A) and (E) were ridiculous.

8. In some instances, it will be easier to work from the answers. Do not
disregard this method because it will at least eliminate some of the choices

and could give you the correct answer. *Sample:*

Find the counting number that is less than 15 and when divided by 3 has a remainder of 1 and divided by 4 has a remainder of 2.

(A) 13   (B) 12   (C) 10   (D) 8   (E) 5

By working from the answers, you eliminate wasting time on other numbers from 1 to 14. Choices (B) and (D) can be immediately eliminated because they are divisible by 4, leaving no remainder. Choices (A) and (E) can also be eliminated because they leave a remainder of 1 when divided by 4. Therefore the correct answer is (C); 10 leaves a remainder of 1 when divided by 3 and a remainder of 2 when divided by 4.

QUANTITATIVE COMPARISON

Ability Tested

Quantitative Comparison tests your ability to use mathematical insight, approximation, simple calculation, or common sense to quickly compare two given quantities.

Basic Skills Necessary

This section requires twelfth-grade competence in high school arithmetic, algebra, and intuitive geometry. Skills in approximating, comparing, and evaluating are also necessary. No advanced mathematics is necessary.

Directions

In this section you will be given two quantities, one in column A and one in column B. You are to determine a relationship between the two quantities and mark—
   (A) if the quantity in column A is greater than the quantity in column B.
   (B) if the quantity in column B is greater than the quantity in column A.
   (C) if the two quantities are equal.
   (D) if the comparison cannot be determined from the information given.

Analysis

The purpose here is to make a comparison; therefore, exact answers are not always necessary. (Remember that you can tell whether you are taller than someone in many cases without knowing that person's height. Comparisons such as this can be made with only partial information—just enough to compare.) (D) is not a possible answer if there are *values* in each column, because you can always compare values.

If you get different relationships, depending on the values you choose for variables, then the answer is always (D). Notice that there are only four possible choices here. *Never* mark (E) on your answer sheet for Quantitative Comparison.

Note that you can add, subtract, multiply, and divide both columns by the same value and the relationship between them will not change. EXCEPTION— You should not multiply or divide each column by negative numbers because then the relationship reverses. Squaring both columns is permissible, as long as each side is positive.

Suggested Approach With Sample Problems

1. This section emphasizes shortcuts, insight, and quick techniques. Long and/or involved mathematical computation is unnecessary and is contrary to the purpose of this section. *Sample:*

Column A	Column B
21 × 43 × 56	44 × 21 × 57

Canceling (or dividing) 21 from each side leaves

43 × 56	44 × 57

The rest of this problem should be done by inspection, because it is obvious that column B is greater than column A without doing any multiplication. You could have attained the correct answer by actually multiplying out each column, but you would then not have enough time to finish the section. The correct answer is (B).

2. The use of partial comparisons can be valuable in giving you insight into finding a comparison. If you cannot simply make a complete comparison, look at each column part by part. *Sample:*

Column A	Column B
$\dfrac{1}{57} - \dfrac{1}{65}$	$\dfrac{1}{58} - \dfrac{1}{63}$

Since finding a common denominator would be too time-consuming, you should first compare the first fraction in each column (partial comparison). Notice that $\frac{1}{57}$ is greater than $\frac{1}{58}$. Now compare the second fractions and notice that $\frac{1}{65}$ is less than $\frac{1}{63}$. Using some common sense and insight, if you start with a larger number and a smaller number, it must be greater than starting with a smaller number and subtracting a larger number, as pointed out below

Larger   **Smaller**

$$\frac{1}{57} - \frac{1}{65} \qquad\qquad \frac{1}{58} - \frac{1}{63}$$

Smaller   **Larger**

The correct answer is (A).

3. Always keep the column in perspective before starting any calculations. Take a good look at the value in each column before starting to work on one column. *Sample:*

Column A   **Column B**

$\sqrt[3]{7^6}$ 2^8

After looking at each column (Note that the answer could not be (D) because there are values in each column), compute the value on the left. Since you are taking a cube root, simply divide the power of 7 by 3 leaving 7^2, or 49. There is no need to take 2 out to the 8th power, just do as little as necessary: $2^2 = 4$, $2^3 = 8$, $2^4 = 16$, $2^5 = 32$. STOP. It is evident that 2^8 is much greater than 49; the correct answer is (B). Approximating can also be valuable while remembering to keep the columns in perspective.

4. If a problem involves variables (without an equation), substitute in the numbers 0, 1, and -1. Then try ½, and 2 if necessary. Using 0, 1, and -1 will often tip off the answer. *Sample:*

Column A   **Column B**

$a + b$ ab

Substituting 0 for a and 0 for b gives

$0 + 0$ $0(0)$

Therefore   0 $=$ 0

Using these values for a and b gives the answer (C). But anytime you multiply two numbers, it is not the same as when you add them, so try some other values.

Substituting 1 for a and −1 for b gives

$$1 + (-1) \qquad\qquad 1(-1)$$

Therefore   0   >   −1

and the answer is now (A).

Anytime you get more than one comparison (different relationships), depending on the values chosen, the correct answer must be (D) (the relationship cannot be determined). Notice that if you had substituted the values a = 4, b = 5; or a = 6, b = 7; or a = 7, b = 9; and so on, you would repeatedly have gotten the answer (B) and might have chosen the incorrect answer.

5. Oftentimes simplifying one or both columns can make an answer evident. *Sample:*

Column A	Column B
a, b, c, all greater than 0	
a(b + c)	ab + ac

Using the distributive property on column A to simplify, gives ab and ac; therefore, the columns are equal.

6. Sometimes you can solve for a column directly, in one step, without solving and substituting. If you have to solve an equation or equations to give the columns values, take a second and see if there is a very simple way to get an answer before going through all of the steps. *Sample:*

Column A	Column B
4x + 2 = 10	
2x + 1	4

Hopefully, you would spot that the easiest way to solve for 2x + 1 is directly by dividing 4x + 2 = 10, by 2, leaving 2x + 1 = 5.

Therefore

5   >   4

Solving for x first in the equation, and then substituting, would also have worked, but would have been more time-consuming. The correct answer is (A).

7. Marking diagrams can be very helpful for giving insight into a problem. Remember that figures and diagrams are meant for positional information only. Just because something "looks" larger, is not enough reason to choose an answer. *Sample:*

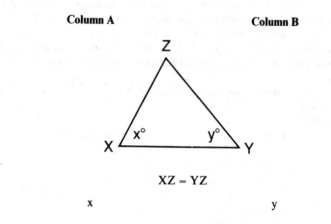

Column A   **Column B**

XZ = YZ

x   y

Even though x appears larger, this is not enough. Mark in the diagrams as shown.

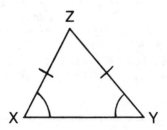

Notice that you should mark things of equal measure with the same markings, and since angles opposite equal sides in a triangle are equal, x = y. The correct answer is (C).

8. If you are given information that is unfamiliar to you and difficult to work with, change the number slightly (but remember what you've changed) to something easier to work with. *Sample:*

Column A   **Column B**

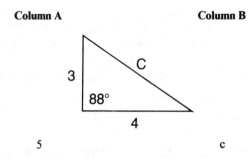

5   c

Since the 88° shown in the figure is unfamiliar to work with, change it to 90° for now, so that you may use the Pythagorean theorem to solve for c.

$$a^2 + b^2 = c^2$$

Solving for c as follows

$$(3)^2 + (4)^2 = c^2$$
$$9 + 16 = c^2$$
$$25 = c^2$$

Therefore

$$5 = c$$

But since you used 90° instead of 88°, you should realize that the side opposite the 88° will be slightly smaller or less than 5. The correct answer is then (A), 5 >c. (Some students may have noticed the 3:4:5 triangle relationship and have not needed the Pythagorean theorem.)

IMPORTANT TERMINOLOGY, FORMULAS, AND GENERAL MATHEMATICAL INFORMATION THAT YOU SHOULD BE FAMILIAR WITH.

COMMON MATH TERMS THAT YOU SHOULD BE FAMILIAR WITH

Natural numbers—the counting numbers: 1, 2, 3, . . .
Whole numbers—the counting numbers beginning with zero: 0, 1, 2, 3, . . .
Integers—positive and negative whole numbers and zero: . . . −3, −2, −1, 0, 1, 2, . . .
Odd numbers—numbers not divisible by 2: 1, 3, 5, 7, . . .

Even numbers—numbers divisible by 2: 0, 2, 4, 6, . . .

Prime number—number divisible by only 1 and itself: 2, 3, 5, 7, 11, 13, . . .

Composite number—number divisible by more than just 1 and itself: 4, 6, 8, 9, 10, 12, 14, 15, . . .

Squares—the result when numbers are multiplied by themselves, $(2 \cdot 2 = 4)$ $(3 \cdot 3 = 9)$: 1, 4, 9, 16, 25, 36, . . .

Cubes—the result when numbers are multiplied by themselves twice, $(2 \cdot 2 \cdot 2 = 8)$, $(3 \cdot 3 \cdot 3 = 27)$: 1, 8, 27, . . .

MATH FORMULAS THAT YOU SHOULD BE FAMILIAR WITH

Triangle

Perimeter = $s_1 + s_2 + s_3$

Area = $\frac{1}{2}bh$

Square

Perimeter = $4s$

Area = $s \cdot s$, or s^2

Rectangle

Perimeter = $2(b + h)$, or $2b + 2h$

Area = bh, or lw

Parallelogram

Perimeter = $2(l + w)$, or $2l + 2w$

Area = bh

Trapezoid

Perimeter = $b_1 + b_2 + s_1 + s_2$

Area = $\frac{1}{2}h(b_1 + b_2)$, or $h\left(\dfrac{b_1 + b_2}{2}\right)$

Circle

Circumference = $2\pi r$, or πd

Area = πr^2

Pythagorean theorem (for right triangles) $a^2 + b^2 = c^2$

The sum of the squares of the legs of a right triangle equals the square of the hypotenuse.

Cube

Volume = $s \cdot s \cdot s = s^3$

Surface area = $s \cdot s \cdot 6$

Rectangular Prism

Volume = $l \cdot w \cdot h$

Surface area = $2(lw) + 2(lh) + 2(wh)$

IMPORTANT EQUIVALENTS THAT CAN SAVE YOU TIME

Memorizing the following can eliminate unnecessary computations:

$\frac{1}{100} = .01 = 1\%$

$\frac{1}{10} = .1 = 10\%$

$\frac{1}{5} = \frac{2}{10} = .2 = .20 = 20\%$

$\frac{3}{10} = .3 = .30 = 30\%$

$\frac{2}{5} = \frac{4}{10} = .4 = .40 = 40\%$

$\frac{1}{2} = \frac{5}{10} = .5 = .50 = 50\%$

$\frac{3}{5} = \frac{6}{10} = .6 = .60 = 60\%$

$\frac{7}{10} = .7 = .70 = 70\%$

$\frac{4}{5} = \frac{8}{10} = .8 = .80 = 80\%$

$\frac{9}{10} = .9 = .90 = 90\%$

$\frac{1}{4} = \frac{25}{100} = .25 = 25\%$

$\frac{3}{4} = \frac{75}{100} = .75 = 75\%$

$\frac{1}{3} = .33\frac{1}{3} = 33\frac{1}{3}\%$

$\frac{2}{3} = .66\frac{2}{3} = 66\frac{2}{3}\%$

$\frac{1}{8} = .125 = .12\frac{1}{2} = 12\frac{1}{2}\%$

$\frac{3}{8} = .375 = .37\frac{1}{2} = 37\frac{1}{2}\%$

$\frac{5}{8} = .625 = .62\frac{1}{2} = 62\frac{1}{2}\%$

$\frac{7}{8} = .875 = .87\frac{1}{2} = 87\frac{1}{2}\%$

$\frac{1}{6} = .16\frac{2}{3} = 16\frac{2}{3}\%$

$\frac{5}{6} = .83\frac{1}{3} = 83\frac{1}{3}\%$

$1 = 1.00 = 100\%$

$2 = 2.00 = 200\%$

$3\frac{1}{2} = 3.5 = 3.50 = 350\%$

MEASURES

Customary System, or English System

Length
12 inches (in) = 1 foot (ft)
3 feet = 1 yard (yd)
36 inches = 1 yard
1760 yards = 1 mile (mi)
5280 feet = 1 mile
$5\frac{1}{2}$ yards = 1 rod

Area
144 square inches (sq in) = 1 square foot (sq ft)
9 square feet = 1 square yard (sq yd)

Weight
16 ounces (oz) = 1 pound (lb)
2000 pounds = 1 ton (T)

Capacity
8 fluid ounces (fl oz) = 1 cup (c)
2 cups = 1 pint (pt)
2 pints = 1 quart (qt)
4 quarts = 1 gallon (gal)
8 dry quarts = 1 peck
4 pecks = 1 bushel

Time
365 days = 1 year
52 weeks = 1 year
10 years = 1 decade
100 years = 1 century

Metric System, or The International System of Units
(SI, *Le Système International d'Unités*)

Length—meter
   Kilometer (km) = 1000 meters (m)
   Hectometer (hm) = 100 meters
   Dekameter (dam) = 10 meters

   Meter
   10 decimeters (dm) = 1 meter
   100 centimeters (cm) = 1 meter
   1000 millimeters (mm) = 1 meter

Volume—liter
   Common measures
   1000 milliliters (ml, or mL) = 1 liter (l, or L)
   1000 liters = 1 kiloliter (kl, or kL)

Mass—gram
   Common measures
      1000 milligrams (mg) = 1 gram (g)
      1000 grams = 1 kilogram (kg)
      1000 kilograms = 1 metric ton (t)

WORDS AND PHRASES THAT CAN BE HELPFUL IN SOLVING PROBLEMS

Words that signal an operation:

ADDITION
- Sum
- Total
- Plus
- Increase
- More than
- Greater than

MULTIPLICATION
- Of
- Product
- Times
- At (Sometimes)
- Total (Sometimes)

SUBTRACTION
- Difference
- Less
- Decreased
- Reduced
- Fewer
- Have left

DIVISION
- Quotient
- Divisor
- Dividend
- Ratio
- Parts

GEOMETRY TERMS AND BASIC INFORMATION

Angles

Vertical angles—Formed by two intersecting lines, across from each other, always equal
Adjacent angles—Next to each other, share a common side and vertex
Right angle—Measures 90 degrees
Obtuse angle—Greater than 90 degrees
Acute angle—Less than 90 degrees
Straight angle, or line—Measures 180 degrees
Angle bisector—Divides an angle into two equal angles
Supplementary angles—Two angles whose total is 180 degrees
Complementary angles—Two angles whose total is 90 degrees

Lines

Two points determine a line
Parallel lines—Never meet
Perpendicular lines—Meet at right angles

Polygons

Polygon—A many-sided (more than two) closed figure
Regular polygon—A polygon with all sides and all angles equal
Triangle—Three-sided polygon; the interior angles total 180 degrees
    Equilateral triangle—All sides equal
    Isosceles triangle—Two sides equal
    Scalene triangle—All sides of different lengths
    Right triangle—A triangle containing a right angle
In a triangle—Angles opposite equal sides are equal.
In a triangle—The longest side is across from the largest angle, and the shortest side is across from the smallest angle.
In a triangle—The sum of any two sides of a triangle is larger than the third side.
In a triangle—An exterior angle is equal to the sum of the remote two angles.
Median of a triangle—A line segment that connects the vertex and the midpoint of the opposite side.
Quadrilateral—Four-sided polygon; the interior angles total 360 degrees.
    Parallelogram—A quadrilateral with opposite sides parallel
      Rectangle—A parallelogram with all right angles
      Rhombus—A parallelogram with equal sides
      Square—A parallelogram with equal sides and all right angles
    Trapezoid—A quadrilateral with two parallel sides

Pentagon—A five-sided polygon
Hexagon—A six-sided polygon
Octagon—An eight-sided polygon

Circles

Radius of a circle—A line segment from the center of the circle to the circle itself.
Diameter of a circle—A line segment that starts and ends on the circle and goes through the center.
Chord—A line segment that starts and ends on the circle
Arc—A part of the circle

Additional Study Aids

For additional review and practice in math, you will find that *Cliffs Math Review for Standardized Tests* will provide you with the help you need. Unlike other general math reviews, this book focuses on *standardized test math* and gives you a practical, personalized test-preparation program. *Cliffs Math Review for Standardized Tests* is available at your local bookstore, or you may order it from Cliffs Notes, Inc., by sending in the coupon you'll find at the back of this book.

INTRODUCTION TO THE TEST OF STANDARD WRITTEN ENGLISH

The Test of Standard Written English is a supplement to the SAT that consists of two types of questions; English Usage and Sentence Correction. The TSWE is 30 minutes in length and contains 50 to 55 questions. It is scored separately from the SAT on a scale from 20 to 80, but scores of above 60 appear only as 60+, as this test is not meant to differentiate between higher levels of standard written English ability. An average score on the TSWE is about 43.

A CAREFUL ANALYSIS OF EACH TYPE OF TEST OF STANDARD WRITTEN ENGLISH QUESTION FOLLOWS.

ABILITY TESTED

This section tests your ability to recognize errors in Standard Written English.

BASIC SKILLS NECESSARY

Knowledge of some basic grammar will help in this section. Review the rules of corrections that have been emphasized in your high school English classes. A summary of the more important rules is given below.

USAGE

Directions

Some of the following sentences are correct. Others contain problems in grammar, usage, idiom, and diction (word choice). There is not more than one error in any sentence.

If there is an error, it will be underlined and lettered. Find the one underlined part that must be changed to make the sentence correct, and choose the corresponding letter on your answer sheet. Mark (E) if the sentence contains no error.

Analysis

1. You are looking for errors in Standard Written English, the kind of English used in most textbooks. Do not evaluate a sentence in terms of the spoken English we all use.

2. When deciding whether an underlined portion is correct or not, assume that *all other parts of the sentence are correct.*

SENTENCE CORRECTION

Directions

Some part of each sentence below is underlined; sometimes the whole sentence is underlined. Five choices for rephrasing the underlined part follow each sentence; the first choice (A) repeats the original, and the other four are different. If choice (A) seems better than the alternatives, choose answer (A); if not, choose one of the others.

For each sentence, consider the requirements of Standard Written English. Your choice should be a correct and effective expression, not awkward or ambiguous. Focus on grammar, word choice, sentence construction, and punctuation. If a choice changes the meaning of the original sentence, do not select it.

Analysis

1. Several alternatives to an underlined portion may be correct; you are to pick the *best* (most clear and exact) one.
2. *Any* alternative which changes the meaning of the sentence should not be chosen, no matter how clear or correct it is.

SUGGESTED APPROACH WITH SAMPLES

1. Look for pronoun errors first. Focus upon words like *he, him, she, her, we, us, they, them, who, whom, whoever, whomever, you, it, which,* or *that.*
Example A—Usage
We rewarded the workers whom, according to the manager,
                          A   B
had done the most imaginative job. No error.
  C   D   E

It is likely that *whom* is an error because it's a pronoun, and pronouns are error-prone. Try replacing *whom* with either *him* or *them: them . . . had done the most imaginative job.* This sounds wrong, a clue that *whom* is wrong. To test whether *who* is correct instead, try substituting *he* or *they: they . . . had done the most imaginative job.* This sounds right.

Remember, if *him* or *them* sounds right when substituted, *whom* is correct; if *he* or *they* sounds right when substituted, *who* is correct.

Example B—Sentence Correction

1. The Rotary Club applauded Tom and I for our work helping the handicapped in town find secure jobs.
   (A) The Rotary Club applauded Tom and I
   (B) The Rotary club applauded Tom and I
   (C) The Rotary Club applauded me and Tom
   (D) The Rotary Club applauded Tom and me
   (E) The Rotary Club applauded both of us

Focus on *I,* because it's a pronoun. To test whether *I* is correct, remove *Tom and.* The result is, *The Rotary Club applauded . . . I. Me* would sound better, and in fact (D) is the correct choice. (E) changes the meaning of the sentence.

2. If the sentence contains no pronouns or if the pronouns are correct, focus on the *verb.*

Example A—Usage

Here on the table is an apple and three pears. No error.
  A   B   C   D   E

Focus on the verb *is* and ask yourself what the subject is. In this sentence, the subject (*an apple and three pears*) *follows* the verb. Since the subject is plural, the verb must be plural—*are* instead of *is.*

Example B—Sentence Correction

The trunk containing costumes, makeup and props were left at the stage entrance of the theater.
   (A) costumes, makeup and props were left
   (B) costumes, makeup and props were all left
   (C) costumes, makeup and props was left
   (D) costumes, makeup and props to be left
   (E) costumes, makeup and props left

The verb is *were left.* Since the subject is singular (*trunk*) the verb must be singular—*was* instead of *were.* Don't assume that the subject immediately precedes the verb; in this case, the subject and verb are some distance apart.

3. Another common error is faulty parallelism. Look for a series of items separated by commas and make sure each item has the same *form.*

Example A—Usage

He <u>liked</u> swimming, <u>weight lifting</u> and <u>to run</u>. <u>No error</u>.
   A   B   C   D   E

To run is incorrect; it should be an *-ing* word like the other items.

Example B—Sentence Correction

To strive, to seek, to find, <u>and not yielding</u> are the heroic goals of Ulysses in Tennyson's famous poem.

(A) To strive, to seek, to find, and not yielding
(B) To strive, to seek, to find, and to yield
(C) To strive, to seek, to find, and not to yield
(D) To strive, to seek, to find, and yet to yield
(E) Striving, seeking, finding and yielding

Not yielding is incorrect; it should have the *to* _____ form of the other items. (C) is the best choice; (B), (E), and (D) are correct, but they change the meaning of the sentence.

    4. Another verb error happens when the verb tense (past, present, future) is inconsistent. If there are two verbs in the sentence, make sure the verb tense of each is appropriate.

Example A—Usage

He walked <u>for</u> miles <u>and</u> finally <u>sees</u> a <u>sign</u> of civilization. <u>No error</u>.
         A   B   C D   E

Walked describes the past; *sees* describes the present. *Sees* should be changed to *saw* so that the whole sentence describes the past.

Example B—Sentence Correction

<u>If he would have worked</u> harder, he could have gone to the movies.

(A) If he would have worked   (D) If he had worked
(B) If he worked   (E) After working
(C) Working

In general, if a sentence contains two *would haves,* two *should haves,* two *could haves,* or any combination of these terms (in this case *would have* and *should have*), one of the verbs should be changed to *had,* to indicate that one of the actions (*working*) occurred earlier than the other (going to the movies). (D) is correct.

SUMMARY

Generally, watch out for pronouns, verbs, and awkward larger structures (illustrated by errors like faulty parallelism). Other common errors are explained in the answers section following the practice tests.

Part III: Practice-Review-Analyze-Practice

Two Full-Length Practice Tests

This section contains two full-length practice simulation SAT's with Tests of Standard Written English. The practice tests are followed by complete answers, explanations, and analysis techniques. The format, levels of difficulty, question structure, and number of questions are similar to those on the actual SAT and TSWE. The actual SAT and TSWE are copyrighted and may not be duplicated and these questions are not taken directly from the actual tests.

When taking these exams, try to simulate the test conditions by following the time allotments carefully. Remember the total test is 3 hours, divided into six sections of 30 minutes each.

PRACTICE TEST NO. 1

ANSWER SHEET FOR SAT and TSWE PRACTICE TEST NO. 1
(Remove This Sheet and Use It to Mark Your Answers)

START WITH NUMBER 1 FOR EACH NEW SECTION OF THE TEST

SECTION I

1 Ⓐ Ⓑ Ⓒ Ⓓ Ⓔ	26 Ⓐ Ⓑ Ⓒ Ⓓ Ⓔ
2 Ⓐ Ⓑ Ⓒ Ⓓ Ⓔ	27 Ⓐ Ⓑ Ⓒ Ⓓ Ⓔ
3 Ⓐ Ⓑ Ⓒ Ⓓ Ⓔ	28 Ⓐ Ⓑ Ⓒ Ⓓ Ⓔ
4 Ⓐ Ⓑ Ⓒ Ⓓ Ⓔ	29 Ⓐ Ⓑ Ⓒ Ⓓ Ⓔ
5 Ⓐ Ⓑ Ⓒ Ⓓ Ⓔ	30 Ⓐ Ⓑ Ⓒ Ⓓ Ⓔ
6 Ⓐ Ⓑ Ⓒ Ⓓ Ⓔ	31 Ⓐ Ⓑ Ⓒ Ⓓ Ⓔ
7 Ⓐ Ⓑ Ⓒ Ⓓ Ⓔ	32 Ⓐ Ⓑ Ⓒ Ⓓ Ⓔ
8 Ⓐ Ⓑ Ⓒ Ⓓ Ⓔ	33 Ⓐ Ⓑ Ⓒ Ⓓ Ⓔ
9 Ⓐ Ⓑ Ⓒ Ⓓ Ⓔ	34 Ⓐ Ⓑ Ⓒ Ⓓ Ⓔ
10 Ⓐ Ⓑ Ⓒ Ⓓ Ⓔ	35 Ⓐ Ⓑ Ⓒ Ⓓ Ⓔ
11 Ⓐ Ⓑ Ⓒ Ⓓ Ⓔ	36 Ⓐ Ⓑ Ⓒ Ⓓ Ⓔ
12 Ⓐ Ⓑ Ⓒ Ⓓ Ⓔ	37 Ⓐ Ⓑ Ⓒ Ⓓ Ⓔ
13 Ⓐ Ⓑ Ⓒ Ⓓ Ⓔ	38 Ⓐ Ⓑ Ⓒ Ⓓ Ⓔ
14 Ⓐ Ⓑ Ⓒ Ⓓ Ⓔ	39 Ⓐ Ⓑ Ⓒ Ⓓ Ⓔ
15 Ⓐ Ⓑ Ⓒ Ⓓ Ⓔ	40 Ⓐ Ⓑ Ⓒ Ⓓ Ⓔ
16 Ⓐ Ⓑ Ⓒ Ⓓ Ⓔ	41 Ⓐ Ⓑ Ⓒ Ⓓ Ⓔ
17 Ⓐ Ⓑ Ⓒ Ⓓ Ⓔ	42 Ⓐ Ⓑ Ⓒ Ⓓ Ⓔ
18 Ⓐ Ⓑ Ⓒ Ⓓ Ⓔ	43 Ⓐ Ⓑ Ⓒ Ⓓ Ⓔ
19 Ⓐ Ⓑ Ⓒ Ⓓ Ⓔ	44 Ⓐ Ⓑ Ⓒ Ⓓ Ⓔ
20 Ⓐ Ⓑ Ⓒ Ⓓ Ⓔ	45 Ⓐ Ⓑ Ⓒ Ⓓ Ⓔ
21 Ⓐ Ⓑ Ⓒ Ⓓ Ⓔ	
22 Ⓐ Ⓑ Ⓒ Ⓓ Ⓔ	
23 Ⓐ Ⓑ Ⓒ Ⓓ Ⓔ	
24 Ⓐ Ⓑ Ⓒ Ⓓ Ⓔ	
25 Ⓐ Ⓑ Ⓒ Ⓓ Ⓔ	

SECTION II

1 Ⓐ Ⓑ Ⓒ Ⓓ Ⓔ	26 Ⓐ Ⓑ Ⓒ Ⓓ Ⓔ
2 Ⓐ Ⓑ Ⓒ Ⓓ Ⓔ	27 Ⓐ Ⓑ Ⓒ Ⓓ Ⓔ
3 Ⓐ Ⓑ Ⓒ Ⓓ Ⓔ	28 Ⓐ Ⓑ Ⓒ Ⓓ Ⓔ
4 Ⓐ Ⓑ Ⓒ Ⓓ Ⓔ	29 Ⓐ Ⓑ Ⓒ Ⓓ Ⓔ
5 Ⓐ Ⓑ Ⓒ Ⓓ Ⓔ	30 Ⓐ Ⓑ Ⓒ Ⓓ Ⓔ
6 Ⓐ Ⓑ Ⓒ Ⓓ Ⓔ	31 Ⓐ Ⓑ Ⓒ Ⓓ Ⓔ
7 Ⓐ Ⓑ Ⓒ Ⓓ Ⓔ	32 Ⓐ Ⓑ Ⓒ Ⓓ Ⓔ
8 Ⓐ Ⓑ Ⓒ Ⓓ Ⓔ	33 Ⓐ Ⓑ Ⓒ Ⓓ Ⓔ
9 Ⓐ Ⓑ Ⓒ Ⓓ Ⓔ	34 Ⓐ Ⓑ Ⓒ Ⓓ Ⓔ
10 Ⓐ Ⓑ Ⓒ Ⓓ Ⓔ	35 Ⓐ Ⓑ Ⓒ Ⓓ Ⓔ
11 Ⓐ Ⓑ Ⓒ Ⓓ Ⓔ	
12 Ⓐ Ⓑ Ⓒ Ⓓ Ⓔ	
13 Ⓐ Ⓑ Ⓒ Ⓓ Ⓔ	
14 Ⓐ Ⓑ Ⓒ Ⓓ Ⓔ	
15 Ⓐ Ⓑ Ⓒ Ⓓ Ⓔ	
16 Ⓐ Ⓑ Ⓒ Ⓓ Ⓔ	
17 Ⓐ Ⓑ Ⓒ Ⓓ Ⓔ	
18 Ⓐ Ⓑ Ⓒ Ⓓ Ⓔ	
19 Ⓐ Ⓑ Ⓒ Ⓓ Ⓔ	
20 Ⓐ Ⓑ Ⓒ Ⓓ Ⓔ	
21 Ⓐ Ⓑ Ⓒ Ⓓ Ⓔ	
22 Ⓐ Ⓑ Ⓒ Ⓓ Ⓔ	
23 Ⓐ Ⓑ Ⓒ Ⓓ Ⓔ	
24 Ⓐ Ⓑ Ⓒ Ⓓ Ⓔ	
25 Ⓐ Ⓑ Ⓒ Ⓓ Ⓔ	

ANSWER SHEET FOR SAT and TSWE PRACTICE TEST NO. 1
(Remove This Sheet and Use It to Mark Your Answers)

START WITH NUMBER 1 FOR EACH NEW SECTION OF THE TEST

SECTION III

1 Ⓐ Ⓑ Ⓒ Ⓓ Ⓔ	26 Ⓐ Ⓑ Ⓒ Ⓓ Ⓔ
2 Ⓐ Ⓑ Ⓒ Ⓓ Ⓔ	27 Ⓐ Ⓑ Ⓒ Ⓓ Ⓔ
3 Ⓐ Ⓑ Ⓒ Ⓓ Ⓔ	28 Ⓐ Ⓑ Ⓒ Ⓓ Ⓔ
4 Ⓐ Ⓑ Ⓒ Ⓓ Ⓔ	29 Ⓐ Ⓑ Ⓒ Ⓓ Ⓔ
5 Ⓐ Ⓑ Ⓒ Ⓓ Ⓔ	30 Ⓐ Ⓑ Ⓒ Ⓓ Ⓔ
6 Ⓐ Ⓑ Ⓒ Ⓓ Ⓔ	31 Ⓐ Ⓑ Ⓒ Ⓓ Ⓔ
7 Ⓐ Ⓑ Ⓒ Ⓓ Ⓔ	32 Ⓐ Ⓑ Ⓒ Ⓓ Ⓔ
8 Ⓐ Ⓑ Ⓒ Ⓓ Ⓔ	33 Ⓐ Ⓑ Ⓒ Ⓓ Ⓔ
9 Ⓐ Ⓑ Ⓒ Ⓓ Ⓔ	34 Ⓐ Ⓑ Ⓒ Ⓓ Ⓔ
10 Ⓐ Ⓑ Ⓒ Ⓓ Ⓔ	35 Ⓐ Ⓑ Ⓒ Ⓓ Ⓔ
11 Ⓐ Ⓑ Ⓒ Ⓓ Ⓔ	36 Ⓐ Ⓑ Ⓒ Ⓓ Ⓔ
12 Ⓐ Ⓑ Ⓒ Ⓓ Ⓔ	37 Ⓐ Ⓑ Ⓒ Ⓓ Ⓔ
13 Ⓐ Ⓑ Ⓒ Ⓓ Ⓔ	38 Ⓐ Ⓑ Ⓒ Ⓓ Ⓔ
14 Ⓐ Ⓑ Ⓒ Ⓓ Ⓔ	39 Ⓐ Ⓑ Ⓒ Ⓓ Ⓔ
15 Ⓐ Ⓑ Ⓒ Ⓓ Ⓔ	40 Ⓐ Ⓑ Ⓒ Ⓓ Ⓔ
16 Ⓐ Ⓑ Ⓒ Ⓓ Ⓔ	41 Ⓐ Ⓑ Ⓒ Ⓓ Ⓔ
17 Ⓐ Ⓑ Ⓒ Ⓓ Ⓔ	42 Ⓐ Ⓑ Ⓒ Ⓓ Ⓔ
18 Ⓐ Ⓑ Ⓒ Ⓓ Ⓔ	43 Ⓐ Ⓑ Ⓒ Ⓓ Ⓔ
19 Ⓐ Ⓑ Ⓒ Ⓓ Ⓔ	44 Ⓐ Ⓑ Ⓒ Ⓓ Ⓔ
20 Ⓐ Ⓑ Ⓒ Ⓓ Ⓔ	45 Ⓐ Ⓑ Ⓒ Ⓓ Ⓔ
21 Ⓐ Ⓑ Ⓒ Ⓓ Ⓔ	46 Ⓐ Ⓑ Ⓒ Ⓓ Ⓔ
22 Ⓐ Ⓑ Ⓒ Ⓓ Ⓔ	47 Ⓐ Ⓑ Ⓒ Ⓓ Ⓔ
23 Ⓐ Ⓑ Ⓒ Ⓓ Ⓔ	48 Ⓐ Ⓑ Ⓒ Ⓓ Ⓔ
24 Ⓐ Ⓑ Ⓒ Ⓓ Ⓔ	49 Ⓐ Ⓑ Ⓒ Ⓓ Ⓔ
25 Ⓐ Ⓑ Ⓒ Ⓓ Ⓔ	50 Ⓐ Ⓑ Ⓒ Ⓓ Ⓔ

SECTION IV

1 Ⓐ Ⓑ Ⓒ Ⓓ Ⓔ	26 Ⓐ Ⓑ Ⓒ Ⓓ Ⓔ
2 Ⓐ Ⓑ Ⓒ Ⓓ Ⓔ	27 Ⓐ Ⓑ Ⓒ Ⓓ Ⓔ
3 Ⓐ Ⓑ Ⓒ Ⓓ Ⓔ	28 Ⓐ Ⓑ Ⓒ Ⓓ Ⓔ
4 Ⓐ Ⓑ Ⓒ Ⓓ Ⓔ	29 Ⓐ Ⓑ Ⓒ Ⓓ Ⓔ
5 Ⓐ Ⓑ Ⓒ Ⓓ Ⓔ	30 Ⓐ Ⓑ Ⓒ Ⓓ Ⓔ
6 Ⓐ Ⓑ Ⓒ Ⓓ Ⓔ	31 Ⓐ Ⓑ Ⓒ Ⓓ Ⓔ
7 Ⓐ Ⓑ Ⓒ Ⓓ Ⓔ	32 Ⓐ Ⓑ Ⓒ Ⓓ Ⓔ
8 Ⓐ Ⓑ Ⓒ Ⓓ Ⓔ	33 Ⓐ Ⓑ Ⓒ Ⓓ Ⓔ
9 Ⓐ Ⓑ Ⓒ Ⓓ Ⓔ	34 Ⓐ Ⓑ Ⓒ Ⓓ Ⓔ
10 Ⓐ Ⓑ Ⓒ Ⓓ Ⓔ	35 Ⓐ Ⓑ Ⓒ Ⓓ Ⓔ
11 Ⓐ Ⓑ Ⓒ Ⓓ Ⓔ	36 Ⓐ Ⓑ Ⓒ Ⓓ Ⓔ
12 Ⓐ Ⓑ Ⓒ Ⓓ Ⓔ	37 Ⓐ Ⓑ Ⓒ Ⓓ Ⓔ
13 Ⓐ Ⓑ Ⓒ Ⓓ Ⓔ	38 Ⓐ Ⓑ Ⓒ Ⓓ Ⓔ
14 Ⓐ Ⓑ Ⓒ Ⓓ Ⓔ	39 Ⓐ Ⓑ Ⓒ Ⓓ Ⓔ
15 Ⓐ Ⓑ Ⓒ Ⓓ Ⓔ	40 Ⓐ Ⓑ Ⓒ Ⓓ Ⓔ
16 Ⓐ Ⓑ Ⓒ Ⓓ Ⓔ	
17 Ⓐ Ⓑ Ⓒ Ⓓ Ⓔ	
18 Ⓐ Ⓑ Ⓒ Ⓓ Ⓔ	
19 Ⓐ Ⓑ Ⓒ Ⓓ Ⓔ	
20 Ⓐ Ⓑ Ⓒ Ⓓ Ⓔ	
21 Ⓐ Ⓑ Ⓒ Ⓓ Ⓔ	
22 Ⓐ Ⓑ Ⓒ Ⓓ Ⓔ	
23 Ⓐ Ⓑ Ⓒ Ⓓ Ⓔ	
24 Ⓐ Ⓑ Ⓒ Ⓓ Ⓔ	
25 Ⓐ Ⓑ Ⓒ Ⓓ Ⓔ	

CUT HERE

ANSWER SHEET FOR SAT and TSWE PRACTICE TEST NO. 1
(Remove This Sheet and Use It to Mark Your Answers)

START WITH NUMBER 1 FOR EACH NEW SECTION OF THE TEST

SECTION V

1 Ⓐ Ⓑ Ⓒ Ⓓ Ⓔ	21 Ⓐ Ⓑ Ⓒ Ⓓ Ⓔ
2 Ⓐ Ⓑ Ⓒ Ⓓ Ⓔ	22 Ⓐ Ⓑ Ⓒ Ⓓ Ⓔ
3 Ⓐ Ⓑ Ⓒ Ⓓ Ⓔ	23 Ⓐ Ⓑ Ⓒ Ⓓ Ⓔ
4 Ⓐ Ⓑ Ⓒ Ⓓ Ⓔ	24 Ⓐ Ⓑ Ⓒ Ⓓ Ⓔ
5 Ⓐ Ⓑ Ⓒ Ⓓ Ⓔ	25 Ⓐ Ⓑ Ⓒ Ⓓ Ⓔ
6 Ⓐ Ⓑ Ⓒ Ⓓ Ⓔ	
7 Ⓐ Ⓑ Ⓒ Ⓓ Ⓔ	
8 Ⓐ Ⓑ Ⓒ Ⓓ Ⓔ	
9 Ⓐ Ⓑ Ⓒ Ⓓ Ⓔ	
10 Ⓐ Ⓑ Ⓒ Ⓓ Ⓔ	
11 Ⓐ Ⓑ Ⓒ Ⓓ Ⓔ	
12 Ⓐ Ⓑ Ⓒ Ⓓ Ⓔ	
13 Ⓐ Ⓑ Ⓒ Ⓓ Ⓔ	
14 Ⓐ Ⓑ Ⓒ Ⓓ Ⓔ	
15 Ⓐ Ⓑ Ⓒ Ⓓ Ⓔ	
16 Ⓐ Ⓑ Ⓒ Ⓓ Ⓔ	
17 Ⓐ Ⓑ Ⓒ Ⓓ Ⓔ	
18 Ⓐ Ⓑ Ⓒ Ⓓ Ⓔ	
19 Ⓐ Ⓑ Ⓒ Ⓓ Ⓔ	
20 Ⓐ Ⓑ Ⓒ Ⓓ Ⓔ	

SECTION VI

1 Ⓐ Ⓑ Ⓒ Ⓓ Ⓔ	26 Ⓐ Ⓑ Ⓒ Ⓓ Ⓔ
2 Ⓐ Ⓑ Ⓒ Ⓓ Ⓔ	27 Ⓐ Ⓑ Ⓒ Ⓓ Ⓔ
3 Ⓐ Ⓑ Ⓒ Ⓓ Ⓔ	28 Ⓐ Ⓑ Ⓒ Ⓓ Ⓔ
4 Ⓐ Ⓑ Ⓒ Ⓓ Ⓔ	29 Ⓐ Ⓑ Ⓒ Ⓓ Ⓔ
5 Ⓐ Ⓑ Ⓒ Ⓓ Ⓔ	30 Ⓐ Ⓑ Ⓒ Ⓓ Ⓔ
6 Ⓐ Ⓑ Ⓒ Ⓓ Ⓔ	31 Ⓐ Ⓑ Ⓒ Ⓓ Ⓔ
7 Ⓐ Ⓑ Ⓒ Ⓓ Ⓔ	32 Ⓐ Ⓑ Ⓒ Ⓓ Ⓔ
8 Ⓐ Ⓑ Ⓒ Ⓓ Ⓔ	33 Ⓐ Ⓑ Ⓒ Ⓓ Ⓔ
9 Ⓐ Ⓑ Ⓒ Ⓓ Ⓔ	34 Ⓐ Ⓑ Ⓒ Ⓓ Ⓔ
10 Ⓐ Ⓑ Ⓒ Ⓓ Ⓔ	35 Ⓐ Ⓑ Ⓒ Ⓓ Ⓔ
11 Ⓐ Ⓑ Ⓒ Ⓓ Ⓔ	
12 Ⓐ Ⓑ Ⓒ Ⓓ Ⓔ	
13 Ⓐ Ⓑ Ⓒ Ⓓ Ⓔ	
14 Ⓐ Ⓑ Ⓒ Ⓓ Ⓔ	
15 Ⓐ Ⓑ Ⓒ Ⓓ Ⓔ	
16 Ⓐ Ⓑ Ⓒ Ⓓ Ⓔ	
17 Ⓐ Ⓑ Ⓒ Ⓓ Ⓔ	
18 Ⓐ Ⓑ Ⓒ Ⓓ Ⓔ	
19 Ⓐ Ⓑ Ⓒ Ⓓ Ⓔ	
20 Ⓐ Ⓑ Ⓒ Ⓓ Ⓔ	
21 Ⓐ Ⓑ Ⓒ Ⓓ Ⓔ	
22 Ⓐ Ⓑ Ⓒ Ⓓ Ⓔ	
23 Ⓐ Ⓑ Ⓒ Ⓓ Ⓔ	
24 Ⓐ Ⓑ Ⓒ Ⓓ Ⓔ	
25 Ⓐ Ⓑ Ⓒ Ⓓ Ⓔ	

CUT HERE

SECTION I: VERBAL ABILITY

Time: 30 Minutes
45 Questions

In this section, choose the best answer for each question and blacken the corresponding space on the answer sheet.

Antonyms

DIRECTIONS

Each word in CAPITAL LETTERS is followed by five words or phrases. The correct choice is the word or phrase whose meaning is most nearly *opposite* to the meaning of the word in capitals. You may be required to distinguish fine shades of meaning. Look at all choices before marking your answer.

1. DRAB
   (A) pure
   (B) bright
   (C) holy
   (D) clear
   (E) trifling

2. BENEDICTION
   (A) yell
   (B) scream
   (C) howl
   (D) curse
   (E) threat

3. VALOR
   (A) cowardice
   (B) valuation
   (C) temerity
   (D) invasion
   (E) bravery

4. BISECT
   (A) divide
   (B) intersect
   (C) trisect
   (D) join
   (E) cut

5. DISPARITY
   (A) excess
   (B) hopefulness
   (C) sensitivity
   (D) coma
   (E) likeness

6. CYCLIC
   - (A) linear
   - (B) square
   - (C) hexagonal
   - (D) rectangular
   - (E) spiral

7. COVENANT
   - (A) condemnation
   - (B) breach
   - (C) disillusion
   - (D) inference
   - (E) argument

8. JAUNTY
   - (A) eager
   - (B) sedentary
   - (C) cheerful
   - (D) morose
   - (E) aghast

9. PASTORAL
   - (A) urban
   - (B) musical
   - (C) religious
   - (D) impious
   - (E) hopeful

10. FRUGAL
    - (A) parsimonious
    - (B) extravagant
    - (C) diligent
    - (D) resourceful
    - (E) lethal

11. EQUINOX
    - (A) iniquity
    - (B) inequity
    - (C) solstice
    - (D) equivocal
    - (E) winter

12. PATRONYMIC
    - (A) matronly
    - (B) patriarchal
    - (C) brotherlike
    - (D) democratic
    - (E) new-made

13. VALEDICTORY
    - (A) salutation
    - (B) entreaty
    - (C) beginning
    - (D) valiance
    - (E) contradiction

14. LITHE
    - (A) stiff
    - (B) deceased
    - (C) indifferent
    - (D) liquid
    - (E) rare

15. SANGUINE
    - (A) abrupt
    - (B) insecure
    - (C) mildly assured
    - (D) insensitive
    - (E) overly defensive

Sentence Completion

DIRECTIONS

Each blank in the following sentences indicates that something has been omitted. Consider the lettered words beneath the sentence and choose the word or set of words that best fits the whole sentence.

16. Trying unsuccessfully the past hour to fall asleep, Dana wished her parrot were just a bit less _____ .
    - (A) playful
    - (B) colorful
    - (C) distressed
    - (D) vocal
    - (E) sleepy

17. Illness is often something to be _____, but it may provide _____ for rest, growth, and change.
    - (A) applauded . . . time
    - (B) anticipated . . . arguments
    - (C) dreaded . . . opportunity
    - (D) encouraged . . . meaning
    - (E) reconciled . . . excitement

18. Although the story told is one of mounting violence, an occasional _____ moment relieves the mood.
    - (A) angry
    - (B) melancholy
    - (C) rehearsed
    - (D) tender
    - (E) fabricated

19. Her research was so _____ that not even one tiny bit of evidence was left _____ .
    - (A) minute . . . showing
    - (B) arduous . . . imperiled
    - (C) impeccable . . . recorded
    - (D) essential . . . documented
    - (E) thorough . . . unexplored

20. The chairperson was noted for not being obstinate; on the contrary, the members praised his _____.
    - (A) resistance
    - (B) experience
    - (C) coherence
    - (D) verbosity
    - (E) flexibility

Reading Comprehension

DIRECTIONS

Questions follow each of the passages below. Using only the stated or implied information in each passage, answer the question.

Questions 21 through 25 refer to the following passage.

From the U.S. Supreme Court now comes an extraordinary decision permitting inquiries into the "state of mind" of journalists and the editorial process of news organizations. This is perhaps the most alarming evidence so far of a determination by the nation's highest court
(5) to weaken the protection of the First Amendment for those who gather and report the news.

The court last year upheld the right of police to invade newspaper offices in search of evidence, and reporters in other cases have gone to jail to protect the confidentiality of their notebooks. Under the recent
(10) 6-3 ruling in a libel case, they now face a challenge to the privacy of their minds.

Few would argue that the First Amendment guarantees absolute freedom of speech or freedom of the press. Slander and libel laws stand to the contrary as a protection of an individual's reputation against the
(15) irresponsible dissemination of falsehoods. The effect of this latest decision, however, is to make the libel suit, or the threat of one, a clear invasion by the courts into the private decision-making that constitutes news and editorial judgment.

In landmark decisions of 1964 and 1967, the Supreme Court estab-
(20) lished that public officials or public figures bringing libel actions must prove that a damaging falsehood was published with "actual malice"— that is, with knowledge that the statements were false, or with reckless disregard of whether they were true or not.

Justice Byron R. White, writing for the new majority in the new
(25) ruling, says it is not enough to examine all the circumstances of publication that would indicate whether there was malicious intent or not. It is proper and constitutional, he says, for "state-of-mind evidence" to be introduced. The court is thus ordering a CBS television producer to answer questions about the thought processes that went into the
(30) preparation and airing of a segment of *60 Minutes*.

That six justices of the Supreme Court fail to see this as a breach of the First Amendment is frightening. The novelist George Orwell may have been mistaken only in the timing of his vision of a Big Brother government practicing mind-control.

21. This article deals principally with
    (A) the U.S. Supreme Court's decisions
    (B) explaining the First Amendment to the Constitution
    (C) an attack on the freedom of the press
    (D) slander and libel laws
    (E) Big Brother in government

22. How many justices would have to change their minds to reverse this decision?
    (A) one   (D) four
    (B) two   (E) five
    (C) three

23. This writer feels the Supreme Court is wrong in this case because
    (A) newspapers were unsophisticated when the First Amendment was written
    (B) reporters are entitled to special rights
    (C) it challenges the privacy of a journalist's mind
    (D) Judge White has himself been accused of slander and libel
    (E) the Supreme Court is capable of malicious intent

24. What does "actual malice" (line 21) mean?
    I. knowledge that the statements were false
    II. reckless disregard of whether the statements were true or not
    III. libel

    (A) I only   (D) I or II
    (B) II only   (E) I or III
    (C) III only

25. According to the passage, if a rock star were to file a libel suit against a newspaper, claiming that the newspaper had falsely represented the star and the star's husband, in order to win the suit in the Supreme Court, the rock star must
    (A) show that the newspaper didn't know it was reporting a falsehood
    (B) demonstrate that the newspaper meant to print the truth
    (C) argue that the newspaper was given false information
    (D) defend her right to privacy
    (E) prove that the newspaper didn't care whether its article was true or not

Questions 26 through 30 are based on the following passage.

Concerning the origin of the soul, Augustine's view differs from that of the Greek philosophers. He does not believe that souls are eternal or that they have an existence prior to their union with the body. He holds that souls are created by God, although it is not entirely clear whether he means that a soul is created simultaneously with the birth of each infant or the soul of the newborn child is generated from the souls of the parents at the same time that the new body is developed. In either case it is the creative activity of God that is involved. Although the souls do not exist prior to their union with the body, they will survive the death of the physical body, in which case they will again be united with some other type of body, the nature of which we do not know. It is in this sense only that Augustine believes in the immortality of the soul. His argument in support of this belief is similar to the one used by Plato. Because the soul is capable of knowing truth which is eternal it must possess qualities that are more than merely temporal.

Souls are free insofar as they have the power to choose between right and wrong courses of action. Hence man is to some degree at least responsible for his fate. He cannot place the blame for his sins on God, nature, or even Satan. The responsibility lies in himself. The temptations are there through no fault of his own, but yielding to these temptations is another matter and one for which he can justly be blamed. The nature of man's freedom was, however, a very difficult one for him to explain, and he was never able to do so without becoming involved in inconsistencies. One of the reasons for this was his belief in predestination along with the idea that God knows what man will do in the future.

Although man was created in the image of God and without any evil being present in this nature, he now finds himself in a miserable predicament. As Augustine contemplates his own nature as well as that of his fellow men, he sees wickedness and corruption on every hand. Man is a sinful creature and there is nothing that is wholly good about him. How did this come about? The answer is to be found in original sin, which mankind inherited from Adam. In what sense can it be said that Adam's descendants are responsible for what he did long ago? It is in this connection that Augustine makes use of the Platonic relationship between the universal and the individual. If Adam is regarded as a particular human being, it would make no sense at all to blame his descendants for the mistakes that he made. But Adam is interpreted to mean the universal man rather than a particular individual. Since the universal necessarily includes all of the particulars belonging to the class, they are involved in whatever the universal does.

The total corruption of human nature as taught by Augustine did not mean that man is incapable of doing any good deeds. It meant that each part of his nature is infected with an evil tendency. In contrast to the Greek notion of a good mind and an evil body, he held that both mind and body had been made corrupt as a result of the fall. This corruption is made manifest in the lusts of the flesh and also in the activities of the mind. So far as the mind is concerned, the evil tendency is present in both the intellect and in the will. In the intellect it is expressed in the sin of pride, and in the will there is the inclination to follow that which is pleasant at the moment rather than to obey the demands of reason.

26. According to Augustine, one of the symptoms of human corruption is
    (A) man's exclusive pursuit of pleasure
    (B) man's periodic attempts to do good deeds
    (C) man's refusal to connect the universal with the particular
    (D) Adam
    (E) Eve

27. Augustine thinks that the soul is
    (A) eternal
    (B) eternal, but not immortal
    (C) immortal, but not eternal
    (D) transient
    (E) capable of sin

28. Augustine could not declare man to be wholly free because
    (A) man is shackled by Adam's sin
    (B) God knows man's every move before it is made
    (C) the question of freedom is a political one
    (D) he himself was not free
    (E) anything that is free is not worth much

29. According to the passage, the desires of the flesh are controlled by
    (A) Augustine's theory   (D) the will
    (B) the intellect   (E) none of these
    (C) God

30. Pride is a function of
    (A) Augustine's theory   (D) the soul
    (B) the intellect   (E) the will
    (C) God

Sentence Completion

DIRECTIONS

Each blank in the following sentences indicates that something has been omitted. Consider the lettered words beneath the sentence and choose the word or set of words that best fits the whole sentence.

31. Acknowledging the _____ and realities that separate us from each other can also enable us to _____ the complex fabric of our society.
   (A) differences . . . appreciate
   (B) truths . . . combat
   (C) traditions . . . resolve
   (D) similarities . . . enrich
   (E) fears . . . complete

32. The clothes she designs for men are conservative, but her fashions for women are more _____ .
   (A) liberal   (D) expensive
   (B) flamboyant   (E) conventional
   (C) tasteless

33. That "less is more" is a(n) _____ upon which all of the governor's conservation program is based.
   (A) hope   (D) image
   (B) question   (E) paradox
   (C) enigma

34. By showing that the trainer's voice _____ gave commands to the horse, he was able to _____ the ruse that contended an animal could add and subtract.
   (A) ostensibly . . . confirm
   (B) never . . . debunk
   (C) covertly . . . unmask
   (D) unwittingly . . . prove
   (E) potentially . . . defend

35. With characteristic understatement, Webster called his client's embezzlement of four million dollars a regretted _____ .
   (A) peccadillo   (D) theft
   (B) crime   (E) enormity
   (C) atrocity

Analogies

DIRECTIONS

In each question below, you are given a related pair of words or phrases. Select the lettered pair that *best* expresses a relationship similar to that in the original pair of words.

36. TUNE : PIANO ::
   (A) essay : pencil   (D) ripen : fruit
   (B) focus : camera   (E) examine : biologist
   (C) transmit : plague

37. ISLAND : OCEAN : :
    (A) tree : forest
    (B) automobile : highway
    (C) radio : sound
    (D) star : zodiac
    (E) oasis : desert

38. SQUARE : CUBE : :
    • (A) triangle : hexagon
    (B) trapezoid : quadrangle
    (C) circle : sphere
    (D) pentagon : pentagram
    (E) addition : subtraction

39. SERUM : SYRINGE : :
    (A) ship : sail
    ' (B) fish : net
    (C) nail : hammer
    (D) battery : bulb
    (E) hope : despair

40. ZIRCON : DIAMOND : :
    (A) gold : silver
    • (B) garnet : ruby
    (C) oyster : pearl
    (D) necklace : bracelet
    (E) emerald : sapphire

41. STRIDE : SAUNTER : :
    (A) hear : listen
    • (B) eat : grow
    (C) flow : meander
    (D) race : dawdle
    (E) restrict : relax

42. REQUEST : REQUIREMENT : :
    (A) solicitation : contribution
    • (B) hope : faith
    (C) aspiration : inspiration
    (D) inquiry : interrogation
    (E) question : answer

43. PLAN : INTRIGUE : :
    (A) move : slink
    • (B) fear : doubt
    (C) run : hasten
    (D) eat : devour
    (E) boil : seeth

44. COMPLAISANT : COURTESY : :
    (A) offensive : smile
    (B) wise : riches
    (C) eager : inaction
    (D) vain : correctness
    (E) voracious : gluttony

45. GAUCHE : GRACE : :
    (A) impecunious : wealth
    (B) greedy : fool
    (C) prejudiced : bigotry
    (D) conservative : reserve
    (E) proud : vanity

STOP. IF YOU FINISH BEFORE TIME IS CALLED, CHECK YOUR WORK ON THIS SECTION ONLY. DO NOT WORK ON ANY OTHER SECTION IN THE TEST.

SECTION II: MATHEMATICAL ABILITY

Time: 30 Minutes
35 Questions

DIRECTIONS

Solve each problem in this section by using the information given and your own mathematical calculations. Then select the *one* correct answer of the five choices given. Use the available space on the page for scratchwork.

Data That May Be Used as Reference for This Section

The area formula for a circle of radius r is: $A = \pi r^2$
The circumference formula is: $C = 2\pi r$
A circle is composed of 360°.
A straight angle measures 180°.

Triangle: The sum of the angles of a triangle is 180°.
If angle ADB is a right angle, then

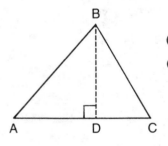

(1) The area of triangle ABC is $\dfrac{AC \times BD}{2}$

(2) $AD^2 + BD^2 = AB^2$

Symbol References:
= is equal to	≥ is greater than or equal to
≠ not equal to	≤ is less than or equal to
> is greater than	‖ is parallel to
< is less than	⊥ is perpendicular to

NOTE: Some problems may be accompanied by figures or diagrams. These figures are drawn as accurately as possible, EXCEPT when it is stated in a specific problem that the figure is not drawn to scale. The figures are meant to provide information useful in solving the problem or problems but are not meant to be measured.

Unless otherwise stated or indicated, all figures lie in a plane.

All numbers used are real numbers.

1. Find .25% of 12

   (A) ³⁄₁₀₀   (B) ³⁄₁₀   (C) ⅓   (D) 3   (E) 300

2. If $2x + 13$ represents an odd number, what must the next consecutive odd number be?

   (A) $2x + 15$ (B) $2x + 14$ (C) $3x + 13$ (D) $3x + 15$
   (E) cannot be determined

3. In the series 8, 9, 12, 17, 24, ... the next number would be

   (A) 41   (B) 35   (C) 33   (D) 30   (E) 29

4. If $x = -1$, then $x^4 + x^3 + x^2 + x - 3 =$
   (A) -13 (B) -7 (C) -3 (D) -2 (E) 1

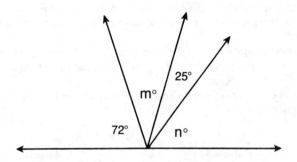

5. In the figure, what is the number of degrees in the sum of $m + n$?
   (A) 103   (B) 97   (C) 93   (D) 83
   (E) cannot be determined

$$\begin{array}{r} \square\ \square\ 4 \\ \times\ \ \ 8 \\ \hline 5\ \ 3\ \ 9\ \square \end{array}$$

6. The sum of the digits in the three boxes equals
   (A) 5   (B) 7   (C) 9   (D) 13   (E) 15

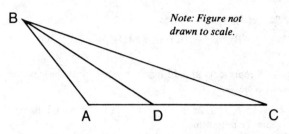

Note: Figure not
drawn to scale.

7. In the figure AB = AD and BD = CD. If ∠C measures 19°, what is the measure of ∠A in degrees?

(A) 75   (B) 94   (C) 104   (D) 142
(E) cannot be determined

Quantitative Comparison

DIRECTIONS

In this section you will be given two quantities, one in column A and one in column B. You are to determine a relationship between the two quantities and mark—

(A) if the quantity in column A is greater than the quantity in column B.
(B) if the quantity in column B is greater than the quantity in column A.
(C) if the quantities are equal.
(D) if the comparison cannot be determined from the information that is given.

	Column A	Column B
8.	$3^2 + 4 \times 10^2 - 4^2$	$3^2 - 4 \times 10^2 - 4^2$

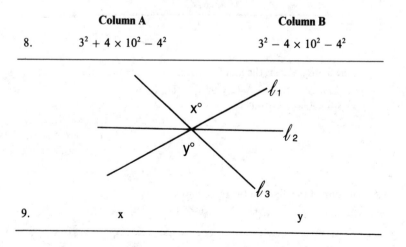

| 9. | x | y |

Column A	Column B

$$x > 0$$

10.	$3x^2$	$2x^3$

11.	$\dfrac{3}{7} \times \dfrac{2}{5} \times \dfrac{5}{8}$	$\dfrac{2}{5} \times \dfrac{4}{11} \times \dfrac{5}{8}$

$$5y = 10$$
$$3x + 2y = 10$$

12.	x	y

13.	Area of circle with diameter 8	Area of square with side 7

$$1 < x + y < 5$$

14.	x	y

15.	number of seconds in two hours	number of hours in 50 weeks

$$\dfrac{a}{6} = \dfrac{b}{4}$$

16.	2a	3b

17.	$1 + \dfrac{1}{2} + \dfrac{1}{4} + \dfrac{1}{16} + \dfrac{1}{32} + \dfrac{1}{64}$	2

18.	Number of ways to arrange four books on a shelf.	12

$$x > y > 0$$

19.	$\sqrt{x} - \sqrt{y}$	$\sqrt{x - y}$

$$0 < y < 1$$

20.	$4y^2 - 4y + 1$	$(2y + 1)^2$

Column A	**Column B**

Questions 21–22 refer to the diagram below

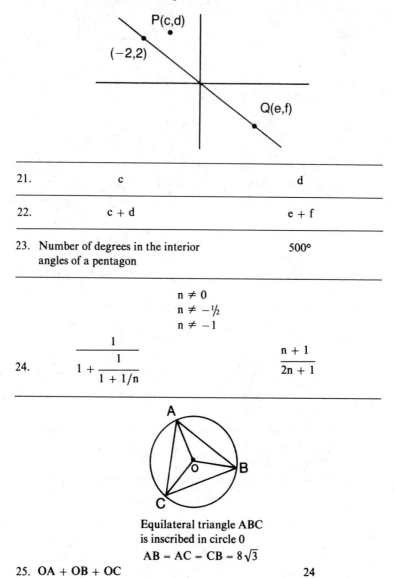

	Column A	**Column B**
21.	c	d
22.	c + d	e + f
23.	Number of degrees in the interior angles of a pentagon	500°

$$n \neq 0$$
$$n \neq -\tfrac{1}{2}$$
$$n \neq -1$$

24. $\dfrac{1}{1 + \dfrac{1}{1 + 1/n}}$ $\dfrac{n + 1}{2n + 1}$

Equilateral triangle ABC
is inscribed in circle 0
AB = AC = CB = $8\sqrt{3}$

25. OA + OB + OC   24

Solve each of the reamining problems in this section and blacken the corresponding space on the answer sheet.

26. The length of a rectangle is 3x and its perimeter is 10x + 8. What is the width of the rectangle?
    (A) 2x + 4   (D) 4x + 4
    (B) 2x + 8   (E) cannot be determined
    (C) 4x + 8

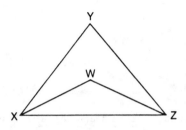

27. WX and WZ are angle bisectors of the base angles of isoscles △ XYZ. If ∠ Y = 80°, find the degree measure of ∠ XWZ.
    (A) 65   (D) 130
    (B) 80   (E) cannot be determined
    (C) 100

28. If $m^2 + n^2 = 12$ and $mn = 9$ then $(m + n)^2 =$
    (A) 12   (D) 42
    (B) 24   (E) cannot be determined
    (C) 30

29. If $n! = n \cdot (n - 1) \cdot (n - 2) \cdot (n - 3) \ldots 2 \cdot 1$, find the value of

$$\frac{(6!)(4!)}{(5!)(3!)}$$

    (A) 5/4   (D) 24
    (B) 8/5   (E) 1152
    (C) 10

30. One angle of a triangle is 68°. The other two angles are in the ratio of 3:4. Find the number of degrees in the smallest angle of the triangle.
    (A) 16   (B) 34   (C) 48   (D) 64   (E) 68

Columns

A	B	C	D	E
3	4	5	7	2
6	8	6	3	5
2	2	7	9	9
1	6	9	2	3
9	9	3	6	7

31. Which column in the chart above contains 3 primes and all the integral positive factors of 18, greater then 1 but less than 18?

    (A) A   (B) B   (C) C   (D) D   (E) E

32. If $\sqrt{\dfrac{81}{x}} = \dfrac{63}{35}$, then x =

    (A) 5   (B) 9   (C) 25   (D) 50   (E) 53

33. If a pipe can drain a tank in t hours, what part of the tank does it drain in 3 hours?

    (A) 3t   (B) $\dfrac{t}{3}$ (C) t + 3   (D) $\dfrac{3}{t}$ (E) t − 3

34. What is the area of a square in square inches if its perimeter is 10 feet?
    (A) 6.25   (B) 25   (C) 60   (D) 600   (E) 900

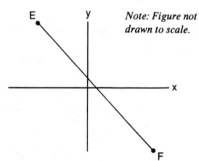

Note: Figure not drawn to scale.

35. If point E has coordinates (−3, 5) and point F has coordinates (6, −7), then length of EF =
    (A) 21   (B) 15   (C) 7   (D) 5   (E) 3

STOP. IF YOU FINISH BEFORE TIME IS CALLED, CHECK YOUR WORK ON THIS SECTION ONLY. DO NOT WORK ON ANY OTHER SECTION IN THE TEST.

SECTION III: TEST OF STANDARD WRITTEN ENGLISH

Time: 30 Minutes
50 Questions

In this section, choose the best answer for each question and blacken the corresponding space on the answer sheet.

Usage

DIRECTIONS

Some of the following sentences are correct. Others contain problems in grammar, usage, idiom, or diction (word choice). There is not more than one error in any sentence.

If there is an error, it will be underlined and lettered. Find the one underlined part that must be changed to make the sentence correct, and choose the corresponding letter on your answer sheet. Mark (E) if the sentence contains no error.

1. The box of <u>nuts and bolts</u> <u>were</u> too heavy for the little boy to
             A   B
   carry <u>by himself,</u> so he asked <u>his</u> mother for some help. <u>No error.</u>
        C   D   E

2. <u>Not</u> able to keep a secret, <u>he announced</u> the stupidity <u>of his friend</u>
    A   B   C
   to the <u>whole</u> class. <u>No error.</u>
         D   E

3. Because he <u>had not listened</u> to the <u>whether</u> forecast, Fred <u>found himself</u>
               A   B   C
   standing in a <u>downpour</u> without an umbrella. <u>No error.</u>
              D   E

4. <u>When</u> one wishes to be polite, <u>they</u> must <u>refrain</u> from eating food with
    A   B   C
   his hands <u>when a knife</u> and fork have been provided. <u>No error.</u>
             D   E

5. <u>Laying</u> on the back porch, the <u>old dog</u> snored loudly, bothering <u>those</u>
    A   B   C

<u>of us</u> who were trying to play checkers <u>nearby</u>. <u>No error.</u>
  C   D   E

6. <u>Today's</u> teenagers usually don't like any music <u>which</u> is played by
    A   B
the <u>Guy Lombardo Orchestra</u>, because the <u>orchestra's arrangements</u>
         C   D
make even new songs sound "old." <u>No error.</u>
                                  E

7. During the examination, <u>two of the three hours</u> will be <u>allotted</u>
                             A   B
for <u>writing;</u> the third hour <u>would be</u> for editing your work. <u>No error.</u>
   C   D   E

8. <u>Adam and Eve</u> walked <u>slow</u> out of paradise, <u>hanging their heads</u>
   A   B   C
in sorrow <u>and</u> wondering about the future. <u>No error.</u>
       D   E

9. <u>Working at a full-time job,</u> <u>helping to support a family,</u> and
         A   B
<u>a college education</u> added up to a <u>tremendous burden</u> for Tom,
     C   D
<u>No error.</u>
 E

10. Hoping <u>to reserve</u> a room at an inexpensive hotel, Bill <u>phoned</u>
         A   B
many <u>lodgings</u> before he concluded that cheap accommodations <u>were</u>
     C   D
<u>impossible</u> to find. <u>No error.</u>
   D   E

11. Speaking to <u>his</u> employees, <u>who he</u> believed to be <u>both trustworthy</u>
         A   B   C
and efficient, the manager praised <u>their</u> accomplishments highly.
                               D
<u>No error.</u>
 E

12. "<u>Who</u> cares whether poor people <u>can</u> take care <u>of theirselves</u> or <u>not?</u>"
    A   B   C   D
<u>asked</u> the rich old woman while munching her caviar dreamily.
 D
<u>No error.</u>
 E

13. Jogging around the track, the runner became sore and tired.
          A   B   C   D

No error.
E

14. Required subjects rarely interest high school students, who flock
          A   B   C

to electives which offer practical guidelines for living in this

completed world. No error.
      D   E

15. A recent Rutgers University study show that cancer is more prevalent
                     A   B   C

on the East Coast than on the West Coast. No error.
          D   E

16. Diving about the pool, the young swimmer displayed talents which
          A   B

should qualify him for competition in the 1984 Summer Olympics.
      C   D

No error.
E

17. Smelling sweetly, the bouquet of roses thrilled the young woman,
          A   B

whose love for flowers was well known. No error.
      C   D   E

18. To keep calm, to think clearly, and answering all the questions
                                   A

which are easy for him are three goals of any effective and well-
      B   C   D

informed test taker. No error.
                  E

19. The bowls of candy sitting atop the television was out of the
                 A   B   C

baby's reach, so she cried and cried. No error.
                D   E

20. If the chairman would have organized the program more intelligently,
    A   B   C

he could have included several more interesting presentations. No error.
      D   E

Sentence Correction

DIRECTIONS

Some part of each sentence below is underlined; sometimes the whole sentence is underlined. Five choices for rephrasing the underlined part follow each sentence; the first choice (A) repeats the original, and the other four are different. If choice (A) seems better than the alternatives, choose answer (A); if not, choose one of the others.

For each sentence, consider the requirements of Standard Written English. Your choice should be a correct and effective expression, not awkward or ambiguous. Focus on grammar, word choice, sentence construction, and punctuation. If a choice changes the meaning of the original sentence, do not select it.

21. A great controversy surrounds the Middle East situation, some people being pro-Arab as opposed to Israelis.
    (A) some people being pro-Arab as opposed to Israelis.
    (B) some pro-Arab and many pro-Israel.
    (C) with some people supporting the Arabs and opposed to the Israelis.
    (D) Arabs on one side and Israelis on the other.
    (E) Arabs versus Israelis.

22. My best friend, Julie, she has always been able to help me out of confusion or depression.
    (A) Julie, she has always been able to help me out of confusion or depression.
    (B) Julie, has always been able to help me out of confusion or depression.
    (C) Julie, has always been able to help me, confused or depressed.
    (D) Julie, out of confusion or depression, has always been able to help me.
    (E) Julie, she had always been willing to help me out of confusion or depression.

23. You can fool some of the people all of the time; as long as there are people, there will be fools.
    (A) as long as there are people, there will be fools.
    (B) as there are people, there will be fools.
    (C) because there are people, there will be fools.
    (D) as long as there are people, there are fools.
    (E) as long as there will be people, there will be fools.

24. <u>Last Thursday, it was decided by the citizens to</u> oppose any changes in the tax law.
    (A) Last Thursday, it was decided by the citizens to
    (B) Last Thursday, the citizens were to
    (C) Last Thursday, it was decided that the citizens
    (D) Thursday, it was decided by the citizens to
    (E) Last Thursday, the citizens decided to

25. <u>She was as pretty</u>, if not prettier than, any other girl at the party.
    (A) She was as pretty
    (B) She was more pretty than
    (C) She was as pretty as
    (D) She was prettier
    (E) She was a girl as pretty

26. Dickens's novels, <u>like many writers, are largely autobiographical.</u>
    (A) like many writers, are largely autobiographical.
    (B) like those of many novelists, are largely autobiographical.
    (C) like many novelists, are largely autobiographical.
    (D) like those of many writers, are largely autobiographical.
    (E) like so many others, are largely autobiographical.

27. It is futile to discuss this issue further, because <u>neither you nor I are going to agree upon anything today</u>.
    (A) neither you nor I are going to agree upon anything today.
    (B) neither you nor I am going to agree upon anything today.
    (C) neither you nor I is going to agree upon anything today.
    (D) neither of us are going to agree upon anything today.
    (E) neither you or I am going to agree upon anything today.

28. <u>If the room would have been brighter</u>, I would have been able to read for a while before bedtime.
    (A) If the room would have been brighter
    (B) If the room was brighter
    (C) If rooms are brighter
    (D) If the room could have been brighter
    (E) If the room had been brighter

29. Struggling with every word, <u>the essay was completed by John</u> at the expense of several hours sleep.
    (A) the essay was completed by John
    (B) John completed the essay
    (C) the essay John completed
    (D) the essay completed itself
    (E) the essay itself was completed

30. Because she worked the night shift, <u>arriving at 10 P.M. and leaving at 6 A.M.</u>
    - (A) arriving at 10 P.M. and leaving at 6 A.M.
    - (B) having arrived at 10 P.M. and leaving at 6 A.M.
    - (C) she arrived at 10 P.M. and left at 6 A.M.
    - (D) with an arrival at 6 and a departure at 10
    - (E) from 10 P.M. to 6 A.M.

31. <u>Fewer rainfall means less traffic accidents</u>, according to several experts on highway safety.
    - (A) Fewer rainfall means less traffic accidents
    - (B) Less rainfall means less traffic accidents
    - (C) Less rainfall means the least traffic accidents
    - (D) Less rainfall means fewer traffic accidents
    - (E) Fewer rainfalls means less traffic accidents

32. The President, in addition to a throng of advisors, <u>are puzzling over the breakneck speed at which the rate of inflation is raising.</u>
    - (A) are puzzling over the breakneck speed at which the rate of inflation is raising.
    - (B) are puzzling over the breakneck speed at which the rate of inflation is raising.
    - (C) is puzzling over the breakneck speed at which the rate of inflation is raising.
    - (D) is puzzling over the breakneck speed at which the rate of inflation is rising.
    - (E) all puzzle over the breakneck speed at which the rate of inflation is raising.

33. <u>Having won the state championship</u>, the brawny female wrestler began training for the national competition.
    - (A) Having won the state championship
    - (B) Intending to win the state championship
    - (C) To win the state championship
    - (D) As soon as she had won the state championship
    - (E) After the state championship

34. <u>The shouts of the onlookers who surrounded Jim and I</u> embarrassed us so much that we decided not to fight with each other.
    - (A) The shouts of the onlookers who surrounded Jim and I
    - (B) The shouts of the onlookers who surrounded Jim and me
    - (C) The onlookers shouting at Jim and I
    - (D) The onlookers shouting at Jim and me
    - (E) The shouting of onlookers surrounding Jim and I

35. I needed to and would have purchased a new suit if I had found one that
was not months out of style.
    (A) I needed to and would have purchased
    (B) I needed a new suit and would have bought it
    (C) I needed to purchase and would have purchased
    (D) I needed purchasing and would have purchased
    (E) I would have purchased what I needed

36. The new recruits are liable from making tactical errors, but we do hope
that their mistakes will disappear after a few weeks.
    (A) are liable from making tactical errors
    (B) are liable from making tactical mistakes
    (C) are liable to make tactical errors
    (D) are liable to make tactical mistakes
    (E) are liable about making tactical errors

37. After laying down all morning, Mary still felt queasy, so she made an
appointment to see the doctor.
    (A) After laying down all morning
    (B) After resting all morning
    (C) After being laid down all morning
    (D) After having lain down all morning
    (E) After lying down all morning

38. Hoping for a contract renewal, the young actor walked into the boss's
office self-confidently.
    (A) Hoping for a contract renewal
    (B) Hoping to have his contract renewed
    (C) Hoping that the boss would renew his contract
    (D) Hopefully
    (E) Hoping for the best

39. Running down the street, her face tingled in the cold morning air.
    (A) her face tingled in the cold morning air.
    (B) she felt her face tingle in the cold morning air.
    (C) she tingled in the cold morning air.
    (D) tingling in the cold morning air.
    (E) she also tingled from the cold.

40. Obviously effected by his new position, the once friendly man became
cold, distant, and greedy.
    (A) Obviously effected by his position
    (B) Effected by his position
    (C) Obvious and affected by his position
    (D) Obviously affected by his position
    (E) His new position effecting him

Usage

DIRECTIONS

Some of the following sentences are correct. Others contain problems in grammar, usage, idiom, or diction (word choice). There is not more than one error in any sentence.

If there is an error, it will be underlined and lettered. Find the one underlined part that must be changed to make the sentence correct, and choose the corresponding letter on your answer sheet. Mark (E) if the sentence contains no error.

41. <u>Him and I</u> will take full responsibility for <u>each other</u> on the camping
        A   B
    trip, <u>using</u> the <u>"buddy system"</u> to insure each other's safety. <u>No error.</u>
          C   D   E

42. The only <u>people</u> in the movie <u>theater</u> on that stormy Monday night
              A   B
    <u>were</u> the usher and <u>me.</u> <u>No error.</u>
      C   D   E

43. After <u>finding</u> the problem, the <u>mechanic</u> cleaned the carburetor
          A   B
    <u>thoroughly,</u> hoping that a clean carburetor would <u>eliminate</u> the
        C   D
    the automobile's stalling problems. <u>No error.</u>
                                  E

44. <u>Us</u> citizens need to speak out on national <u>as well as</u> local issues,
     A   B
    because a strong, efficient federal government <u>will have</u> its effect
                                           C
    <u>on the quality</u> of our city. <u>No error.</u>
        D   E

45. <u>Because of the traffic on the highway,</u> speeds <u>have decreased</u>
          A   B
    to such an extent that <u>they</u> must endure <u>bumper-to-bumper</u> congestion.
                       C   D
    <u>No error.</u>
      E

46. He wore <u>a wig</u> that was <u>far more</u> attractive <u>than</u> the <u>other men</u>
            A   B   C   D
    who had their own hair. <u>No error.</u>
                     E

47. The <u>anger of</u> the opposing candidates <u>was obvious,</u> but <u>neither</u> <u>of</u>
          A   B   C   D
them insulted the other. <u>No error.</u>
  D   E

48. If the dog <u>had lain</u> there without snarling, the visitor <u>wouldn't</u>
                  A   B
have been tempted <u>to provoke</u> him into biting. <u>No error.</u>
  C   D   E

49. If <u>one reads</u> the newspaper carefully everyday, you <u>will be surprised</u>
          A   B
at the <u>improvement</u> in your <u>overall</u> reading skills. <u>No error.</u>
          C   D   E

50. An <u>in-depth analysis</u> of a person's dreams, when <u>done systematically,</u>
          A   B
can <u>frequently</u> indicate <u>their</u> fears, loves, and desires. <u>No error.</u>
      C   D   E

STOP. IF YOU FINISH BEFORE TIME IS CALLED, CHECK YOUR
WORK ON THIS SECTION ONLY. DO NOT WORK ON ANY
OTHER SECTION IN THE TEST.

SECTION IV: VERBAL ABILITY

Time: 30 Minutes
40 Questions

In this section, choose the best answer for each question and blacken the corresponding space on the answer sheet.

Antonyms

DIRECTIONS

Each word in CAPITAL LETTERS is followed by five words or phrases. The correct choice is the word or phrase whose meaning is most nearly *opposite* to the meaning of the word in capitals. You may be required to distinguish fine shades of meaning. Look at all choices before marking your answer.

1. NEMESIS
   (A) colleague
   (B) player
   (C) denominator
   (D) savior
   (E) nominee

2. FUSE
   (A) diffuse
   (B) separate
   (C) suffuse
   (D) segregate
   (E) relegate

3. VERTICAL
   (A) diagonal
   (B) horizontal
   (C) flat
   (D) verticillate
   (E) divergent

4. FIDELITY
   (A) faithlessness
   (B) distemper
   (C) deceitfulness
   (D) truthlessness
   (E) divorce

5. COLLOQUIAL
   (A) slang
   (B) formal
   (C) slack
   (D) jive
   (E) hip

6. IMPELLED
    (A) unaware
    (B) compelled
    (C) reluctant
    (D) recalcitrant
    (E) modest

7. EXTROVERT
    (A) pervert
    (B) introvert
    (C) adversary
    (D) reactionary
    (E) subversive

8. TRACTABLE
    (A) retractable
    (B) refractory
    (C) refreshing
    (D) retrainable
    (E) retrenched

9. PLETHORA
    (A) supply
    (B) alliance
    (C) enigma
    (D) modicum
    (E) shortage

10. DIPSOMANIAC
    (A) pyromaniac
    (B) bibliomaniac
    (C) teetotaler
    (D) violator
    (E) excavator

Sentence Completion

DIRECTIONS

Each blank in the following sentences indicates that something has been omitted. Consider the lettered words beneath the sentence and choose the word or set of words that best fits the whole sentence.

11. Because eating habits have been linked to various diseases, the government has developed a guideline for proper _____ .
    (A) exercise
    (B) nutrition
    (C) hypoglycemia
    (D) therapy
    (E) health

12. One of the eagerly awaited promises of the new lifestyle was the _____ of false _____ for judging human behavior.
    (A) creation . . . requirements
    (B) articulation . . . services
    (C) abolition . . . criteria
    (D) establishment . . . measures
    (E) proliferation . . . inducements

13. This treatise is concerned only with the processes unique to the period in question; therefore, no attempt has been made to _____ phenomena _____ to that era.
    (A) include . . . unrelated
    (B) omit . . . irrelevant
    (C) re-create . . . fictional
    (D) substantiate . . . essential
    (E) evaluate . . . pertinent

14. In order to _____ their opposition, the _____ of the state legislature passed a law limiting the money a first-time candidate could spend on the election but set no limits on their own expenditures.
    (A) denigrate . . . members
    (B) vilify . . . office-holders
    (C) undermine . . . incumbents
    (D) incapacitate . . . candidates
    (E) languish . . . legislators

15. Eager to improve anyone and everyone, Mr. Martin delivered a _____ on the evils of drink to men sitting nearby.
    (A) soliloquy   (D) homily
    (B) commendation   (E) paean
    (C) declamation

Analogies

DIRECTIONS

In each question below, you are given a related pair of words or phrases. Select the lettered pair that *best* expresses a relationship similar to that in the original pair of words.

16. PATTERN : DRESSMAKER ::
    (A) rule : carpenter   (D) canvas : sailmaker
    (B) recipe : chef   (E) novel : novelist
    (C) composer : musician

17. CLOTHES : LUGGAGE ::
    (A) baggage car : train   (D) airmail : postman
    (B) package : post office   (E) plant : flowerpot
    (C) documents : briefcase

18. DECADE : CENTURY ::
    (A) month : year   (D) gram : kilogram
    (B) dime : dollar   (E) minute : hour
    (C) yard : mile

19. JURY : VERDICT ::
    (A) team : game
    (B) lawyer : trial
    (C) doctor : cure
    (D) dogcatcher : muzzle
    (E) diners : table

20. SMOCK : ARTIST ::
    (A) hoe : gardener
    (B) badge : policeman
    (C) shoulder pads : football
        player
    (D) eyeglasses : reader
    (E) detergent : washing machine

21. SUPINE : PRONE ::
    (A) lying : reclining
    (B) dark : light
    (C) straight : narrow
    (D) open : overt
    (E) pensive : thoughtful

22. TUBER : PLANT ::
    (A) leaf : tree
    (B) foundation : building
    (C) fang : tiger
    (D) hope : expectation
    (E) lime : citrus

23. ABBOT : MONASTERY ::
    (A) nun : convent
    (B) conductor : orchestra
    (C) priest : diocese
    (D) author : book
    (E) runner : marathon

24. ACCRETE : DIMINISH ::
    (A) wax : wane
    (B) divide : subtract
    (C) decline : erode
    (D) augment : increase
    (E) tremble : waver

25. PROVINCE : CANTON ::
    (A) state : county
    (B) shire : country
    (C) city : capitol
    (D) segment : section
    (E) senate : senator

Reading Comprehension

DIRECTIONS

Questions follow each of the passages below. Using only the stated or implied information in each passage, answer the questions.

Questions 26 through 29 are based on the following passage.

Certain writers in the past have tended to regard everything in eighteenth-century opera before Gluck as being somewhat in the nature

of a necessary but regrettable episode, declining about the middle of the
century to a hopelessly low state of affairs, which Gluck, practically
(5) single-handed, redeemed through his so-called reforms—the very word
carrying with it an aura of moral uplift, implying that something bad
was replaced by something better. This point of view—a relic of the
evolutionary philosophy of history—has had the consequence of leading
to the neglect of early and middle eighteenth-century Italian opera
(10) composers, a failure to appreciate their real merits and the quality of
their music in relation to its period and the circumstances for which it
was composed. The situation has been aggravated by the fact that
Italian scholars have so far not made much of the music of their own
composers available in modern editions. The German musicologists have
(15) concerned themselves chiefly with either composers of German birth or
composers who were active in Germany, and even here they have been
more attentive to those aspects of the music which appeal to Germans
than to the fundamentally vocal and melodic traits characteristic of
Italy. The result is that the importance of Gluck, great as it unquestion-
(20) ably is, has been exaggerated by an inadequate idea both of the real
nature of the situation against which he was striving and of the
contributions of other composers who to some extent anticipated his
doctrines.

26. Which of the following best states the main point of the passage?
    (A) The study of music should not be influenced by nationalistic
        concerns.
    (B) The originality and importance of Gluck's music has been underes-
        timated.
    (C) The originality and importance of Italian eighteenth-century music
        has been underestimated.
    (D) Gluck should be assessed with a full knowledge of his predecessors
        and contemporaries.
    (E) To understand music, we must first understand the period and
        circumstances in which it was composed.

27. The phrase "the evolutionary philosophy of history" in line 8 refers to the
    idea that
    (A) things are always changing
    (B) things get better and better
    (C) the fittest survives in time
    (D) history is cyclical
    (E) moral improvement is steady

28. According to the passage, the Italian music of the early and middle eighteenth century
    (A) is not readily accessible in modern editions
    (B) is orchestral rather than vocal
    (C) is superior to the music of eighteenth-century German composers
    (D) had little or no influence on the music of Gluck
    (E) has been carefully studied by Italian musicologists

29. Which of the following facts about Gluck can we infer from the passage?

    I. Gluck was an opera composer of the middle eighteenth century.
    II. Gluck was an Italian.
    III. Gluck's importance in musical history is uncertain.

    (A) I only   (D) I and II
    (B) II only   (E) I and III
    (C) III only

Questions 30 through 33 are based on the following passage.

John Patric, a right-wing, anti-labor writer, wrote glowing articles for the *National Geographic* on two of Hitler's earliest targets, Hungary and Czechoslovakia, and for nearly ten years before the outbreak of World War II, it appears that the *National Geographic* couldn't get enough of Fascist Italy. While most of these articles carefully avoided outright political commentary, the articles no doubt fostered tourist travel by portraying Mussolini's Italy as a nation reborn. And in this glorification came, to at least some degree, acceptance.

In March 1940, John Patric—whose articles had so much praise for Mussolini's Rome three years earlier—and the *National Geographic* were back in Italy, again gushing about the public-works projects of Mussolini in "Italy, from Roman Ruins to Radio." By the time this article ran, Hitler and Mussolini had announced their formal alliance, the "Pact of Steel," almost nine months earlier; Hitler had annexed Czechoslovakia and defeated and annexed Poland; Britain, South Africa, and Canada had declared war on Germany while the United States and Italy were officially neutral. Finland had been defeated by the Soviets; and work had begun on the Auschwitz death camp.

Scarcely more than three years later, Allied military men would be fighting and dying throughout Mussolini's scenic, historic, and hospitable land, and utilizing the many public works of Sicily and Italy in their own way.

30. The primary focus of the passage is on
    (A) the quality of the articles appearing in *National Geographic*
    (B) the anti-Fascist stance of *National Geographic* articles
    (C) the *National Geographic's* support of a Fascist country
    (D) the development of travel writing
    (E) Europe on the eve of World War II

31. On which of the following topics would John Patric have been most likely
    to write sympathetically?
    (A) the British Labor Party   (D) Republican Spain
    (B) the Soviet Union   (E) Fascist Spain
    (C) the defeat of Finland

32. According to the passage, by 1940 Italy
    (A) was no longer praised by the *National Geographic*
    (B) was an ally of Hitler's Germany
    (C) was an ally of the United States
    (D) had attacked Poland and Czechoslovakia
    (E) had declared war on Great Britain

33. In the last paragraph the author refers to American soldiers using the
    "public works" of Italy in order to
    (A) demonstrate the lasting achievements of Mussolini
    (B) underplay the horror of war
    (C) mock the views of the *National Geographic*
    (D) avoid offending readers sympathetic to Italy
    (E) demonstrate how quickly attitudes can change

Questions 34 through 37 are based on the following passage.

Vanity was the beginning and end of Sir Walter Elliot's character:
vanity of person and of situation. He had been remarkably handsome in
his youth, and at fifty-four was still a very fine man. Few women could
think more of their personal appearance than he did, nor could the valet
of any new-made lord be more delighted with the place he held in
society. He considered the blessing of beauty as inferior only to the
blessing of a baronetcy; and the Sir Walter Elliot, who united these gifts,
was the constant object of his warmest respect and devotion.

His good looks and his rank had one fair claim on his attachment,
since to them he must have owed a wife of very superior character to
anything deserved by his own. Lady Elliot had been an excellent woman,
sensible and amiable, whose judgment and conduct, if they might be
pardoned the youthful infatuation which made her Lady Elliot, had
never required indulgence afterwards. She had humoured, or softened,
or concealed his failings, and promoted his real respectability for

seventeen years; and though not the very happiest being in the world herself, had found enough in her duties, her friends, and her children, to attach her to life, and make it no matter of indifference to her when she was called on the quit them. Three girls, the two eldest sixteen and fourteen, was an awful legacy for a mother to bequeath, an awful charge rather, to confide to the authority and guidance of a conceited, silly father. She had, however, one very intimate friend, a sensible, serving woman, who had been brought, by strong attachment to herself, to settle close by her, in the village of Kellynch; and on her kindness and advice Lady Elliot mainly relied for the best help and maintenance of the good principles and instruction which she had been anxiously giving her daughters.

This friend and Sir Walter did *not* marry, whatever might have been anticipated on that head by their acquaintance. Thirteen years had passed away since Lady Elliot's death, and they were still near neighbours and intimate friends, and one remained a widower, the other a widow.

That Lady Russell, of steady age and character, and extremely well provided for, should have no thought of a second marriage, needs no apology to the public, which is rather apt to be unreasonably discontented when a woman *does* marry again, than when she does *not;* but Sir Walter's continuing in singleness requires explanation. Be it known, then, that Sir Walter, like a good father (having met with one or two private disappointments in very unreasonable applications), prided himself on remaining single for his dear daughter's sake. For one daughter, his eldest, he would really have given up anything, which he had not been very much tempted to do. Elizabeth had succeeded at sixteen to all that was possible of her mother's rights and consequence; and being very handsome, and very like himself, her influence had always been great, and they had gone on together most happily. His two other children were of very inferior value. Mary had acquired a little artificial importance by becoming Mrs. Charles Musgrove; but Anne, with an elegance of mind and sweetness of character, which must have placed her high with any people of real understanding, was nobody with either father or sister; her word had not weight, her convenience was always to give way—she was only Anne.

34. The passage is primarily concerned with
   (A) how Sir Walter Elliot learned to accept the responsibilities of parenthood
   (B) the family and friends of Sir Walter Elliot
   (C) the vices of the English aristocracy
   (D) the limitations of Sir Walter Elliot
   (E) the importance of marriage in eighteenth-century England

35. The two characters mentioned in the passage of whom the author seems most to disapprove are
    (A) Sir Walter Elliot and Anne Elliot
    (B) Sir Walter Elliot and Elizabeth Elliot
    (C) Sir Walter Elliot and Lady Russell
    (D) Sir Walter and Lady Elliot
    (E) Mary Elliot Musgrove and Anne Elliot

36. The style and content of the passage indicate that it is most likely an excerpt from a(n)
    (A) novel
    (B) social history
    (C) psychological study
    (D) essay
    (E) political history

37. With which of the following proverbs would Sir Walter Elliot be most likely to agree?
    (A) Handsome is as handsome does.
    (B) Variety is the spice of life.
    (C) Beauty is only skin deep.
    (D) *Noblesse oblige.*
    (E) Blood will tell.

Questions 38 through 40 are based on the following passage.

There are a number of ideas about the origin of comets that place the site in the realm of the giant planets and the time of the recent past, astronomically speaking. One idea is that comets are ejected from super-volcanoes on the outer planets. This is certainly consistent with the composition of comets; the major planets and many of their satellites do have icy interiors. However the tremendous gravitational field of the major planets would require the comets to be accelerated to great speeds before they could escape.

In the 1960s Russian astronomers suggested that volcanic activity in the satellites of the major planets could be responsible for comet formation. The *Voyager* spacecraft found volcanic activity on Jupiter's moon Io. The volcanoes on Io have a very high sulphur content. Until recently, this was taken as a good argument against the hypothesis, since comets have not shown any sulphur concentration. However, recent spectroscopic observations of comets have revealed the weak presence of diatonic sulphur. But there is growing evidence that Io has virtually no ice. No signs of volcanic activity occur on the other satellites observed by *Voyager.*

Another possible site for comet formation could be the rings of Saturn. A possible ejection mechanism could be a close encounter between chunks of ice in the rings. From a dynamical point of view, this is possible; however, the encounter would have to be so close that the bodies would probably merely collide, and a close quantitative analysis of any of these ejection ideas makes them seem highly unlikely.

38. The best title for the passage would be
    (A) The Origin of Comets
    (B) The Volcanic Origin of Comets
    (C) The Origin of Comets and the Rings of Saturn
    (D) The Origin of Comets: An Unanswered Question
    (E) The Satellite Origin of Comets

39. From the passage, we can infer that a plausible site of comet origin would have to offer
    (A) large deposits of sulphur
    (B) volcanoes and ice
    (C) high gravitational fields
    (D) low gravitational fields
    (E) hydrogen and oxygen

40. The satellites of major planets are more likely sites of origin for comets than the rings of Saturn because of their
    (A) higher gravitational fields
    (B) rich sources of sulphur
    (C) high oxygen supply
    (D) icy interiors
    (E) volcanic activity

STOP. IF YOU FINISH BEFORE TIME IS CALLED, CHECK YOUR WORK ON THIS SECTION ONLY. DO NOT WORK ON ANY OTHER SECTION IN THE TEST.

SECTION V: MATHEMATICAL ABILITY

Time: 30 Minutes
25 Questions

DIRECTIONS

Solve each problem in this section by using the information given and your own mathematical calculations. Then select the *one* correct answer of the five choices given. Use the available space on the page for scratchwork.

Data That May Be Used as Reference for This Section

The area formula for a circle of radius r is: $A = \pi r^2$
The circumference formula is: $C = 2\pi r$
A circle is composed of 360°.
A straight angle measures 180°.

Triangle: The sum of the angles of a triangle is 180°.
If angle ADB is a right angle, then

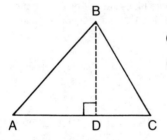

(1) The area of triangle ABC is $\dfrac{AC \times BD}{2}$

(2) $AD^2 + BD^2 = AB^2$

Symbol References:
= is equal to	≥ is greater than or equal to
≠ not equal to	≤ is less than or equal to
> is greater than	‖ is parallel to
< is less than	⊥ is perpendicular to

NOTE: Some problems may be accompanied by figures or diagrams. These figures are drawn as accurately as possible, EXCEPT when it is stated in a specific problem that the figure is not drawn to scale. The figures are meant to provide information useful in solving the problem or problems but are not meant to be measured.

All numbers used are real numbers.

1. If $3m + n = 7$, then $9m + 3n =$
   (A) $\frac{7}{9}$ (B) $\frac{7}{3}$ (C) 10   (D) 21   (E) 63

2. If $\frac{1}{5}$ of a number is 2, what is $\frac{1}{2}$ of the number?
   (A) 10   (B) 5   (C) 2   (D) 1
   (E) cannot be determined

3. If a book costs $5.70 after a 40% discount, what was its original price?
   (A) $2.28   (B) $6.10   (C) $7.98   (D) $9.12
   (E) $9.50

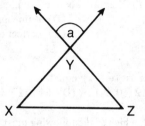

4. In △XYZ, XY = 10, YZ = 10, and ∠a = 84°. Find the degree measure of ∠Z.
   (A) 96°   (B) 84°   (C) 48°   (D) 42°
   (E) cannot be determined

5. $\dfrac{2/3 - 1/2}{1/6 + 1/4 + 2/3} =$
   (A) $\frac{2}{13}$ (B) $\frac{2}{9}$ (C) $\frac{13}{20}$ (D) $1\frac{1}{13}$ (E) $3\frac{1}{4}$

6. What is the ratio of $\frac{3}{10}$ to $\frac{5}{8}$?
   (A) $\frac{3}{16}$ (B) $\frac{12}{25}$ (C) $\frac{37}{40}$ (D) $\frac{25}{12}$ (E) $\frac{16}{3}$

7. If D is between A and B on $\overleftrightarrow{AB}$, which of the following must be true?
   (A) AD = DB   (B) DB = AB − AD   (C) AD = AB + DB
   (D) DB = AD + AB   (E) AB = AD = BD

8. What would be the closest approximation to $\sqrt{83}$?
   (A) 8.3   (B) 8.9   (C) 9.1   (D) 9.7   (E) 41.5

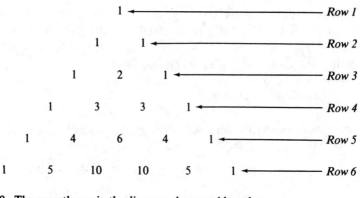

9. The seventh row in the diagram above could not have any
   (A) even numbers   (D) prime numbers
   (B) odd numbers   (E) perfect cube numbers
   (C) perfect numbers

10. If $x - 4 = y$, what must $(y - x)^3$ equal?
    (A) -64 (B) -12 (C) 12   (D) 64   (E) cannot be determined

11. If $a > b$, and $ab > 0$, which of the following must be true?

    I. $a > 0$
    II. $b > 0$
    III. $\dfrac{a}{b} > 0$

    (A) I only   (B) II only   (C) III only   (D) I and II
    (E) none must be true.

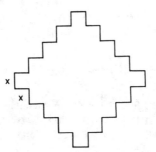

12. In the figure, all line segments meet at right angles and each segment
    has a length of x. What is the area of the figure in terms of x?
    (A) $25x$ (B) $36x$ (C) $36x^2$ (D) $41x^2$ (E) $41x^3$

13. In a class of 40 students there are 24 girls. What percent of the class are boys?

    (A) 16   (B) 24   (C) 40   (D) 50   (E) 60

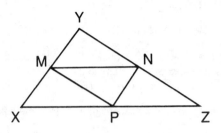

14. In △ XYZ, points M, N, and P are midpoints. If XY = 10, YZ = 15 and XZ = 17, what is the perimeter of △ MNP?

    (A) 10⅔   (B) 14   (C) 16   (D) 21   (E) cannot be determined

15. The average of 9 numbers is 7 and the average of 7 other numbers is 9. What is the average of all 16 numbers?

    (A) 8   (B) 7⅞   (C) 7½   (D) 7¼
    (E) cannot be determined

16. If a and b are integers, which of the following conditions is sufficient

$$\text{for } \frac{a^2 - b^2}{a - b} = a + b \text{ to be true?}$$

    (A) $a > 0$ (B) $a < 0$ (C) $a > b$ (D) $b > 0$ (E) $b < 0$

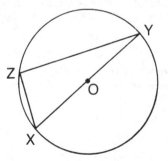

17. In circle O, XY is a diameter, OX = 8.5, and YZ = 15. What is the area of △ XYZ in square units?

    (A) 40   (B) 60   (C) 120   (D) 127.5   (E) cannot be determined

18. If x, y, and z are consecutive positive integers greater than 1, not necessarily in that order, then which of the following is (are) true?

I. $x > z$ III. $yz > xz$
II. $x + y > z$ IV. $xy > y + z$

(A) I   (B) II   (C) II and III   (D) III and IV   (E) II and IV

19. If the length and width of a rectangle are increased by x units, its perimeter is increased by how many units?
(A) 4x   (B) 2x   (C) x^2 (D) x   (E) cannot be determined

20. Mary will be y years old x years from now. How old will she be z years from now?
(A) $y - x + z$ (B) $y + x + z$ (C) $y + x - z$
(D) $y - x - z$ (E) $x + z - y$

21. A speed of 75 miles per hour is approximately equivalent to how many feet per second?
(A) 22   (B) 100   (C) 110   (D) 120   (E) 440

22. The area of a square is 72 square feet. What is the length of a diagonal of the square?
(A) 36 feet   (B) $18\sqrt{2}$ feet   (C) 12 feet   (D) $6\sqrt{2}$ feet
(E) cannot be determined

23. A girl runs k miles in n hours. How many miles will she run in x hours at the same rate?

(A) knx   (B) $\dfrac{k}{n}$ (C) $\dfrac{kx}{n}$ (D) kx   (E) $\dfrac{kn}{x}$

24. If the diameter of circle R is 30% of the diameter of circle S, the area of circle R is what percent of the area of circle S?
(A) 9%   (B) 15%   (C) 30%   (D) 60%
(E) cannot be determined

25 If the average of two numbers is y and one of the numbers is equal to z, then the other number is equal to

(A) $2z - y$ (B) $\dfrac{y + z}{2}$ (C) $z - y$ (D) $2y - z$

(E) cannot be determined

STOP. IF YOU FINISH BEFORE TIME IS CALLED, CHECK YOUR WORK ON THIS SECTION ONLY. DO NOT WORK ON ANY OTHER SECTION IN THE TEST.

SECTION VI: MATHEMATICAL ABILITY

Time: 30 Minutes
35 Questions

DIRECTIONS

Solve each problem in this section by using the information given and your own mathematical calculations. Then select the *one* correct answer of the five choices given. Use the available space on the page for scratchwork.

Data That May Be Used as Reference for This Section

The area formula for a circle of radius r is: $A = \pi r^2$
The circumference formula is: $C = 2\pi r$
A circle is composed of 360°.
A straight angle measures 180°.

Triangle: The sum of the angles of a triangle is 180°.
If angle ADB is a right angle, then

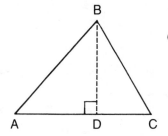

(1) The area of triangle ABC is $\dfrac{AC \times BD}{2}$

(2) $AD^2 + BD^2 = AB^2$

Symbol References:
$=$ is equal to	$\geq$ is greater than or equal to
$\neq$ not equal to	$\leq$ is less than or equal to
$>$ is greater than	$\parallel$ is parallel to
$<$ is less than	$\perp$ is perpendicular to

NOTE: Some problems may be accompanied by figures or diagrams. These figures are drawn as accurately as possible, EXCEPT when it is stated in a specific problem that the figure is not drawn to scale. The figures are meant to provide information useful in solving the problem or problems but are not meant to be measured.

Unless otherwise stated or indicated, all figures lie in a plane.

All numbers used are real numbers.

1. If $2x - 5 = 9$, then $3x + 2 =$
   (A) 44   (B) 23   (C) 16   (D) 14   (E) 7

2. What percent of $\frac{2}{3}$ is $\frac{1}{2}$?
   (A) 300%   (B) 133⅓%   (C) 75%   (D) 50%   (E) 33⅓%

3. If $x = 3$, $y = 4$, and $z = -1$, find the value of $2x + 3y^2 - z$.
   (A) 151   (B) 149   (C) 55   (D) 53   (E) 19

4. If a store purchases several items for $1.80 per dozen and sells them at 3 for $.85, what is their profit on 6 dozen of these items.?
   (A) $4.20   (B) $5.70   (C) $9.60   (D) $10.60
   (E) $20.40

5. A square 4 inches on a side is cut up into smaller squares 1 inch on a side. What is the maximum number of such squares that can be formed?
   (A) 4   (B) 8   (C) 16   (D) 36   (E) 64

6. Which of the following fractions is the largest?
   (A) $\frac{25}{52}$ (B) $\frac{31}{60}$ (C) $\frac{19}{40}$ (D) $\frac{51}{103}$ (E) $\frac{43}{90}$

7. If a number is divisible by 7 but is not divisible by 21 then the number cannot be divisible by
   (A) 2   (B) 3   (C) 5   (D) 8   (E) 10

Quantitative Comparison

DIRECTIONS

In this section you will be given two quantities, one in column A and one in column B. You are to determine a relationship between the two quantities and mark—
   (A) if the quantity in column A is greater than the quantity in column B.
   (B) if the quantity in column B is greater than the quantity in column A.
   (C) if the quantities are equal.
   (D) if the comparison cannot be determined from the information that is given.

Column A	Column B
8. 35% of 50	50% of 35

	Column A		Column B

$$x^2 = 36$$

9.	6		x
10.	$3\sqrt{2}$		$\sqrt{17}$

Questions 11–14 refer to the diagram.

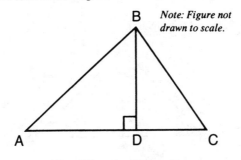

Note: Figure not drawn to scale.

$$AD = BD = 6, \angle ADB = 90°$$

11.	AB	BC
12.	$\angle$BAD	$\angle$ABD
13.	$\angle$DBC + $\angle$BCD	90°
14.	AB + BC	AC
15.	$(2.3)^{10}$	$(.23)^{100}$

$$a = b$$
$$a < c$$

16.	2a	b + c
17.	$\frac{1}{3} \times \frac{2}{5} \times \frac{1}{8}$	$.33 \times .4 \times .125$

$$a > b > c$$

18.	a – b – c	a + b – c

	Column A	Column B

19. Volume of cube with side 6   Volume of rectangular prism with two dimensions less than 6

$$5x + y = 2$$
$$x + 3y = 6$$

20.   x   y

Questions 21–22 refer to the diagram.

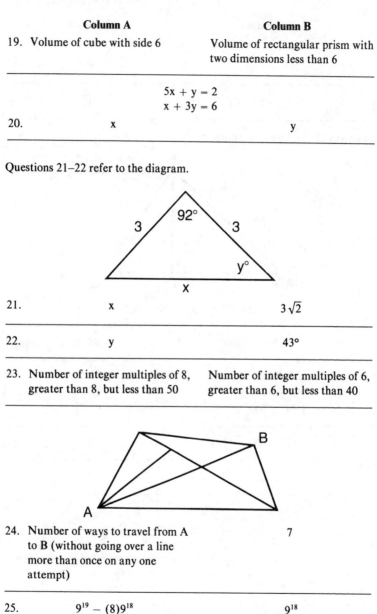

21.   x $3\sqrt{2}$

22.   y   43°

23. Number of integer multiples of 8, greater than 8, but less than 50   Number of integer multiples of 6, greater than 6, but less than 40

24. Number of ways to travel from A to B (without going over a line more than once on any one attempt)   7

25. $9^{19} - (8)9^{18}$ 9^{18}

Solve each of the remaining problems in this section and blacken the corresponding space on the answer sheet.

26. The length of a rectangle is $6l$ and the width is $4w$. What is its perimeter?
    (A) $24lw$ (B) $20lw$ (C) $10lw$ (D) $12l + 8w$
    (E) $6l + 4w$

27. How many times will the digit 6 appear between 1 and 100?
    (A) 10   (B) 11   (C) 18   (D) 19   (E) 20

28. If $x(y - z) = t$, then $y =$
    (A) $\dfrac{t}{x} + z$ (B) $\dfrac{tz}{x}$ (C) $t + x - z$ (D) $\dfrac{t + z}{x}$
    (E) $t - x + z$

29. The angles of a quadrilateral are in the ratio of $2 : 3 : 4 : 6$. Find the degree measure of its largest angle.
    (A) 72   (B) 120   (C) 144   (D) 150
    (E) cannot be determined

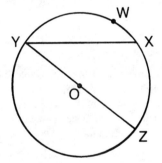

30. On the circle with center O, arc YWX equals 100°. Find the degree measure of ∠XYZ.
    (A) 130   (B) 100   (C) 80   (D) 50   (E) 40

31. How many 1-gallon containers of water would be needed to fill 200 pint bottles?
    (A) 20   (B) 25   (C) 33⅓   (D) 50   (E) 100

32. If $\dfrac{x^2 - 5x + 7}{x^2 - 4x + 10} = 1$, then $x =$
    (A) -3 (B) ⅓   (C) ⁷⁄₁₀   (D) ¹⁷⁄₉
    (E) cannot be determined

33. Simplify $\sqrt{125} - \sqrt{45} - \sqrt{20}$.
    (A) $6\sqrt{5}$ (B) 10   (C) $2\sqrt{15}$ (D) $4\sqrt{5}$ (E) 0

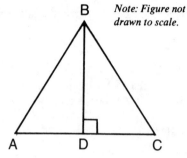

Note: Figure not drawn to scale.

34. In the figure, BD ⊥ AC, AB = 34, BD = 30, and BC = 34. Find AC.
    (A) 8   (B) 18   (C) 30   (D) 32   (E) 34

Figure 1   Figure 2   Figure 3

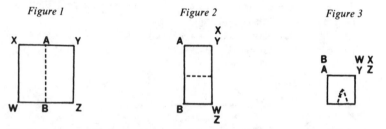

35. In figure 1 above, a square piece of paper is folded along dotted line AB
    so that X is on top of Y and W is on top of Z (figure 2). The paper is then
    folded again so that B is on top of A, and WZ is on top of XY (figure 3).
    A small triangle is cut out of the folded paper as shown in figure 3. If the
    paper is unfolded, which of the following could be the result?

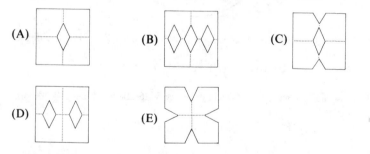

STOP. IF YOU FINISH BEFORE TIME IS CALLED, CHECK YOUR
WORK ON THIS SECTION ONLY. DO NOT WORK ON ANY
OTHER SECTION IN THE TEST.

ANSWER KEY FOR PRACTICE TEST NO. 1

Mathematics sections II, V, and VI in this Answer Key are coded so that you can quickly determine the math area on which you may need to concentrate your study time. AR = arithmetic, AL = algebra, and G = geometry.

Section I		Section II	Section III	
1. B	41. C	1. A (AR)	1. B	41. A
2. D	42. D	2. A (AL)	2. E	42. D
3. A	43. A	3. C (AR)	3. B	43. E
4. D	44. E	4. C (AL)	4. B	44. A
5. E	45. A	5. D (G)	5. A	45. C
6. A		6. E (AR)	6. E	46. D
7. B		7. C (G)	7. D	47. E
8. D		8. A (AR)	8. B	48. E
9. A		9. C (G)	9. C	49. A
10. B		10. D (AL)	10. E	50. D
11. C		11. A (AR)	11. B	
12. E		12. C (AL)	12. C	
13. A		13. A (G)	13. E	
14. A		14. D (AL)	14. D	
15. B		15. B (AR)	15. B	
16. D		16. C (AL)	16. A	
17. C		17. B (AR)	17. A	
18. D		18. A (AR)	18. A	
19. E		19. B (AL)	19. C	
20. E		20. B (AL)	20. B	
21. C		21. B (G)	21. C	
22. B		22. A (G)	22. B	
23. C		23. A (G)	23. A	
24. D		24. C (AL)	24. E	
25. E		25. C (G)	25. C	
26. A		26. A (G)	26. D	
27. C		27. D (G)	27. B	
28. B		28. C (AL)	28. E	
29. E		29. D (AL)	29. B	
30. B		30. C (G)	30. C	
31. A		31. D (AR)	31. D	
32. B		32. C (AL)	32. D	
33. E		33. D (AL)	33. A	
34. C		34. E (G)	34. B	
35. A		35. B (G)	35. C	
36. B			36. C	
37. E			37. E	
38. C			38. A	
39. C			39. B	
40. B			40. D	

ANSWER KEY FOR PRACTICE TEST NO. 1 (continued)

Section IV	Section V	Section VI
1. D	1. D (AL)	1. B (AL)
2. B	2. B (AL)	2. C (AR)
3. B	3. E (AR)	3. C (AL)
4. A	4. C (G)	4. C (AR)
5. B	5. A (AR)	5. C (G)
6. C	6. B (AR)	6. B (AR)
7. B	7. B (G)	7. B (AR)
8. B	8. C (AR)	8. C (AR)
9. E	9. D (AR)	9. D (AL)
10. C	10. A (AL)	10. A (AL)
11. B	11. C (AL)	11. D (G)
12. C	12. D (G)	12. C (G)
13. A	13. C (AR)	13. C (G)
14. C	14. D (G)	14. A (G)
15. D	15. B (AL)	15. A (AR)
16. B	16. C (AL)	16. B (AL)
17. C	17. B (G)	17. A (AR)
18. B	18. B (AL)	18. D (AL)
19. C	19. A (G)	19. D (G)
20. C	20. A (AL)	20. B (AL)
21. B	21. C (AR)	21. A (G)
22. B	22. C (G)	22. A (G)
23. B	23. C (AL)	23. C (AR)
24. A	24. A (G)	24. A (G)
25. D	25. D (AL)	25. C (AL)
26. D		26. D (G)
27. B		27. E (AR)
28. A		28. A (AL)
29. A		29. C (G)
30. C		30. E (G)
31. E		31. B (AR)
32. B		32. A (AL)
33. C		33. E (AL)
34. D		34. D (G)
35. B		35. D (G)
36. A		
37. E		
38. D		
39. D		
40. E		

HOW TO SCORE YOUR EXAM

1. Add the total number of correct responses for each Verbal Section.
2. Add the total number of incorrect responses (only those attempted or marked in) for each Verbal Section.
3. The total number of incorrect responses should be divided by 4, giving the adjustment factor.
4. Subtract this adjustment factor from the total number of correct responses to obtain a raw score in the Verbal Section.
5. This score is then scaled from 200 to 800.
6. Repeat this process for the Mathematical Section, but remember to divide the total of the incorrect QUANTITATIVE COMPARISON responses by 3, instead of 4.
7. The Mathematical Ability Raw Score is then scaled from 200 to 800.

Example:
A. If the total number of correct answers was 40 out of a possible 85.
B. And 20 problems were attempted but missed.
C. Dividing the 20 by 4 gives an adjustment factor of 5.
D. Subtracting this adjustment factor of 5 from the original 40 correct gives a raw score of 35.
E. This raw score is then scaled to range of 200 to 800.

ANALYZING YOUR TEST RESULTS

The charts on the following pages should be used to carefully analyze your results and spot your strengths and weaknesses. The complete process of analyzing each subject area and each individual problem should be completed for each Practice Test. These results should then be reexamined for trends in types of errors (repeated errors) or poor results in specific subject areas. THIS REEXAMINATION AND ANALYSIS IS OF TREMENDOUS IMPORTANCE TO YOU IN ASSURING MAXIMUM TEST PREPARATION BENEFIT.

PRACTICE TEST NO. 1: VERBAL ABILITY ANALYSIS SHEET

SECTION I: VERBAL ABILITY

	Possible	Completed	Right	Wrong
Antonyms	15			
Sentence Completion	5			
Reading Comprehension	10			
Sentence Completion	5			
Analogies	10			
SUBTOTAL	45			

SECTION IV: VERBAL ABILITY

	Possible	Completed	Right	Wrong
Antonyms	10			
Sentence Completion	5			
Analogies	10			
Reading Comprehension	15			
SUBTOTAL	40			
OVERALL VERBAL ABILITY TOTALS	85			

RAW SCORE = NUMBER RIGHT MINUS ONE-FOURTH POINT FOR EACH ONE ATTEMPTED BUT MISSED. (NO POINTS SUBTRACTED FOR BLANK ANSWERS.)

PRACTICE TEST NO. 1: MATHEMATICAL ABILITY ANALYSIS SHEET

SECTION II: MATHEMATICAL ABILITY

	Possible	Completed	Right	Wrong
Math Ability	17			
Arithmetic	(4)			
Algebra	(6)			
Geometry	(7)			
Quantitative Comparison	18			
Arithmetic	(5)			
Algebra	(7)			
Geometry	(6)			
Subtotal	35			

SECTION V: MATHEMATICAL ABILITY

	Possible	Completed	Right	Wrong
Math Ability	25			
Arithmetic	(7)			
Algebra	(10)			
Geometry	(8)			
Subtotal	25			

SECTION VI: MATHEMATICAL ABILITY

	Possible	Completed	Right	Wrong
Math Ability	17			
Arithmetic	(6)			
Algebra	(5)			
Geometry	(6)			
Quantitative Comparison	18			
Arithmetic	(4)			
Algebra	(6)			
Geometry	(8)			
SUBTOTAL	35			
OVERALL MATHEMATICAL ABILITY TOTALS	95			

RAW SCORE = NUMBER RIGHT MINUS ONE-FOURTH POINT FOR EACH ONE ATTEMPTED BUT MISSED. (NO POINTS SUBTRACTED FOR BLANK ANSWERS.)

PRACTICE TEST NO. 1: TEST OF STANDARD WRITTEN ENGLISH ANALYSIS SHEET

SECTION III: TSWE

	Possible	Completed	Right	Wrong
Usage	30			
Sentence Correction	20			
OVERALL TSWE TOTALS	50			

WHY??????????????????????????????????

ANALYSIS: TALLY SHEET FOR PROBLEMS MISSED

One of the most important parts of test preparation is analyzing WHY! you missed a problem so that you can reduce the number of mistakes. Now that you have taken the practice test and corrected your answers, carefully tally your mistakes by marking them in the proper column.

REASON FOR MISTAKE

	Total Missed	Simple Mistake	Misread Problem	Lack of Knowledge
SECTION I: VERBAL ABILITY				
SECTION IV: VERBAL ABILITY				
SUBTOTAL				
SECTION II: MATH ABILITY				
SECTION V: MATH ABILITY				
SECTION VI: MATH ABILITY				
SUBTOTAL				
TOTAL MATH AND VERBAL				

Reviewing the above data should help you determine WHY you are missing certain problems. Now that you have pinpointed the type of error, take the next practice test focusing on avoiding your most common type.

COMPLETE ANSWERS AND EXPLANATIONS FOR
PRACTICE TEST NO. 1

SECTION I: VERBAL ABILITY

Antonyms

1. (B) As an adjective, *drab* means *dull, monotonous.* The opposite here is *bright.*

2. (D) A *benediction* (*bene = good; dic = to speak*) is a blessing, a speaking well of. To speak badly of is to *curse.*

3. (A) *Valor* (*val = to be strong, to be well, to have worth*) means *courage.* Its opposite is *cowardice.*

4. (D) *Bisect* (*bi = two; sec = to cut*) means *to cut into two.* Its opposite is *join.*

5. (E) A *disparity* is a difference; its opposite is *likeness.*

6. (A) *Cyclic* means *moving in circles.* Its opposite is *linear,* which means *moving in a straight line.*

7. (B) A *covenant* (*co = together; ven = come*) is a solemn mutual agreement. A *breach* is a violation of such an agreement.

8. (D) The adjective *jaunty* means *sprightly.* The opposite is *morose,* which means *gloomy.*

9. (A) The adjective *pastoral* is used to refer to rural life as peaceful and natural. The opposite here is *urban,* which refers to a city environment.

10. (B) *Frugal* means *thrifty* or *economical. Extravagant* is the opposite.

11. (C) The *equinox* (*equi = equal*) refers to the times of year when day and night are equal. *Solstice* refers to the times of year when day and night are most unequal.

12. (E) *Patronymic* (*pater = father; onoma = name*) refers to a name which is derived, or made from, the name of a father or ancestor. Its opposite is *new-made.*

13. (A) A *valedictory* (*dic = to say*) is a farewell speech. A *salutation* (*salus = health, greeting*) usually refers to words of welcome. *Beginning* is not the best choice because it does not as specifically refer to words.

14. (A) The adjective *lithe* means *flexible* or *supple.* Its opposite is *stiff.*

15. (B) *Sanguine* means *confident* or *secure.* The opposite is *insecure.*

Sentence Completion

16. (D), *vocal.* While choice (A), *playful,* is a possible choice, choice (D) is better. It is consistent with Dana's unsuccessful attempts at falling asleep, as a *vocal* parrot would keep her awake.

17. (C), *dreaded . . . opportunity.* The first completion should probably be negative because it defines *illness.* The second part of the sentence begins with the signal word *but.* It should be opposite in connotation from the first part of the sentence. The completion which yields a logical positive connotation is *opportunity.*

18. (D), *tender.* The signal word *although* indicates that the first phrase (before the comma) should be opposite to the second phrase (after the comma). Since the first phrase establishes a mood of *violence,* the best opposite for the second phrase is a *tender* moment.

19. (E), *thorough . . . unexplored.* None of the other choices makes sense within the context of the sentence.

20. (E), *flexibility. On the contrary* indicates that the phrase following should be opposite to the initial part of the sentence. *Flexibility* is the best opposite for *obstinate.*

Reading Comprehension

21. (C) In both the introductory and final paragraphs, the writer is concerned with attacks on the First Amendment, and throughout the article emphasizes this with a detailed look at what he or she thinks is an attack on a particular group, the press, that is guaranteed a certain amount of freedom by that amendment. Because of this, choices (A) and (B) are much too broad, and choices (D) and (E) are supporting ideas rather than principal ideas; *slander and libel laws* and *Big Brother in government* are mentioned only briefly.

22. (B) The second paragraph says a *6–3 ruling.* So if two justices change their minds, we would have a 4–5 ruling for the other side.

23. (C) The last sentence of the second paragraph says that reporters *now face a challenge to the privacy of their minds,* and the last sentence in the passage is a statement against *mind-control.* All other choices are not explicitly supported by material in the passage.

24. (D) I or II. As is stated in the fourth paragraph, actual malice is *with knowledge that the statements were false, or with reckless disregard of whether they were true or not.*

25. (E) As mentioned in lines 19–23, the Supreme Court held that in order to win a libel suit, a party must show *malicious intent:* reckless disregard, or not caring whether the facts were true or not.

26. (A) The fourth paragraph describes Augustine's ideas about man's evil tendency, which contributes to the *corruption of human nature.* This evil tendency is associated *in the will* with *the inclination to follow that which is pleasant.* Adam (D) and Eve (E) became corrupt, but they cannot be described as *symptoms* because they are people.

27. (C) The first paragraph says that Augustine does not *believe that souls are eternal* and later states that souls are immortal, that *they will survive the death of the physical body.* Choice (E) is incorrect because it is the intellect and the will which are capable of sin, not the soul. (See the fourth paragraph.)

28. (B) The second paragraph states that one of the difficulties Augustine had explaining *the nature of man's freedom* involved *the idea that God knows what man will do in the future.* Choice (A) is correct according to certain religions, but it is not stated in the passage as an obstacle to man's freedom.

29. (E) According to the passage (fourth paragraph), the intellect and the will (choices B and D) are parts of the mind, not the flesh. Choices (A) and (C) are obviously inconsistent with the passage.

30. (B) The fourth paragraph says, *In the intellect it* [the evil tendency] *is expressed in the sin of pride.*

Sentence Completion

31. (A) *differences . . . appreciate. Differences* matches with *complex fabric of our society.* In choice (D), *similarities* does not make sense with *separate us.*

32. (B), *flamboyant.* Again the *but* indicates that the adjective must contrast (with *conservative*). One opposite is *flamboyant,* which means *showy, ornate.* While *liberal* (A) contrasts with *conservative* in the political sense, in speaking of fashion, it is not as good a choice as *flamboyant.*

33. (E), *paradox.* Here, the right word must describe the phrase *less is more.* The correct choice is *paradox,* a seeming self-contradiction (*less/ more*).

34. (C), *covertly . . . unmask.* The missing verb here has *ruse (trick, deceit)* as its object, so either *debunk* or *unmask* will fit. The missing adverb refers to a signal that is part of the ruse. This, we must suppose, is *covertly (secretly)*.

35. (A), *peccadillo.* The word for the crime must be an *understatement.* A *peccadillo (slight fault* or petty event) is certainly an understated description of a four-million-dollar robbery.

Analogies

36. (B) Before it can perform well, a *piano* must be *tuned.* (*Tune* here is a verb not a noun.) Similarly, a *camera* must be *focused.* You might be tempted to choose (D) *ripen : fruit,* but this is not as good a choice because both a piano and a camera are mechanical items.

37. (E) An *island* is land surrounded by the waters of the *ocean;* an *oasis* is a place of water surrounded by the dry sands of a *desert.*

38. (C) The two-dimensional *square* becomes the three-dimensional *cube* as a two-dimensional *circle* can become a three-dimensional *sphere.*

39. (C) The *syringe* is the device by which a *serum* is injected into the body. The best analogy here is *hammer* and *nail.*

40. (B) A *zircon* is a mineral which can resemble a *diamond,* but is far less costly. Similarly, a *garnet* is a red semiprecious stone that resembles a *ruby.*

41. (C) The verbs *stride, saunter* describe a deliberate motion and then a careless, slower sort of motion. The same progress exists in the *flow, meander* verbs to describe the motion of water.

42. (D) The difference between *request* and *requirement* is the element of force or compulsion in *requirement.* A similar difference is approximated in the move from *inquiry* to *interrogation.*

43. (A) Both words here are verbs. To *intrigue* is to *plan* or scheme secretly or underhandedly. The relationship is similar to that of *move* and *slink.*

44. (E) *Complaisant* means *polite* or *obliging,* and *courtesy* is a quality of a person who is *complaisant* as *gluttony* is likely in a person who is *voracious.*

45. (A) The adjective *gauche* means *awkward* or *without grace.* Similarly, an *impecunious* person is *without wealth.*

SECTION II: MATHEMATICAL ABILITY

1. (A) $\dfrac{\text{percent}}{100} = \dfrac{\text{is Number}}{\text{of Number}}$

   $\dfrac{.25}{100} = \dfrac{x}{12}$ (cross multiplying)

   $100x = 3.00$

   $\dfrac{100x}{100} = \dfrac{3.00}{100}$

   $x = .03$, or $\dfrac{3}{100}$

2. (A) Since the difference between any two consecutive odd numbers is 2, the next odd number after $2x + 13$ would be

   $(2x + 13) + 2 = 2x + 15$

3. (C) In the series $8, 9, 12, 17, 24 \ldots$

   $9 - 8 = 1$ $17 - 12 = 5$
   $12 - 9 = 3$ $24 - 17 = 7$

   Hence the difference between the next term and 24 must be 9 or

   $x - 24 = 9$
   and $x = 33$

   Hence the next term in the series must be 33.

4. (C) If $x = -1$, $x^4 + x^3 + x^2 + x - 3$
   $= (-1)^4 + (-1)^3 + (-1)^2 + (-1) - 3$
   $= 1 + (-1) + 1 + (-1) - 3$
   $= 0 + 1 + (-1) - 3$
   $= 1 + (-1) - 3$
   $= 0 - 3$
   $= -3$

5. (D) Since the sum of the angles is 180° we have

   $m + n + 72 + 25 = 180$
   $m + n + 97 \qquad = 180$
   $m + n \qquad\quad = 180 - 97$
   $m + n \qquad\quad = 83$

   Hence the sum of $m + n$ is 83°.

6. (E) For the multiplication problem to work correctly, the figures must be

$$
\begin{array}{r}
\boxed{6}\ \boxed{7}\ 4 \\
\times\ \ \ \ 8 \\
\hline
5\ \ 3\ \ 9\ \ \boxed{2}
\end{array}
$$

Thus, the sum of the boxed digits is 15.

7. (C) Since BD = CD, ∠CBD = ∠C = 19°

Hence ∠BDC = 180 − (∠CBD − ∠C)
= 180 − (19 + 19)
= 180 − 38
∠BDC = 142°

Then ∠BDA = 180 − ∠BDC
= 180 − 142
∠BDA = 38°
Since AB = AD, ∠ABD = ∠BDA = 38°

Hence ∠A = 180 − (∠BDA + ∠ABD)
= 180 − (38 + 38)
= 180 − 76
∠A = 104°

Quantitative Comparison Answers 8-25

8. (A) By inspection, since both sides are exactly the same except in column A you are adding $4 \cdot 10^2$ and in column B you are subtracting $4 \cdot 10^2$. Therefore column A is greater. Solving for values would give

$$
\begin{array}{ll}
3^2 + 4 \cdot 10^2 - 4^2 & \quad 3^2 + 4 \cdot 10^2 - 4^2 \\
9 + 4 \cdot 100 - 16 & \quad 9 - 4 \cdot 100 - 16 \\
9 + 400 - 16 & \quad 9 - 400 - 16 \\
409 - 16 & \quad -391 - 16 \\
393 & \quad > \quad -407
\end{array}
$$

9. (C) Angles x and y are vertical angles formed by two intersecting lines; therefore they are equal. Vertical angles are always equal.

10. (D) Trying some small values is required here, keeping in mind that x must be greater than 0. Let x = 1 then

$3(1)^2$ $2(1)^2$
$3(1)$ $2(1)$
3 $>$ 2

In this case column A is greater. Now try another value for x. Let x = 2 then

$3(2)^3$ $2(2)^3$
$3(4)$ $2(8)$
12 $<$ 16

In this case column B is greater. Since there are different answers depending on the values chosen, the correct answer is (D)—cannot be determined.

11. (A) Since both sides have the factors 2/5 and 5/8, you may eliminate them from each column. Now compare

3/7 and 4/11 by

cross multiplying upward and you get 33   28 . Since

33 is greater than 28, 3/7 > 4/11

12. (C) Solving the top equation of 5y = 10 gives y = 2. Then substituting y = 2 into the second equation

leaves 3x + 2(2) = 10
solving 3x + 4 = 10
            3x = 6

Therefore x = 2 and columns A and B are equal.

13. (A) Area of circle with diameter 8 is computed by finding the radius, which is half of the diameter and substituting into this equation $A = \pi r^2$. Since the radius is 4, and π is about 3.14

$\pi(4)^2$ Area of square with
3.14×16 side 7 is
50.24 $>$ 49

14. (D) If x = 2 and y = 2, then the condition is satisfied. If x = 3 and y = 1, the condition is also satisfied. In one situation the columns are equal, in the other, column A is greater; therefore no comparison is possible.

15. **(B)** Number of seconds in   Number of hours in
        two hours.   fifty weeks

        $60^{min} \times 60^{sec} \times 2\ hr$ $24^{hrs} \times 7^{days} \times 50\ weeks$
        7200 $<$ 8400

16. **(C)** To solve $a/6 = b/4$

Cross multiply, giving $4a = 6b$
then divide by 2
leaves $2a = 3b$

17. **(B)** The easiest method is by inspection (and/or addition). Column A is approaching 2, but will not get here. Mathematically getting a common denominator and adding gives

$1 + 1/2 + 1/4 + 1/16 + 1/32 + 1/64$, or

$1 + 32/64 + 16/64 + 4/64 + 2/64 + 1/64$

$1 + 55/64$

and $1\ 55/64 < 2$

18. **(A)** To find the number of ways four books can be arranged on a shelf, you multiply $4 \times 3 \times 2 \times 1$ and get 24, which is greater than column B.

19. **(B)** Substitute $x = 9$ and $y = 4$ (Note these are square numbers and they can make solving easier when dealing with square roots).

       $\sqrt{x} - \sqrt{y}$ $\sqrt{x - y}$
       $\sqrt{9} - \sqrt{4}$ $\sqrt{9 - 4}$
       $3 - 2$ $\sqrt{5}$
then   1 $<$ 2.23

Now try $x = 16$ and $y = 1$

$\sqrt{16} - \sqrt{1}$ $\sqrt{16 - 1}$
$4 - 1$ $\sqrt{15}$
3         $<$ 3.87

Column B will always be greater.

20. **(B)** First multiply out column B getting

$4y^2 - 4y + 1$ $(2y + 1)^2$
$4y^2 - 4y + 1$ $4y^2 + 4y + 1$

Now subtract out from both sides getting

−4y   +4y

Divide both sides by 4 getting

−y   +y

Since y is a positive number between 0 and 1, column B is greater than column A.

21. (B) Since d is above the x axis, it must be positive and c, being to the left of the y axis, must be negative. Therefore $c < d$, since all negatives are less than all positives.

22. (A) Since point P is above the line containing points $(-2, 2)$, then d (actual distance) is greater than $|c|$; therefore $c + d$ is a positive number. Point Q is on the line, therefore e and f are additive inverses of each other, totaling 0. All positive numbers are greater than 0, then $c + d > e + f$.

23. (A) To find the number of degrees in the interior angles of a pentagon use the formula $180 \times (n - 2)$, where n is the number of sides, therefore $180 \times (5 - 2) = 180 \times 3 = 540$

$540° > 500°$

Another method would be to draw the pentagon and break it into triangles connecting vertices, (lines cannot cross) as shown below.

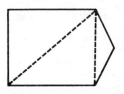

Multiplying the number of triangles (3) by 180 (degrees in a triangle) gives the same result, 540°.

24. (C) Simplifying the complex fraction in column A as follows

$$\cfrac{1}{1 + \cfrac{1}{1 + 1/n}} = \cfrac{1}{1 + \cfrac{1}{n/n + 1/n}} = \cfrac{1}{1 + \cfrac{1}{(n + 1)/n}} = \cfrac{1}{1 + \cfrac{n}{n + 1}}$$

$$= \cfrac{1}{\cfrac{n+1}{n+1}+\cfrac{n}{n+1}} = \cfrac{1}{\cfrac{n+1+n}{n+1}} = \cfrac{1}{\cfrac{2n+1}{n+1}} = \cfrac{n+1}{2n+1}$$

$$= \frac{n+1}{2n+1}$$

Alternate method would involve substituting simple numbers into each expression.

25. (C) Extend line CO as shown.

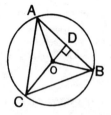

You now have triangle OBD, which is a 30°–60°–90° triangle. Since all 30°–60°–90° triangles are in proportion $1 - \sqrt{3} - 2$, and since side DB = half of 8 $\sqrt{3}$, or 4 $\sqrt{3}$, then side OB = 8. Therefore OB + OA + OC = 8 + 8 + 8 = 24.

26. (A) The perimeter of a rectangle with length l and width w is $2l + 2w$.

Since the perimeter of the rectangle is 10x + 8 and its length is 3x we have

$$\text{Perimeter} = 2l + 2w$$
$$10x + 8 = 2(3x) + 2w$$
$$10x + 8 = 6x + 2w$$
$$10x + 8 - 6x = 6x + 2w - 6x$$
$$4x + 8 = 2w$$

$$\frac{4x+8}{2} = \frac{2w}{2}$$

$$2x + 4 = w$$

Hence the width of the rectangle is 2x + 4.

27. **(D)** In isosceles △XYZ, ∠X = ∠Z.

Since ∠Y = 80, we have

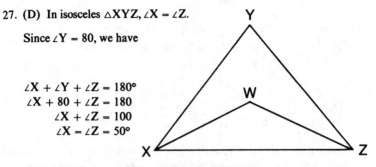

$$\angle X + \angle Y + \angle Z = 180°$$
$$\angle X + 80 + \angle Z = 180$$
$$\angle X + \angle Z = 100$$
$$\angle X = \angle Z = 50°$$

Since WX bisects ∠YXZ and WZ bisects ∠YZX, we have

$$\angle YXW = \angle WXZ = \angle YZW = \angle WZX = 25°$$

Hence on △XWZ,

$$\angle XWZ + \angle WXZ + \angle WZX = 180°$$
$$\angle XWZ + 25 + 25 = 180$$
$$\angle XWZ + 50 = 180$$
$$\angle XWZ = 130°$$

28. **(C)** $(m + n)^2 = (m + n)(m + n)$
$$= m^2 + mn + mn + n^2$$
$$= m^2 + 2mn + n^2$$
$$= (m^2 + n^2) + (2mn)$$

Since $m^2 + n^2 = 12$ and $mn = 9$ we have

$$(m^2 + n^2) + (2mn) = 12 + 2(9)$$
$$= 12 + 18$$
$$= 30$$

29. **(D)**

$$\frac{(6!)\,(4!)}{(5!)\,(3!)} = \frac{(6 \cdot \cancel{5} \cdot \cancel{4} \cdot \cancel{3} \cdot \cancel{2} \cdot \cancel{1}) \cdot (4 \cdot \cancel{3} \cdot \cancel{2} \cdot \cancel{1})}{(\cancel{5} \cdot \cancel{4} \cdot \cancel{3} \cdot \cancel{2} \cdot \cancel{1}) \cdot (\cancel{3} \cdot \cancel{2} \cdot \cancel{1})}$$
$$= \frac{6 \cdot 4}{1} = 24$$

30. **(C)** Let 3x = one angle and 4x = other angle

3x + 4x + 68 = 180	x = 16
7x + 68 = 180	3x = 48
7x = 112	4x = 64

Hence the smallest angle of the triangle is 48°.

31. (D)

Columns

A	B	C	D	E
3	4	5	7	2
6	8	6	3	5
2	2	7	9	9
1	6	9	2	3
9	9	3	6	7

Column D contains 3 primes (2, 3, and 7) and all the integral positive factors of 18, greater than 1 but less than 18 (2, 3, 6, and 9). Note that column A does not contain 3 primes (1 is not a prime number).

32. (C) $\sqrt{\dfrac{81}{x}} = \dfrac{63}{35} = \dfrac{9}{5}$

Squaring both sides we get

$$\dfrac{81}{x} = \dfrac{81}{25}$$

Hence x = 25

33. (D) Since it takes the pipe t hours to drain the tank completely, it will drain 1/t part of the tank each hour.

Hence in three hours, it will drain 3 (1/t), or 3/t, part of the tank.

34. (E) Perimeter = 10 feet
            = (10) (12) inches
            = 120 inches

Perimeter = 4s   (s = length of side)

4s = 120

$\dfrac{4s}{4} = \dfrac{120}{4}$

s = 30 inches

Area = s^2
       = $(30)^2$
       = (30)(30)
       = 900 square inches

35. **(B)** If two points have coordinates (x_1, y_1) and (x_2, y_2), the distance, d, between these points is defined to be

$$d = \sqrt{(x_1 - x_2)^2 + (y_1 - y_2)^2}$$

Since E has coordinates $(-3, 5)$ and F had coordinates $(6, -7)$, the distance between E and F is

$$EF = \sqrt{(-3 - 6)^2 + [5 - (-7)]^2}$$
$$= \sqrt{(-9)^2 + (12)^2}$$
$$= \sqrt{81 + 144}$$
$$= \sqrt{225}$$

$$EF = 15$$

SECTION III: TEST OF STANDARD WRITTEN ENGLISH

Usage

1. (B) The subject is singular, *box,* so the verb must be singular, *was,* instead of *were.*

2. (E) This sentence contains no error.

3. (B) *Whether* is a homonym (sounds like) the correct word—*weather.*

4. (B) *They* is meant to refer back to *one;* since *one* is singular, *they* (a plural) is incorrect. The correct pronoun is *one* or *he.*

5. (A) *Laying* means *putting in place;* the meaning required here is *resting,* so the correct word is *lying.*

6. (E) This sentence contains no error.

7. (D) The second verb, *would be,* must be the same tense as the first verb, *will be.* So *would be* must be changed to *will be.*

8. (B) *Slow* is an adjective, and since it is meant to describe an action (walking), it must be changed to an adverb, *slowly.*

9. (C) An error in parallelism occurs with *a college education,* which may be corrected by adding an *-ing* word, *completing.* So the correct, parallel phrase is *completing a college education.*

10. (E) This sentence contains no error.

11. (B) *Who* should be changed to *whom.*

12. (C) *Theirselves* is not a standard English word.

13. (E) This sentence contains no error.

14. (D) *Completed* is the wrong word; a correct choice would be *complex.*

15. (B) The subject is singular, *study,* so the verb must also be singular, *shows* instead of *show.*

16. (A) *Diving about* doesn't make sense; *diving into* does.

17. (A) For the bouquet of roses to smell *sweetly,* the roses must have little noses! To avoid the mistaken impression that roses are able to smell, *sweetly* should be changed to *sweet.*

18. (A) *Answering* is not parallel; *to answer* is.

19. (C) The subject is plural, *bowls,* so the verb must be plural—*were* instead of *was.*

20. (B) The first half of the sentence describes an earlier action than the second half, so the verb tense in the first half must be different—*had* instead of *would have.*

Sentence Correction

21. (C) *As opposed to* does not provide a clear connection between *pro-Arab* and *Israelis,* especially insofar as these terms refer to *people.* (B), (D), and (E) change the meaning of the sentence; the rephrasing in (C) is both balanced and clear.

22. (B) *She* is unnecessary. Eliminating it restores the clarity and flow of the sentence.

23. (A) None of the rephrasings is as clear and effective as the original.

24. (E) *It* is vague; we can't say exactly what it refers to. Generally, the whole underlined part is too wordy. (E) eliminates both the vague *it* and the awkward wordiness; it is a direct and economical rephrasing.

25. (C) One *as* in a sentence should usually be followed by another *as* (*as pretty as*) when the sentence is expressing a comparison.

26. (D) You cannot logically compare *novels* (things) to *writers* (persons). But you *can* compare novels to novels; including *those of* achieves this comparison.

27. (B) In a *neither . . . nor* sentence, the noun or pronoun closest to the verb often signals what the verb should be. In this case, *I* is closest, and the verb that fits with *I* is *am.*

28. (E) This is a verb tense error (see Introduction to the Test of Standard Written English); *would have* should be changed to *had.*

29. (B) This is a dangling modifier. The sentence seems to say that the essay did the struggling! (B) eliminates this problem, clearly associating *John* with the opening phrase about struggling.

30. (C) The original sentence is a fragment; so are choices (B), (D), and (E).

31. (D) *Fewer* is used correctly to refer to items that are *countable* (people, apples, accidents), and *less* is used correctly to refer to items which are *uncountable* (time, emotion, rainfall). Here their uses are mixed up; (D) corrects the mixup.

32. (D) The subject is singular, *the President;* therefore, the verb must be singular—*is* instead of *are.* Also, *raising* is misused; the correct choice is *rising.*

33. (A) This sentence contains no error. Although the other choices are grammatically correct, they change the meaning of the original.

34. (B) This is a pronoun error; *I* should be changed to *me.*

35. (C) The original sentence has both *needed to* and *would have* connecting with *purchased.* Since *needed to purchased* is ungrammatical, we must supply *needed to* with an appropriate verb—*purchase.*

36. (C) *Liable from making* is not idiomatic; that is, it doesn't sound right to most native English speakers. *Liable to make* is idiomatically correct.

37. (E) *Laying* means *putting in place;* the correct verb here is *lying,* which means *resting.*

38. (A) This sentence contains no error.

39. (B) This sentence contains a dangling modifier. It seems to say that her face itself is running down the street! (B) makes it clear that *she* is running down the street. (C) and (E) unnecessarily change the meaning of the sentence.

40. (D) *Effected* (resulting from) is the wrong word for this sentence. *Affected* (influenced) carries the correct meaning.

Usage

41. (A) *Him and I* is ungrammatical; *He and I* is correct.

42. (D) *Me* should be changed to *I.*

43. (E) This sentence contains no error.

44. (A) *Us* should be changed to *we.*

45. (C) The pronoun *they* has no reference. It should be corrected by replacing it with either the word *drivers* or *we.*

46. (D) The wig cannot be more attractive than the other men; a wig cannot be compared to men, but it can be compared to *the wigs of other men.*

47. (E) This sentence contains no error.

48. (E) This sentence contains no error. *Had lain,* referring to *resting,* is used correctly.

49. (A) To make the sentence consistent, *one reads* should be changed to *you read.*

50. (D) *Their* is incorrect. Since it refers to a *person*'s, it should be singular: either *his, her,* or *one's.*

SECTION IV: VERBAL ABILITY

Antonyms

1. (D) *Nemesis* was the name of the Greek goddess of vengeance, and nowadays refers to one who seems inevitably to defeat or frustrate someone else. Its opposite is *savior*, which means *someone who rescues*. A *colleague* is a *fellow worker*, not necessarily a helpful one.

2. (B) To *fuse* is to *unite by melting*. Its opposite is *separate*. *Diffuse* means *not concentrated, spread in different directions*.

3. (B) *Vertical* means *straight up and down*. Its opposite is *horizontal*, meaning *parallel to the plane of the horizon*. *Flat* is not the best choice because a flat surface need not be horizontal.

4. (A) *Fidelity* (*fid = having faith*) means *faithfulness*. So its opposite is *faithlessness*.

5. (B) *Colloquial* (*loqui = to speak*) refers to informal, everyday conversations. Its opposite is *formal*. *Slang* is a type of colloquial usage, not its opposite.

6. (C) To be *impelled* (*pell = push, drive*) is to be motivated or pushed from within. The opposite is *reluctant*.

7. (B) An *extrovert* (*extra = outside; vert = to turn*) is an *outgoing person*. The opposite is *introvert*, describing someone who is "ingoing," interested more in inner feelings than in external events.

8. (B) *Tractable* (*tract = to draw* or *pull*) means *easy to manage*. Its opposite is *refractory*, which means *difficult to manage, stubborn, obstinate*. *Retractable* means *capable of being withdrawn or denied*.

9. (E) *Plethora* generally means an *overabundance;* therefore the opposite is *shortage*. *Modicum* is a possibility, but it is not as extreme as *shortage*.

10. (C) A *dipsomaniac* (*mania = excessive craving*) has an unquenchable desire for alcohol. The opposite, one who drinks no alcohol, is a *teetotaler*.

Sentence Completion

11. (B), *nutrition*. The focus is on *eating habits,* which are linked to diseases; therefore, the best answer refers to such eating habits, or *nutrition*.

12. **(C)**, *abolition . . . criteria. Eagerly awaited promises* indicates something positive is expected. The only positive choice that fits the sentence is the *abolition of false criteria for judging human behavior.*

13. **(A)**, *include . . . unrelated.* Note that the semicolon indicates two related sentences. Since the latter begins with *therefore,* this second sentence should be consistent in meaning with the first sentence. Choice (A) best continues the thought of the first sentence.

14. **(C)**, *undermine . . . incumbents.* Ths missing verb must mean something like *injure* or *weaken,* while the missing noun must refer to the politicians in office and in the position to pass a law. Either (C) or (D) would work as the verb, but *incumbents (current office holders)* makes sense while *candidates (persons seeking office)* does not.

15. **(D)**, *homily.* The missing word must mean something like *speech* or *sermon.* Only *homily* makes sense. A *soliloquy* is impossible because the speaker is not alone.

Analogies

16. **(B)** To make an article of clothing, a *dressmaker* must begin with the *pattern* of the article; in the same way, a *chef* uses a *recipe* to create food.

17. **(C)** As *luggage* is a traveler's equipment for carrying or transporting *clothes,* so a *briefcase* is equipment for transporting *documents.*

18. **(B)** A *decade* is a period of ten years, one-tenth of a *century,* as a *dime* is one-tenth of a *dollar.*

19. **(C)** A *jury's* purpose is to reach a *verdict* as a *doctor's* is to effect a *cure.*

20. **(C)** The *smock* is the protective clothing used by the *painter* as *shoulder pads* are a *football player's* protective clothes.

21. **(B)** *Supine* and *prone* are opposites meaning *lying face up* and *face down.*

22. **(B)** A *tuber* is the fleshy root of certain kinds of *plant* from which the plant grows. The closest parallel here is *foundation* and *building.*

23. **(B)** An *abbot* is a monk who is the head of, not merely a member of, a *monastery.* The closest parallel to this position is the *conductor* of an *orchestra.*

24. **(A)** To *accrete* is to *grow by being added to,* so the two verbs are opposites, like wax *(to increase in size)* and *wane (to decrease).*

25. (D) Both *provinces* and *cantons* are political divisions of countries, of Canada and Switzerland, for example. They are parallel in meaning, like *segment* and *section*. A canton is not a smaller part of a province as a county is of a state.

Reading Comprehension

26. (D) Though the author would probably agree with the ideas in choices (A), (C), and (E), the central concern of this passage is (D).

27. (B) The phrase is defined by the previous sentence: *implying that something bad was replaced by something better.*

28. (A) According to the passage, little of the Italian music of the early and middle eighteenth century has been made *available in modern editions* by Italian musicologists.

29. (A) We can infer I from the first sentence of the passage. Neither II nor III is true.

30. (C) The passage presents the *National Geographic* as sympathetic to Fascist Germany and Italy long after the danger of such an attitude became clear.

31. (E) As a right-wing, anti-labor writer who wrote favorably of Fascist Italy, Patric would also be likely to write favorably on Fascist Spain.

32. (B) The second paragraph states that Hitler and Mussolini had a *formal alliance.*

33. (C) The March 1940 *Geographic* printed articles *gushing* about Mussolini's *public works.* By repeating the words in the third paragraph, the author shows how misguided the *Geographic*'s view of Italy had been.

34. (D) The passage is centrally concerned with the limitations of Sir Walter Elliot, his vanity about his title and good looks, and his failure to value his children properly.

35. (B) The criticism of Sir Walter Elliot is clear. That he especially values his daughter Elizabeth and that she is *very like himself* tells us that the author does not approve of her. The passage praises Lady Elliot, Lady Russell, and Anne Elliot.

36. (A) The passage is from Jane Austen's novel *Persuasion.* The other forms would be much less likely to use the irony or the comedy of this passage or to deal with so many characters.

37. (E) Sir Walter places undue importance on being born with a title. Though he is a nobleman, he is too self-centered to concern himself with the obligation of the nobility (D).

38. (D) The passage raises questions about each of the suggested sites of origin and offers no answer to the question of comet origin.

39. (D) Though ice is evidently necessary, volcanoes are only a possible means of ejection. For a comet to escape from its source, it would have to overcome the gravitational pull.

40. (E) Both have ice, but the ejection mechanism on the rings of Saturn is less certain than volcanic activity on the satellites.

SECTION V: MATHEMATICAL ABILITY

1. (D) Multiplying each side by 3

$$3m + n = 7$$
$$3(3m + n) = 3(7)$$

therefore $9m + 3n = 21$

2. (B) Setting up an equation gives $1/5x = 2$

Multiplying both sides by 5, $5(1/5x) = 2(5)$
then $x = 10$
and ½ of 10 is 5

3. (E) Let x = original price

Then
$$x - .40x = 5.70$$
$$.60x = 5.70$$
$$x = 9.50$$

Hence the book originally cost \$9.50.

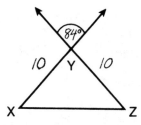

4. (C) Since $XY = YZ = 10$, then $\triangle XYZ$ is an isosceles $\triangle$ and $\angle X = \angle Z$. $\angle Y = 84°$, since it forms a vertical angle with the given angle.

$$\angle X + \angle Y + \angle Z = 180$$
$$\angle X + 84 + \angle Z = 180$$
$$2(\angle Z) + 84 = 180$$
$$2(\angle Z) = 96$$
$$\angle Z = 48$$

Hence the measure of $\angle Z = 48°$.

5. **(A)** Multiply numerator and denominator by 12 (L.C.D.)

$$\frac{12\,(2/3 - 1/2)}{12\,(1/6 + 1/4 + 2/3)} = \frac{8 - 6}{2 + 3 + 8} = 2/13$$

6. **(B)** Ratio of 3/10 to 5/8 $= \dfrac{3/10}{5/8}$

Multiply numerator and denominator by 40 (L.C.D.)

$$\frac{40\,(3/10)}{40\,(5/8)} = 12/25$$

Hence the ratio of 3/10 to 5/8 = 12/25

7. **(B)**

Since D is between A and B on $\overleftrightarrow{AB}$, we know that the sum of the lengths of the smaller segments AD and DB is equal to the length of the larger segment AB.

Hence   AB = AD + DB

          AB − AD = AD + DB − AD

          AB − AD = DB

8. **(C)** Since 83 is a little larger than 81, $\sqrt{83}$ would be a little larger than $\sqrt{81}$ = 9. Hence the correct choice would be approximately 9.1.

9. **(D)** The seventh row will be 1–6–15–20–15–6–1, which contains no prime numbers.

10. **(A)** If x − 4 = y then y − x = −4

Hence $(y - x)^3 = (-4)^3 = -64$

11. **(C)** Since a and b must both be positive or both be negative, choice (C) III is the only answer that *must* be true.

12. **(D)** Breaking the figure into squares of side x by adding lines gives

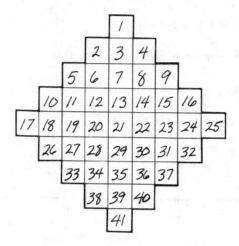

Remember each square has area x^2
then the total area is $41x^2$.

Choice (A), (B), and (E) are not possible as area must be in square units.

13. **(C)** There are $40 - 24 = 16$ boys in the class

$$\frac{\text{is number}}{\text{of number}} = \frac{\text{percent}}{100}$$

$$\frac{16}{40} = \frac{x}{100}$$

$$40x = 1600$$

$$x = 40$$

Hence 40% of the class are boys.

14. (D) Perimeter of △MNP = ½ (perimeter of △XYZ)
                           = ½ (XY − YZ + XZ)
                           = ½ (10 + 15 + 17)
                           = ½ (42)
    Perimeter of △MNP = 21

15. (B) If the average of 9 numbers is 7, then the sum of these numbers must be 9 × 7, or 63.

    If the average of 7 numbers is 9, then the sum of these numbers must be 7 × 9, or 63.

    The sum of all 16 numbers must be 63 + 63, or 126.

    Hence the average of all 16 numbers must be

    $$126 \div 16 = \frac{126}{16} = 7\frac{14}{16} = 7\frac{7}{8}$$

16. (C) For $(a^2 - b^2)/a - b = a + b$ to be true, the denominator $a - b$ cannot equal zero, therefore a cannot equal b; a > b is sufficient for this.

17. (B) ∠XYZ is inscribed in a semicircle and is therefore a right angle.

    Hence △XYZ is a right triangle and the Pythagorean theorem states

    $(XY)^2 = (XZ)^2 + (YZ)^2$
    $(17)^2 = (XZ)^2 + (15)^2$ (XY is a diameter)
    $289 = (XZ)^2 + 225$
    $(XY)^2 = 64$
    $XZ = \sqrt{64}$
    $XZ = 8$

    The area of △XYZ = ½ bh
                     = ½ (XZ)(YZ)
                     = ½ (8)(15)
                     = (4)(15)
                     = 60

18. (B) Adding any two of three consecutive positive integers will always be greater than the other integer, therefore II is true. The others cannot be determined, as they depend on values and/or the order of x, y, and z.

19. (A) Perimeter of rectangle $2l + 2w$

Where l is the length and w is the width.

If the length and width are increased by x, the perimeter will be

$2(l + x) + 2(w + x)$
$= 2l + 2x + 2w + 2x$
$= 2l + 2w + 4x$

Which is an increase of 4x units.

20. (A) Since Mary will be y years old x years from now she is y − x years old now.

Hence z years from now she will be y − x + z years old.

21. (C) 75 miles per hour $= \dfrac{75 \text{ miles}}{1 \text{ Hour}}$

Since 1 mile = 5280 feet

and 1 hour = 60 minutes = 3600 seconds

$\dfrac{75 \text{ miles}}{1 \text{ hour}} = \dfrac{75 \times 5280 \text{ feet}}{1 \times 3600 \text{ seconds}}$

$= 110$ feet per second

22. (C)

Area of square $= \frac{1}{2} \times$ product of diagonals
$= \frac{1}{2} d_1 d_2$
$= \frac{1}{2} d^2$ (since $d_1 = d_2$ in a square)

Hence $\frac{1}{2} d^2 = 72$
$d^2 = 144$
$d = 12$ feet.

23. (C) Distance = rate × time

$d = rt$
$k = rn$

$r = \dfrac{k}{n}$ miles per hour.

Hence $d = rt$

$d = \left(\dfrac{k}{n}\right)(x) = \dfrac{kx}{n}$

24. (A) Ratio of diameters = ratio of radii

$$\frac{d_1}{d_2} = \frac{r_1}{r_2} = \frac{30}{100} = 3/10$$

Ratio of area = (ratio of radii)^2

$$\frac{A_1}{A_2} = \left(\frac{r_1}{r_2}\right)^2$$

$$\frac{A_1}{A_2} = 9/100$$

Hence the area of circle R is 9/100, or 9%, of the area of circle S.

25. (D) Let x = the missing number
    Since the average of x and z is y, we have

$$\frac{1}{2}(x + z) = y$$

$$2 \cdot \frac{1}{2}(x + z) = 2y$$

$$x + z = 2y$$
$$x + z - z = 2y - z$$
$$x = 2y - z$$

SECTION VI: MATHEMATICAL ABILITY

1. (B) Solve for x, $2x - 5 = 9$
$$2x = 14$$
then $$x = 7$$
   Now substitute 7 for x,

   hence $3x + 2 = 3(7) + 2$
$$= 21 + 2$$
$$= 23$$

2. (C) $\dfrac{\text{is number}}{\text{of number}} = \dfrac{\text{percent}}{100}$

$$\frac{1/2}{2/3} = \frac{x}{100}$$

$$\frac{2}{3}x = 50$$

$$x = \frac{150}{2} = 75\%$$

3. (C) $2x + 3y^2 - z = (2)(3) + 3(4^2) - (-1)$
$$= 6 + 3(16) + 1$$
$$= 6 + 48 + 1$$
$$= 55$$

4. (C) The cost for 1 dozen at 3 for $.85 is

   $3 \times 4 = 12 = 1$ dozen $= \$.85 \times 4 = \$3.40$

   Hence 6 dozen will yield

   $\$3.40 \times 6 = \$20.40$

   The cost for 6 dozen at $1.80 per dozen is

   $\$1.80 \times 6 = \$10.80$

   Hence the profit on 6 dozen of these items will be

   $\$20.40 - \$10.80$, or $\$9.60$

5. **(C)** The maximum number of squares 1 inch by 1 inch will be 16.

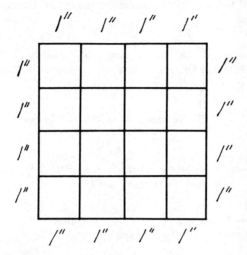

6. **(B)** Since $^{31}/_{60} > ^{1}/_{2}$, while the other four choices are less than $^{1}/_{2}$, $^{31}/_{60}$ is the largest fraction.

7. **(B)** For a number to be divisible by 21, it must be divisible by 3 and by 7, since $21 = 3 \times 7$.

   Hence if a number is divisible by 7 but not by 21, it cannot be divisible by 3.

Quantitative Comparison—Answers 8-25

8. **(C)** This comparison should be made without any actual computation as follows

   35% of 50   50% of 35
   .35 × 50   .50 × 35

   Since 35 × 50 is on each side, and then each column's answer has two decimal places, the quantities are equal.

   Or 35/100 × 50   50/100 × 35
   1/100 × 35 × 50   =   1/100 × 50 × 35

9. **(D)** Solving $x^2 = 36$ gives $+6$ and -6, therefore x can be equal to 6 or less than 6, making no comparison possible.

10. **(A)** Changing the form of column A by squaring 3 and then multiplying it by 2 to get everything under the radical sign, leaves the simple comparison $\sqrt{18} > \sqrt{17}$

11. **(D)** The length of side AB is determinable by using the Pythagorean theorem, but since DC is not known, BC cannot be determined. Note you cannot make a determination by measuring.

12. **(C)** $\angle BAD = \angle ABD$, for angles across from equal sides in a triangle are equal.

13. **(C)** Since there are 180° in a triangle and $\angle BDC$ is 90°, the remaining two angles, $\angle DBC$ and $\angle BCD$, must total 90°.

14. **(A)** AB + BC is greater than AC, since the sum of any two sides of a triangle is greater than the third side.

15. **(A)** In column A a number greater than 1 is multiplied by itself 10 times. The answer will be greater than 1. But in column B a number less than 1 (.23) is multiplied by itself 100 times. The answer in column B will be smaller than 1.

16. **(B)** If $a = b$ and $a < c$, then the following substitutions make the comparison simpler.

$$2a \qquad b + c$$
$$a + a \qquad b + c$$

Since $a = b$, then
$$a + b \qquad b + c$$

now canceling b's from each column

leaves $a \quad < \quad c$.

17. **(A)** Change column A to decimals

$$\frac{1}{3} \times \frac{2}{5} \times \frac{1}{8}$$

gives $.33\frac{1}{3} \times .4 \times .125$ which, by inspection is greater than column B. Another method would be to change column B to all fractions and then compare.

18. (D) You should substitute small numbers following the condition $a > b > c$.
Let $a = 2, b = 1, c = 0$ then

$$\begin{array}{cc} (2) - (1) - 0 & (2) + (1) - 0 \\ 1 & < \quad 3 \end{array}$$

Now try different values. Let $a = 1, b = 0, c = -1$

$$\begin{array}{cc} (1) - (0) - (1) & (1) + (0) - (1) \\ 0 & = \quad 0 \end{array}$$

Since different answers occur depending on the values chosen, the correct answer is (D.) You could have worked this problem by first eliminating a and $-c$ from each side and comparing b and $-b$ with different values.

19. (D) Volume of cube with side 6 is $6 \times 6 \times 6 = 216$. Volume of rectangular prism with two dimensions less than 6 is not determinable because the third dimension is needed. Therefore no comparison can be made.

20. (B) Solving the systems of equations as follows by first multiplying the bottom equation by -5 gives

$$5x + y = 2$$
$$-5x + -15y = -30$$

Now adding equations leaves

$$-14y = -28$$

therefore $y = 2$
substituting $y = 2$ into the original second equation gives

$$x + 3(2) = 6$$
then $x + 6 = 6$
and $x = 0$
therefore $x < y$

21. (A) If the top angle was 90°, then x would be $3\sqrt{2}$. This could be calculated using the Pythagorean theorem,

$$a^2 + b^2 = c^2$$
$$3^2 + 3^2 = x^2$$
$$9 + 9 = x^2$$
$$18 = x^2$$

Therefore $\sqrt{18} = x$

Which simplified is $3\sqrt{2}$. But since the angle was originally larger than 90°, then the side across from 92° must be larger than $3\sqrt{2}$. The correct answer is (A).

22. (A) Since there are 180° in a triangle and 92° in one angle, that leaves 88° to be split equally between two angles. Thus angle y is 44°. (The degrees must be split equally because angles across from equal sides are equal). And the triangle has two equal sides (isosceles). The correct answer is (A).

23. (C) The integer multiples of 8 greater than 8 but less than 50 are 16, 24, 32, 40, and 48. Column A is therefore 5. The integer multiples of 6 greater than 6 but less than 40 are 12, 18, 24, 30, 36. Therefore column B is also 5. The correct answer is (C).

24. (A) The following diagrams show eight ways of going from A to B, and there are more:

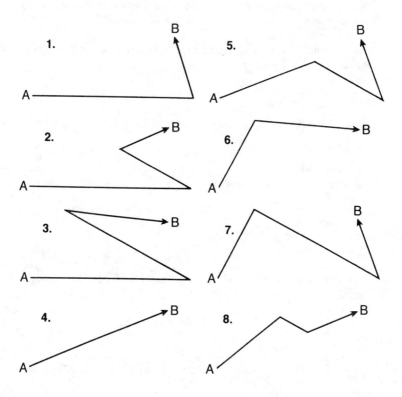

25. (C) It would be much too time consuming to multiply out 9^{19} or 9^{18}. Therefore, the quick way to solve this problem is to factor out column A as follows:

$$9^{19} - (8)9^{18}$$
$$(9^1)(9^{18}) - (8)9^{18}$$
$$(9^1 - 8)(9^{18})$$
$$(1)(9^{18})$$

Thus, they are equal.

26. (D) The perimeter of a rectangle is equal to the sum of the dimensions of its sides. For this rectangle we have

$$\text{Perimeter} = 6l + 4w + 6l + 4w$$
$$= 6l + 6l + 4w + 4w$$
$$= 12l + 8w$$

27. (E) The digit 6 will appear in the "ones" place 10 times between 1 and 100 (6, 16, 26, 36, 46, 56, 66, 76, 86, 96).

The digit 6 will appear in the "tens" place 10 times between 1 and 100 (60, 61, 62, 63, 64, 65, 66, 67, 68, 69).

Hence, the digit 6 will appear 20 times between 1 and 100.

28. (A) if $x(y - z) = t$

$$\frac{\cancel{x_1}(y - z)}{\cancel{x_1}} = \frac{t}{x}$$

$$y - z = \frac{t}{x}$$

$$y - z + z = \frac{t}{x} + z$$

$$y = \frac{t}{x} + z$$

29. (C) Let $2x$ = first angle
$3x$ = second angle
$4x$ = third angle
$6x$ = fourth angle

Since the sum of the measures of the angles in a quadrilateral must be 360°, we have

$$2x + 3x + 4x + 6x = 360°$$
$$15x = 360$$

$$\frac{15x}{15} = \frac{360}{15}$$

$$x = 24°$$
$$2x = 48° = \text{first angle}$$
$$3x = 72° = \text{second angle}$$
$$4x = 96° = \text{third angle}$$
$$6x = 144° = \text{fourth angle}$$

Hence the largest angle of the quadrilateral has a measure of 144°.

30. (E) Since arc YXZ is a semicircle, its measure is 180°.

$$\text{arc } XZ = \text{arc } YXZ - \text{arc } YWX$$
$$= 180° - 100°$$
$$\text{arc } XZ = 80°$$

Since an inscribed angle = ½ (intercepted arc)
we have $\angle XYZ = $ ½ (arc XZ)
$$= \text{½ } (80°)$$
$$= (40°)$$

Hence $\angle XYZ$ has a measure of 40°

31. (B) Since 1 gallon = 4 quarts
and 1 quart = 2 pints
1 gallon = 8 pints

Hence 200 pints would be equivalent to

200 ÷ 8 = 25 gallons.

Hence it would take 25 1-gallon containers to fill 200 pint bottles.

32. (A) Since $\dfrac{x^2 - 5x + 7}{x^2 - 4x + 10} = 1 = \dfrac{1}{1}$

$$x^2 - 5x + 7 = x^2 - 4x + 10 \text{ (cross multiply)}$$
$$x^2 - 5x + 7 - x^2 = x^2 - 4x + 10 - x^2$$
$$-5x + 7 = -4x + 10$$
$$-5x + 7 + 4x = -4x + 10 + 4x$$
$$-x + 7 = 10$$
$$-x + 7 - 7 = 10 - 7$$
$$-x = 3$$
$$x = -3$$

33. (E)

Since $\sqrt{125} = \sqrt{25 \cdot 5} = \sqrt{25} \cdot \sqrt{5} = 5\sqrt{5}$
and $\sqrt{45} = \sqrt{9 \cdot 5} = \sqrt{9} \cdot \sqrt{5} = 3\sqrt{5}$
and $\sqrt{20} = \sqrt{4 \cdot 5} = \sqrt{4} \cdot \sqrt{5} = 2\sqrt{5}$

$$\sqrt{125} - \sqrt{45} - \sqrt{20} = 5\sqrt{5} - 3\sqrt{5} - 2\sqrt{5}$$
$$= 2\sqrt{5} - 2\sqrt{5}$$
$$= 0\sqrt{5}$$
$$= 0$$

34. (D) Since AB = BE = 34, $\triangle$ABC is an isosceles triangle and altitude BD will bisect AC. Since $\triangle$BDC is a right triangle, we use the Pythagorean theorem, which says

$(BC)^2 = (BD)^2 + (CD)^2$
$(34)^2 = (30)^2 + x^2$
$1156 = 900 + x^2$
$x^2 = 1156 - 900$
$x^2 = 256$
$x^2 = \sqrt{256} = 16$

Hence CD = 16 = AD
and   AC = AD + DC
          = 16 + 16
          = 32

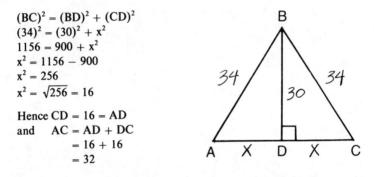

35. (D) Try it yourself with a scissors and square piece of paper.

PRACTICE TEST NO. 2

ANSWER SHEET FOR SAT AND TSWE PRACTICE TEST NO. 2
(Remove This Sheet and Use it to Mark Your Answers)

START WITH NUMBER 1 FOR EACH NEW SECTION OF THE TEST

SECTION I

1 Ⓐ Ⓑ Ⓒ Ⓓ Ⓔ	26 Ⓐ Ⓑ Ⓒ Ⓓ Ⓔ
2 Ⓐ Ⓑ Ⓒ Ⓓ Ⓔ	27 Ⓐ Ⓑ Ⓒ Ⓓ Ⓔ
3 Ⓐ Ⓑ Ⓒ Ⓓ Ⓔ	28 Ⓐ Ⓑ Ⓒ Ⓓ Ⓔ
4 Ⓐ Ⓑ Ⓒ Ⓓ Ⓔ	29 Ⓐ Ⓑ Ⓒ Ⓓ Ⓔ
5 Ⓐ Ⓑ Ⓒ Ⓓ Ⓔ	30 Ⓐ Ⓑ Ⓒ Ⓓ Ⓔ
6 Ⓐ Ⓑ Ⓒ Ⓓ Ⓔ	31 Ⓐ Ⓑ Ⓒ Ⓓ Ⓔ
7 Ⓐ Ⓑ Ⓒ Ⓓ Ⓔ	32 Ⓐ Ⓑ Ⓒ Ⓓ Ⓔ
8 Ⓐ Ⓑ Ⓒ Ⓓ Ⓔ	33 Ⓐ Ⓑ Ⓒ Ⓓ Ⓔ
9 Ⓐ Ⓑ Ⓒ Ⓓ Ⓔ	34 Ⓐ Ⓑ Ⓒ Ⓓ Ⓔ
10 Ⓐ Ⓑ Ⓒ Ⓓ Ⓔ	35 Ⓐ Ⓑ Ⓒ Ⓓ Ⓔ
11 Ⓐ Ⓑ Ⓒ Ⓓ Ⓔ	36 Ⓐ Ⓑ Ⓒ Ⓓ Ⓔ
12 Ⓐ Ⓑ Ⓒ Ⓓ Ⓔ	37 Ⓐ Ⓑ Ⓒ Ⓓ Ⓔ
13 Ⓐ Ⓑ Ⓒ Ⓓ Ⓔ	38 Ⓐ Ⓑ Ⓒ Ⓓ Ⓔ
14 Ⓐ Ⓑ Ⓒ Ⓓ Ⓔ	39 Ⓐ Ⓑ Ⓒ Ⓓ Ⓔ
15 Ⓐ Ⓑ Ⓒ Ⓓ Ⓔ	40 Ⓐ Ⓑ Ⓒ Ⓓ Ⓔ
16 Ⓐ Ⓑ Ⓒ Ⓓ Ⓔ	41 Ⓐ Ⓑ Ⓒ Ⓓ Ⓔ
17 Ⓐ Ⓑ Ⓒ Ⓓ Ⓔ	42 Ⓐ Ⓑ Ⓒ Ⓓ Ⓔ
18 Ⓐ Ⓑ Ⓒ Ⓓ Ⓔ	43 Ⓐ Ⓑ Ⓒ Ⓓ Ⓔ
19 Ⓐ Ⓑ Ⓒ Ⓓ Ⓔ	44 Ⓐ Ⓑ Ⓒ Ⓓ Ⓔ
20 Ⓐ Ⓑ Ⓒ Ⓓ Ⓔ	45 Ⓐ Ⓑ Ⓒ Ⓓ Ⓔ
21 Ⓐ Ⓑ Ⓒ Ⓓ Ⓔ	
22 Ⓐ Ⓑ Ⓒ Ⓓ Ⓔ	
23 Ⓐ Ⓑ Ⓒ Ⓓ Ⓔ	
24 Ⓐ Ⓑ Ⓒ Ⓓ Ⓔ	
25 Ⓐ Ⓑ Ⓒ Ⓓ Ⓔ	

SECTION II

1 Ⓐ Ⓑ Ⓒ Ⓓ Ⓔ
2 Ⓐ Ⓑ Ⓒ Ⓓ Ⓔ
3 Ⓐ Ⓑ Ⓒ Ⓓ Ⓔ
4 Ⓐ Ⓑ Ⓒ Ⓓ Ⓔ
5 Ⓐ Ⓑ Ⓒ Ⓓ Ⓔ
6 Ⓐ Ⓑ Ⓒ Ⓓ Ⓔ
7 Ⓐ Ⓑ Ⓒ Ⓓ Ⓔ
8 Ⓐ Ⓑ Ⓒ Ⓓ Ⓔ
9 Ⓐ Ⓑ Ⓒ Ⓓ Ⓔ
10 Ⓐ Ⓑ Ⓒ Ⓓ Ⓔ
11 Ⓐ Ⓑ Ⓒ Ⓓ Ⓔ
12 Ⓐ Ⓑ Ⓒ Ⓓ Ⓔ
13 Ⓐ Ⓑ Ⓒ Ⓓ Ⓔ
14 Ⓐ Ⓑ Ⓒ Ⓓ Ⓔ
15 Ⓐ Ⓑ Ⓒ Ⓓ Ⓔ
16 Ⓐ Ⓑ Ⓒ Ⓓ Ⓔ
17 Ⓐ Ⓑ Ⓒ Ⓓ Ⓔ
18 Ⓐ Ⓑ Ⓒ Ⓓ Ⓔ
19 Ⓐ Ⓑ Ⓒ Ⓓ Ⓔ
20 Ⓐ Ⓑ Ⓒ Ⓓ Ⓔ
21 Ⓐ Ⓑ Ⓒ Ⓓ Ⓔ
22 Ⓐ Ⓑ Ⓒ Ⓓ Ⓔ
23 Ⓐ Ⓑ Ⓒ Ⓓ Ⓔ
24 Ⓐ Ⓑ Ⓒ Ⓓ Ⓔ
25 Ⓐ Ⓑ Ⓒ Ⓓ Ⓔ

CUT HERE

ANSWER SHEET FOR SAT AND TSWE PRACTICE TEST NO. 2
(Remove This Sheet and Use it to Mark Your Answers)

START WITH NUMBER 1 FOR EACH NEW SECTION OF THE TEST

SECTION III

1 Ⓐ Ⓑ Ⓒ Ⓓ Ⓔ	26 Ⓐ Ⓑ Ⓒ Ⓓ Ⓔ
2 Ⓐ Ⓑ Ⓒ Ⓓ Ⓔ	27 Ⓐ Ⓑ Ⓒ Ⓓ Ⓔ
3 Ⓐ Ⓑ Ⓒ Ⓓ Ⓔ	28 Ⓐ Ⓑ Ⓒ Ⓓ Ⓔ
4 Ⓐ Ⓑ Ⓒ Ⓓ Ⓔ	29 Ⓐ Ⓑ Ⓒ Ⓓ Ⓔ
5 Ⓐ Ⓑ Ⓒ Ⓓ Ⓔ	30 Ⓐ Ⓑ Ⓒ Ⓓ Ⓔ
6 Ⓐ Ⓑ Ⓒ Ⓓ Ⓔ	31 Ⓐ Ⓑ Ⓒ Ⓓ Ⓔ
7 Ⓐ Ⓑ Ⓒ Ⓓ Ⓔ	32 Ⓐ Ⓑ Ⓒ Ⓓ Ⓔ
8 Ⓐ Ⓑ Ⓒ Ⓓ Ⓔ	33 Ⓐ Ⓑ Ⓒ Ⓓ Ⓔ
9 Ⓐ Ⓑ Ⓒ Ⓓ Ⓔ	34 Ⓐ Ⓑ Ⓒ Ⓓ Ⓔ
10 Ⓐ Ⓑ Ⓒ Ⓓ Ⓔ	35 Ⓐ Ⓑ Ⓒ Ⓓ Ⓔ
11 Ⓐ Ⓑ Ⓒ Ⓓ Ⓔ	36 Ⓐ Ⓑ Ⓒ Ⓓ Ⓔ
12 Ⓐ Ⓑ Ⓒ Ⓓ Ⓔ	37 Ⓐ Ⓑ Ⓒ Ⓓ Ⓔ
13 Ⓐ Ⓑ Ⓒ Ⓓ Ⓔ	38 Ⓐ Ⓑ Ⓒ Ⓓ Ⓔ
14 Ⓐ Ⓑ Ⓒ Ⓓ Ⓔ	39 Ⓐ Ⓑ Ⓒ Ⓓ Ⓔ
15 Ⓐ Ⓑ Ⓒ Ⓓ Ⓔ	40 Ⓐ Ⓑ Ⓒ Ⓓ Ⓔ
16 Ⓐ Ⓑ Ⓒ Ⓓ Ⓔ	41 Ⓐ Ⓑ Ⓒ Ⓓ Ⓔ
17 Ⓐ Ⓑ Ⓒ Ⓓ Ⓔ	42 Ⓐ Ⓑ Ⓒ Ⓓ Ⓔ
18 Ⓐ Ⓑ Ⓒ Ⓓ Ⓔ	43 Ⓐ Ⓑ Ⓒ Ⓓ Ⓔ
19 Ⓐ Ⓑ Ⓒ Ⓓ Ⓔ	44 Ⓐ Ⓑ Ⓒ Ⓓ Ⓔ
20 Ⓐ Ⓑ Ⓒ Ⓓ Ⓔ	45 Ⓐ Ⓑ Ⓒ Ⓓ Ⓔ
21 Ⓐ Ⓑ Ⓒ Ⓓ Ⓔ	46 Ⓐ Ⓑ Ⓒ Ⓓ Ⓔ
22 Ⓐ Ⓑ Ⓒ Ⓓ Ⓔ	47 Ⓐ Ⓑ Ⓒ Ⓓ Ⓔ
23 Ⓐ Ⓑ Ⓒ Ⓓ Ⓔ	48 Ⓐ Ⓑ Ⓒ Ⓓ Ⓔ
24 Ⓐ Ⓑ Ⓒ Ⓓ Ⓔ	49 Ⓐ Ⓑ Ⓒ Ⓓ Ⓔ
25 Ⓐ Ⓑ Ⓒ Ⓓ Ⓔ	50 Ⓐ Ⓑ Ⓒ Ⓓ Ⓔ

SECTION IV

1 Ⓐ Ⓑ Ⓒ Ⓓ Ⓔ	26 Ⓐ Ⓑ Ⓒ Ⓓ Ⓔ
2 Ⓐ Ⓑ Ⓒ Ⓓ Ⓔ	27 Ⓐ Ⓑ Ⓒ Ⓓ Ⓔ
3 Ⓐ Ⓑ Ⓒ Ⓓ Ⓔ	28 Ⓐ Ⓑ Ⓒ Ⓓ Ⓔ
4 Ⓐ Ⓑ Ⓒ Ⓓ Ⓔ	29 Ⓐ Ⓑ Ⓒ Ⓓ Ⓔ
5 Ⓐ Ⓑ Ⓒ Ⓓ Ⓔ	30 Ⓐ Ⓑ Ⓒ Ⓓ Ⓔ
6 Ⓐ Ⓑ Ⓒ Ⓓ Ⓔ	31 Ⓐ Ⓑ Ⓒ Ⓓ Ⓔ
7 Ⓐ Ⓑ Ⓒ Ⓓ Ⓔ	32 Ⓐ Ⓑ Ⓒ Ⓓ Ⓔ
8 Ⓐ Ⓑ Ⓒ Ⓓ Ⓔ	33 Ⓐ Ⓑ Ⓒ Ⓓ Ⓔ
9 Ⓐ Ⓑ Ⓒ Ⓓ Ⓔ	34 Ⓐ Ⓑ Ⓒ Ⓓ Ⓔ
10 Ⓐ Ⓑ Ⓒ Ⓓ Ⓔ	35 Ⓐ Ⓑ Ⓒ Ⓓ Ⓔ
11 Ⓐ Ⓑ Ⓒ Ⓓ Ⓔ	36 Ⓐ Ⓑ Ⓒ Ⓓ Ⓔ
12 Ⓐ Ⓑ Ⓒ Ⓓ Ⓔ	37 Ⓐ Ⓑ Ⓒ Ⓓ Ⓔ
13 Ⓐ Ⓑ Ⓒ Ⓓ Ⓔ	38 Ⓐ Ⓑ Ⓒ Ⓓ Ⓔ
14 Ⓐ Ⓑ Ⓒ Ⓓ Ⓔ	39 Ⓐ Ⓑ Ⓒ Ⓓ Ⓔ
15 Ⓐ Ⓑ Ⓒ Ⓓ Ⓔ	40 Ⓐ Ⓑ Ⓒ Ⓓ Ⓔ
16 Ⓐ Ⓑ Ⓒ Ⓓ Ⓔ	
17 Ⓐ Ⓑ Ⓒ Ⓓ Ⓔ	
18 Ⓐ Ⓑ Ⓒ Ⓓ Ⓔ	
19 Ⓐ Ⓑ Ⓒ Ⓓ Ⓔ	
20 Ⓐ Ⓑ Ⓒ Ⓓ Ⓔ	
21 Ⓐ Ⓑ Ⓒ Ⓓ Ⓔ	
22 Ⓐ Ⓑ Ⓒ Ⓓ Ⓔ	
23 Ⓐ Ⓑ Ⓒ Ⓓ Ⓔ	
24 Ⓐ Ⓑ Ⓒ Ⓓ Ⓔ	
25 Ⓐ Ⓑ Ⓒ Ⓓ Ⓔ	

ANSWER SHEET FOR SAT AND TSWE PRACTICE TEST NO. 2
(Remove This Sheet and Use it to Mark Your Answers)

START WITH NUMBER 1 FOR EACH NEW SECTION OF THE TEST

SECTION V

1 Ⓐ Ⓑ Ⓒ Ⓓ Ⓔ
2 Ⓐ Ⓑ Ⓒ Ⓓ Ⓔ
3 Ⓐ Ⓑ Ⓒ Ⓓ Ⓔ
4 Ⓐ Ⓑ Ⓒ Ⓓ Ⓔ
5 Ⓐ Ⓑ Ⓒ Ⓓ Ⓔ
6 Ⓐ Ⓑ Ⓒ Ⓓ Ⓔ
7 Ⓐ Ⓑ Ⓒ Ⓓ Ⓔ
8 Ⓐ Ⓑ Ⓒ Ⓓ Ⓔ
9 Ⓐ Ⓑ Ⓒ Ⓓ Ⓔ
10 Ⓐ Ⓑ Ⓒ Ⓓ Ⓔ
11 Ⓐ Ⓑ Ⓒ Ⓓ Ⓔ
12 Ⓐ Ⓑ Ⓒ Ⓓ Ⓔ
13 Ⓐ Ⓑ Ⓒ Ⓓ Ⓔ
14 Ⓐ Ⓑ Ⓒ Ⓓ Ⓔ
15 Ⓐ Ⓑ Ⓒ Ⓓ Ⓔ
16 Ⓐ Ⓑ Ⓒ Ⓓ Ⓔ
17 Ⓐ Ⓑ Ⓒ Ⓓ Ⓔ
18 Ⓐ Ⓑ Ⓒ Ⓓ Ⓔ
19 Ⓐ Ⓑ Ⓒ Ⓓ Ⓔ
20 Ⓐ Ⓑ Ⓒ Ⓓ Ⓔ
21 Ⓐ Ⓑ Ⓒ Ⓓ Ⓔ
22 Ⓐ Ⓑ Ⓒ Ⓓ Ⓔ
23 Ⓐ Ⓑ Ⓒ Ⓓ Ⓔ
24 Ⓐ Ⓑ Ⓒ Ⓓ Ⓔ
25 Ⓐ Ⓑ Ⓒ Ⓓ Ⓔ

26 Ⓐ Ⓑ Ⓒ Ⓓ Ⓔ
27 Ⓐ Ⓑ Ⓒ Ⓓ Ⓔ
28 Ⓐ Ⓑ Ⓒ Ⓓ Ⓔ
29 Ⓐ Ⓑ Ⓒ Ⓓ Ⓔ
30 Ⓐ Ⓑ Ⓒ Ⓓ Ⓔ
31 Ⓐ Ⓑ Ⓒ Ⓓ Ⓔ
32 Ⓐ Ⓑ Ⓒ Ⓓ Ⓔ
33 Ⓐ Ⓑ Ⓒ Ⓓ Ⓔ
34 Ⓐ Ⓑ Ⓒ Ⓓ Ⓔ
35 Ⓐ Ⓑ Ⓒ Ⓓ Ⓔ

SECTION VI

1 Ⓐ Ⓑ Ⓒ Ⓓ Ⓔ
2 Ⓐ Ⓑ Ⓒ Ⓓ Ⓔ
3 Ⓐ Ⓑ Ⓒ Ⓓ Ⓔ
4 Ⓐ Ⓑ Ⓒ Ⓓ Ⓔ
5 Ⓐ Ⓑ Ⓒ Ⓓ Ⓔ
6 Ⓐ Ⓑ Ⓒ Ⓓ Ⓔ
7 Ⓐ Ⓑ Ⓒ Ⓓ Ⓔ
8 Ⓐ Ⓑ Ⓒ Ⓓ Ⓔ
9 Ⓐ Ⓑ Ⓒ Ⓓ Ⓔ
10 Ⓐ Ⓑ Ⓒ Ⓓ Ⓔ
11 Ⓐ Ⓑ Ⓒ Ⓓ Ⓔ
12 Ⓐ Ⓑ Ⓒ Ⓓ Ⓔ
13 Ⓐ Ⓑ Ⓒ Ⓓ Ⓔ
14 Ⓐ Ⓑ Ⓒ Ⓓ Ⓔ
15 Ⓐ Ⓑ Ⓒ Ⓓ Ⓔ
16 Ⓐ Ⓑ Ⓒ Ⓓ Ⓔ
17 Ⓐ Ⓑ Ⓒ Ⓓ Ⓔ
18 Ⓐ Ⓑ Ⓒ Ⓓ Ⓔ
19 Ⓐ Ⓑ Ⓒ Ⓓ Ⓔ
20 Ⓐ Ⓑ Ⓒ Ⓓ Ⓔ
21 Ⓐ Ⓑ Ⓒ Ⓓ Ⓔ
22 Ⓐ Ⓑ Ⓒ Ⓓ Ⓔ
23 Ⓐ Ⓑ Ⓒ Ⓓ Ⓔ
24 Ⓐ Ⓑ Ⓒ Ⓓ Ⓔ
25 Ⓐ Ⓑ Ⓒ Ⓓ Ⓔ

26 Ⓐ Ⓑ Ⓒ Ⓓ Ⓔ
27 Ⓐ Ⓑ Ⓒ Ⓓ Ⓔ
28 Ⓐ Ⓑ Ⓒ Ⓓ Ⓔ
29 Ⓐ Ⓑ Ⓒ Ⓓ Ⓔ
30 Ⓐ Ⓑ Ⓒ Ⓓ Ⓔ
31 Ⓐ Ⓑ Ⓒ Ⓓ Ⓔ
32 Ⓐ Ⓑ Ⓒ Ⓓ Ⓔ
33 Ⓐ Ⓑ Ⓒ Ⓓ Ⓔ
34 Ⓐ Ⓑ Ⓒ Ⓓ Ⓔ
35 Ⓐ Ⓑ Ⓒ Ⓓ Ⓔ
36 Ⓐ Ⓑ Ⓒ Ⓓ Ⓔ
37 Ⓐ Ⓑ Ⓒ Ⓓ Ⓔ
38 Ⓐ Ⓑ Ⓒ Ⓓ Ⓔ
39 Ⓐ Ⓑ Ⓒ Ⓓ Ⓔ
40 Ⓐ Ⓑ Ⓒ Ⓓ Ⓔ

CUT HERE

SECTION I: VERBAL ABILITY

Time: 30 Minutes
45 Questions

In this section, choose the best answer for each question and blacken the corresponding space on the answer sheet.

Antonyms

DIRECTIONS

Each word in CAPITAL LETTERS is followed by five words or phrases. The correct choice is the word or phrase whose meaning is most nearly *opposite* to the meaning of the word in capitals. You may be required to distinguish fine shades of meaning. Look at all choices before marking your answer.

1. FANTASY
   - (A) substance
   - (B) reality
   - (C) archetype
   - (D) survival
   - (E) image

2. MOPE
   - (A) slur
   - (B) rollick
   - (C) spill
   - (D) enjoy
   - (E) agree

3. FORTHWITH
   - (A) forthcoming
   - (B) consecutively
   - (C) right away
   - (D) after a while
   - (E) instantaneously

4. PRAISE
   - (A) blandishment
   - (B) distinction
   - (C) vilification
   - (D) portrayal
   - (E) celebration

5. FRENZY
   - (A) aberration
   - (B) rehearsal
   - (C) fatigue
   - (D) dementia
   - (E) calm

6. PARDON
   (A) acquit
   (B) punish
   (C) deserve
   (D) claim
   (E) remit

7. CONCILIATORY
   (A) personal
   (B) irrational
   (C) pessimistic
   (D) divisive
   (E) agreeable

8. AMBIGUOUS
   (A) clear
   (B) faulty
   (C) equivocal
   (D) obscure
   (E) secure

9. DISPASSIONATE
   (A) tepid
   (B) affectionate
   (C) partial
   (D) unafraid
   (E) hopeful

10. PRIM
   (A) pert
   (B) orderly
   (C) prissy
   (D) hatless
   (E) enraged

11. DOGMATIC
   (A) categorical
   (B) rhetorical
   (C) doubtful
   (D) skillful
   (E) forceful

12. TRANSIENT
   (A) indifferent
   (B) divergent
   (C) sacrosanct
   (D) permanent
   (E) indefinite

13. CONTUMACIOUS
   (A) compliant
   (B) reciprocal
   (C) pertinacious
   (D) obdurate
   (E) dogged

14. CLOY
   (A) starve
   (B) mold
   (C) club
   (D) flay
   (E) glut

15. VERACITY
   (A) falseness
   (B) subordination
   (C) mercy
   (D) ingenuousness
   (E) complaint

Sentence Completion

DIRECTIONS

Each blank in the following sentences indicates that something has been omitted. Consider the lettered words beneath the sentence and choose the word or set of words that best fits the whole sentence.

16. The trustees reported that the previous year's expenditures had already _____ the budget and that additional spending would be impossible.
    (A) increased
    (B) exceeded
    (C) eased
    (D) restored
    (E) authorized

17. The author has no interest in African _____, so his book is _____ as a guide to the animals of Kenya and Uganda.
    (A) beasts . . . helpful
    (B) flora . . . useless
    (C) creatures . . . instructive
    (D) livestock . . . useful
    (E) fauna . . . valueless

18. The concepts that physicists introduce to explain phenomena are often quite unlike anything that can be _____ from observation of the world around us.
    (A) deduced
    (B) seen
    (C) induced
    (D) implied
    (E) accepted

19. After the smoke and _____ of the city, Mr. Fitzgerald was glad to return to the _____ air and peace of the mountains.
    (A) hubbub . . . turbid
    (B) grime . . . murky
    (C) tranquility . . . effulgent
    (D) composure . . . brisk
    (E) hustle-bustle . . . exhilarating

20. The _____ upon which this fine novel is developed with great _____ and intelligence is that no males live beyond the age of eighteen.
    (A) theory . . . fatuity
    (B) plot . . . understanding
    (C) idea . . . recalcitrance
    (D) promise . . . subtlety
    (E) solution . . . cleverness

Reading Comprehension

DIRECTIONS

Questions follow each of the passages below. Using only the stated or implied information in each passage, answer the questions.

Questions 21 through 25 are based on the following passage.

Geologic processes have not necessarily been uniform in time. Glaciation, for example, has been spasmodic, occurring only at rare intervals during the past. Mountains have been formed at different times in different places and have been unequally spaced in their origin and distribution. The relative arrangement of land and sea has varied considerably, so that maps of the continents would continually be different but not in predictable fashion. The evolution of life has been one-directional and its results cannot be anticipated. Thus, geology has been described as "the historical science." But the principles of cause and effect have been dependable, so that miracles and catastrophes need not be required to account for geologic features. Sudden and drastic events are not ruled out, however, so long as they take place in a natural fashion.

The original meanings of the names given to the intervals of geologic time have been modified, so that they no longer carry much of their original (mostly geographic) significance. Thus, Devonian rocks were first studied in Devonshire, and the Cretaceous rocks were often chalky (*crete* means *chalk*) where originally described. The nature of the fossil record is now given chief emphasis. Eras (representing the main chapters of earth history) are subdivided into periods, and these into epochs.

Formations are named after a type locality, which is where they were first described. Thus, the famous St. Peter sandstone was named for a town in Minnesota. Formations may be divided into members, or they may be combined into groups; members and groups are also given names. Formations are usually sedimentary rocks, but igneous and metamorphic bodies may be similarly named (such as the Pikes Peak granite). The boundary between two beds (strata) is called the bedding plane. The formations of a given locality can be charted as a columnar section, in which the older rock is drawn beneath the younger one as in the normal sequence in the earth.

The original position of bedded rocks (which are always deposited nearly flat) can be determined by such features as mud cracks, ripple marks, raindrop impressions, and the gas cavities in lava. These features show which side of the rock was up and which was down, for some of them occur only at the top or are different at the top.

Parallel strata that are separated by an interval of lost time make up a disconformity. If rocks of two different types (igneous, sedimentary, or metamorphic) are in such contact, the structure is called a nonconformity. When the lower beds were tilted before the upper ones were put down, an angular unconformity resulted.

Rock layers can sometimes be correlated by observing them over a considerable distance, as along a canyon wall, such as across the Grand Canyon. Some rocks appear similar in composition, texture, color, or other features over a wide distance. The more distinctive a bed is, the farther it can be traced with confidence; red sandstone and gray shale, for instance, are often ordinary looking, for there are many rocks like them.

21. According to the passage, in both time and location, geologic processes are
    (A) regularly spaced   (D) rapid
    (B) determined by catastrophe (E) unpredictable
    (C) sudden and drastic

22. With which of the following would the author of the passage be most likely to agree?
    (A) Glaciation depends upon cause and effect.
    (B) In geological history, no events are sudden.
    (C) The time of the occurrence of most geological events is predictable.
    (D) Some geological events can be explained only as miracles.
    (E) The distribution of mountains on the surface of the earth is regular.

23. According to the passage, the turned-up side of a bedded rock might retain
    (A) chalkiness   (D) raindrop impressions
    (B) its original hardness   (E) an ancient fossil
    (C) its original shape

24. Geology has been called the "historical science" because it is
    (A) more scientific than historical
    (B) more predictable than other sciences
    (C) more concerned with the past than with the present
    (D) concerned with a one-directional evolution of life
    (E) more scientific than historical

25. Igneous, sedimentary, and metamorphic are terms distinguishing
    (A) formations of different types
    (B) bedding positions
    (C) rocks of different ages
    (D) red sandstone from gray shale
    (E) the age of rocks

Questions 26 through 30 are based on the following passage.

Many people seem to think that science fiction is typified by the covers of some of the old pulp magazines: the Bug-Eyed Monster, embodying every trait and feature that most people find repulsive, is about to grab, and presumably ravish, a scantily-clad Earth girl. This is unfortunate because it demeans and degrades a worthwhile and even important literary endeavor. In contrast to this unwarranted stereotype, science fiction rarely emphasizes sex, and when it does, it is more discreet than other contemporary fiction. Instead, the basic interest of science fiction lies in the relation between man and his technology and between man and the universe. Science fiction is a literature of change and a literature of the future, and while it would be foolish to claim that science fiction is a major literary genre at this time, the aspects of human life that it considers make it well worth reading and studying— for no other literary form does quite the same things.

The question is: what is science fiction? And the answer must be, unfortunately, that there have been few attempts to consider this question at any length or with much seriousness; it may well be that science fiction will resist any comprehensive definition of its characteristics. To say this, however, does not mean that there are no ways of defining it nor that various facets of its totality cannot be clarified. To begin, the following definition should be helpful: science fiction is a literary sub-genre which postulates a change (for human beings) from conditions as we know them and follows the implications of these changes to a conclusion. Although this definition will necessarily be modified and expanded, and probably changed, in the course of the exploration, it covers much of the basic groundwork and provides a point of departure.

The first point—that science fiction is a literary sub-genre—is a very important one, but one which is often overlooked or ignored in most discussions of science fiction. Specifically, science fiction is a sub-genre of prose fiction, for nearly every piece of science fiction is either a short story or a novel. There are only a very few dramas which could be called science fiction, with Karel Capek's *RUR* (Rossum's Universal Robots) being the only one that is well known; the body of poetry that might be labeled science fiction is only slightly larger. To say that science fiction is a sub-genre of prose fiction is to say that it has all the basic characteristics and serves the same basic functions in much the same way as prose fiction in general—that is, it shares a great deal with all other novels and short stories.

Everything that can be said about prose fiction, in general applies to science fiction. Every piece of science fiction, whether short story or novel, must have a narrator, a story, a plot, a setting, characters, language, and theme. And like any prose, the themes of science fiction are concerned with interpreting man's nature and experience in relation to the world around him. Themes in science fiction are constructed and presented in exactly the same ways that themes are dealt with in any other kind of fiction. They are the result of a particular combination of narrator, story, plot, character, setting, and language. In short, the reasons for reading and enjoying science fiction, and the ways of studying and analyzing it, are basically the same as they would be for any other story or novel.

26. Science fiction is called a literary sub-genre because
    (A) it is not important enough to be a literary genre
    (B) it cannot be made into a dramatic presentation
    (C) it has its limits
    (D) it shares characteristics with other types of prose fiction
    (E) to call it a "genre" would subject it to literary jargon

27. Which of the following does not usually contribute to the theme in a piece of science fiction?
    (A) narrator   (D) setting
    (B) character   (E) rhyme
    (C) plot

28. The view of science fiction encouraged by pulp magazines, while wrong, is nevertheless
    (A) popular   (D) deranged
    (B) elegant   (E) accurate
    (C) fashionable

29. An appropriate title for this passage would be
    (A) On the Inaccuracies of Pulp Magazines
    (B) Man and the Universe
    (C) Toward a Definition of Science Fiction
    (D) A Type of Prose Fiction
    (E) Beyond the Bug-Eyed Monster

30. The author's definition suggests that all science fiction deals with
    (A) monsters
    (B) the same topics addressed by novels and short stories
    (C) the unfamiliar or unusual
    (D) Karel Capek's well-known postulate
    (E) the conflict between science and fiction

Sentence Completion

DIRECTIONS

Each blank in the following sentences indicates that something has been omitted. Consider the lettered words beneath the sentence and choose the word or set of words that best fits the whole sentence.

31. Since the issue is so insignificant, it was surprising that the
_____ among the City Council members was so
_____.
    (A) argument . . . tepid   (D) dispute . . . acrimonious
    (B) disagreement . . . slovenly   (E) ratiocination . . . lurid
    (C) comment . . . trivial

32. _____ for talking too much, the teacher _____ his
    reputation by keeping the class thirty minutes longer than the scheduled
    class time.
    (A) Famous . . . evinced   (D) Illustrious . . . rebutted
    (B) Renowned . . . overturned   (E) Eminent . . . established
    (C) Notorious . . . verified

33. The critic praised the scenery of the film _____ but
    _____ his enthusiasm when he discussed the plot and charac-
    terization.
    (A) heartily . . . expanded   (D) fervidly . . . augmented
    (B) moderately . . . qualified   (E) backhandedly . . . lessened
    (C) effusively . . . tempered

34. The _____ use of washing machines and automobiles in the
    Middle Ages is part of the comedy of this high-spirited film.
    (A) untimely   (D) mistaken
    (B) anachronistic   (E) supposed
    (C) unconvincing

35. His biographer believed that Pierce's _____ was caused by his
    _____ to travel and his refusal to read about any position
    different from his own.
    (A) parochialism . . . reluctance   (D) narrow-mindedness . . . eagerness
    (B) insularity . . . readiness   (E) magnanimity . . . failure
    (C) bigotry . . . zeal

Analogies

DIRECTIONS

In each question below, you are given a related pair of words or phrases.
Select the lettered pair that *best* expresses a relationship similar to that in the
original pair of words.

36. SENATOR : CONGRESS : :
    (A) alcohol : wine   (D) leaf : plant
    (B) governor : state   (E) camera : film crew
    (C) spectator : crowd

37. CHOREOGRAPHER : DANCE ::
    (A) conductor : symphony
  • (B) artist : model
    (C) director : actor
    (D) ingredient : recipe
    (E) playwright : play

38. CONSTELLATION : STAR ::
    (A) quasar : comet
  • (B) sun : milky way
    (C) asteroid : planet
    (D) telescope : astronomer
    (E) solar system : planet

39. LAMB : MUTTON ::
    (A) chicken : turkey
  • (B) veal : beef
    (C) shrub : tree
    (D) root : flower
    (E) beef : cow

40. EARN : FILCH ::
    (A) create : plagiarize
  • (B) injure : maim
    (C) plant : bury
    (D) follow : stalk
    (E) lie : perjure

41. DISLIKE : LOATHE ::
    (A) praise : extol
  • (B) yearn : desire
    (C) insure : rely
    (D) stuff : cram
    (E) hurry : run

42. CREDULOUS : DOUBT ::
    (A) naive : sorrow
  • (B) avaricious : money
    (C) complacent : modesty
    (D) arduous : task
    (E) industrious : employment

43. SLANDER : LIBEL ::
    (A) magazine : book
  • (B) love : admiration
    (C) dance : song
    (D) speech : essay
    (E) felony : misdemeanor

44. GLADIOLUS : APHID ::
    (A) child : toothache
  • (B) home : mortgage
    (C) vulture : carrion
    (D) apple : scale
    (E) river : pollution

45. SURFEIT : DEARTH ::
    (A) reign : election
  • (B) flood : drought
    (C) top : bottom
    (D) teacher : pupil
    (E) hand : finger

STOP. IF YOU FINISH BEFORE TIME IS CALLED, CHECK YOUR WORK ON THIS SECTION ONLY. DO NOT WORK ON ANY OTHER SECTION IN THE TEST.

SECTION II: MATHEMATICAL ABILITY

Time: 30 Minutes
25 Questions

DIRECTIONS

Solve each problem in this section by using the information given and your own mathematical calculations. Then select the *one* correct answer of the five choices given. Use the available space on the page for scratchwork.

Data That May Be Used as Reference for This Section

The area formula for a circle of radius r is: $A = \pi r^2$
The circumference formula is: $C = 2\pi r$
A circle is composed of 360°.
A straight angle measures 180°.

Triangle: The sum of the angles of a triangle is 180°.
If angle ADB is a right angle, then

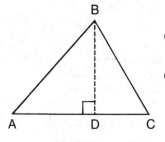

(1) The area of triangle ABC is $\dfrac{AC \times BD}{2}$

(2) $AD^2 + BD^2 = AB^2$

Symbol References:

= is equal to	≧ is greater than or equal to
≠ not equal to	≦ is less than or equal to
> is greater than	‖ is parallel to
< is less than	⊥ is perpendicular to

NOTE: Some problems may be accompanied by figures or diagrams. These figures are drawn as accurately as possible, EXCEPT when it is stated in a specific problem that the figure is not drawn to scale. The figures are meant to provide information useful in solving the problem or problems but are not meant to be measured.

Unless otherwise stated or indicated, all figures lie in a plane.

All numbers used are real numbers.

1. If .0039y = 39, then y =
   (A) 10   (B) 100   (C) 1000   (D) 10,000   (E) 100,000

2. What is the reciprocal of $\dfrac{.25 \times \dfrac{2}{3}}{.06 \times 15}$?
   (A) $\frac{3}{20}$ (B) $\frac{5}{27}$ (C) $\frac{2}{3}$ (D) $\frac{27}{5}$ (E) $\frac{20}{3}$

3. If it takes 18 minutes to fill $\frac{2}{3}$ of a container, how long will it take to fill the rest of the container at the same rate?
   (A) 6 minutes   (B) 9 minutes   (C) 12 minutes
   (D) 27 minutes   (E) 36 minutes

4. A man purchased 4 pounds of steak priced at $3.89 per pound. How much change did he receive from a twenty-dollar bill?
   (A) $44.66   (B) $15.56   (C) $4.46   (D) $4.44
   (E) $4.34

5. If x is between 0 and 1, which of the following statements is true?

   I. $x^2 > 1$
   II. $x^2 > 0$
   III. $x^2 > x$

   (A) I only   (B) II only   (C) III only   (D) I and II
   (E) II and III

6. If $16\frac{1}{2}$ feet equals 1 rod, how many inches are there in 4 rods?
   (A) 2376   (B) 792   (C) 66   (D) 22   (E) $5\frac{1}{2}$

7. If a = p + prt, then r =
   (A) $\dfrac{a-1}{t}$ (B) $\dfrac{a-p}{pt}$ (C) $a - p - pt$ (D) $\dfrac{a}{t}$
   (E) $\dfrac{a+p}{pt}$

8. What is 30% of $\frac{25}{18}$?
   (A) $\frac{5}{108}$ (B) $\frac{5}{12}$ (C) $\frac{25}{54}$ (D) $\frac{25}{6}$ (E) $\frac{125}{3}$

9. How many degrees has the minute hand moved on a clock from 4:00 P.M. to 4:12 P.M.?
   (A) 12   (B) 36   (C) 72   (D) 90
   (E) cannot be determined

10. On the circle with center C, CD ⊥ AB, AB = 24 and CD = 5. Find the radius of the circle.

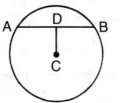

Note: Figure not drawn to scale.

   (A) 19   (B) 17   (C) 13   (D) 7
   (E) cannot be determined

11. If r represents the tens digit and s represents the unit's digit of a two-digit number, then the number would be represented by
   (A) rs   (B) sr   (C) r +   (D) 10r + s   (E) 10s + r

12. Which of the following ordered pairs (a,b) is not a member of the solution set of 2a − 3b = 6?
   (A) (6,2)   (B) (−3,−4)   (C) (3,0)   (D) (4,⅔)
   (E) (0,2)

13. Find the area of the given trapezoid in square inches.

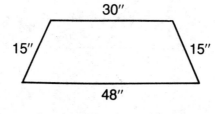

   (A) 108   (B) 234   (C) 468   (D) 585
   (E) cannot be determined

14. Which of the following is the smallest?

    (A) ⅛   (B) $(.3)^2$ (C) ⅓   (D) $\sqrt{.36}$ (E) ¹¹/₁₀₀

15. If $x - y = 15$ and $3x + y = 13$, then y =
    (A) -8 (B) -7 (C) 7   (D) 8
    (E) none of the above

16. If the diagonal of a rectangle is 16, then what is its area in square units?
    (A) 32   (B) 64   (C) 160   (D) 256
    (E) cannot be determined

17. The average of three numbers is 55. The second is 1 more than twice the first, and the third is 4 less than three times the first. Find the largest number.
    (A) 165   (B) 88   (C) 80   (D) 57
    (E) none of the above

18. Find the total surface area in square meters of a rectangular solid whose length is 7 meters, width is 6 meters, and depth is 3 meters.
    (A) $32m^2$ (B) $81m^2$ (C) $126m^2$ (D) $162m^2$
    (E) $252m^2$

19. In the figure, X and Y are the centers of the two circles. If the area of the larger circle is 144π, what is the area of the smaller circle?

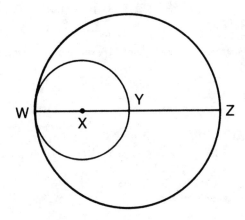

    (A) 72π (B) 36π (C) 24π (D) 12π
    (E) cannot be determined

20. Bob is older than Jane but he is younger than Jim. If Bob's age is b, Jane's age is c, and Jim's is d, then which of the following is true?
    (A) $c < b < d$ (B) $b < c < d$ (C) $b < d < c$
    (D) $c < d < b$ (E) $d < c < b$

21. In a triangle, the ratio of two angles is 5:2, and the third angle is equal to the difference between the other two. Find the number of degrees in the smallest angle.
    (A) 36   (B) $25\frac{5}{7}$ (C) $25\frac{2}{7}$ (D) 18
    (E) cannot be determined

22. If $\frac{a}{b} = \frac{c}{d}$ and a, b, c, and d are positive integers, then which of the following is true?

    (A) $\frac{a}{b} = \frac{d}{c}$ (B) $ac = bd$ (C) $a + d = b + c$

    (D) $\frac{d}{b} = \frac{c}{a}$ (E) $\frac{a}{d} = \frac{c}{b}$

23. The base of an isosceles triangle exceeds each of the equal sides by 8 feet. If the perimeter is 89 feet, find the length of the base in feet.
    (A) 27   (B) $29\frac{2}{3}$ (C) 35   (D) 54
    (E) cannot be determined

24. If $(a,b) \oplus (c,d) = (ac - bd, ad)$ then $(-2,3) \oplus (4,-1) =$
    (A) $(-5,2)$ (B) $(-5,-2)$ (C) $(-11,2)$ (D) $(-11,-2)$
    (E) $(-5,-3)$

25. If m and n are integers and $\sqrt{mn} = 10$, which of the following cannot be a value of $m + n$?
    (A) 25   (B) 29   (C) 50   (D) 52   (E) 101

STOP. IF YOU FINISH BEFORE TIME IS CALLED, CHECK YOUR WORK ON THIS SECTION ONLY. DO NOT WORK ON ANY OTHER SECTION IN THE TEST.

SECTION III: TEST OF STANDARD WRITTEN ENGLISH

Time: 30 Minutes
50 Questions

In this section, choose the best answer for each question and blacken the corresponding space on the answer sheet.

Usage

DIRECTIONS

Some of the following sentences are correct. Others contain problems in grammar, usage, idiom, or diction (word choice). There is not more than one error in any sentence.

If there is an error, it will be underlined and lettered. Find the one underlined part that must be changed to make the sentence correct, and choose the corresponding letter on your answer sheet. Mark (E) if the sentence contains no error.

1. Between he and his wife there have been nothing but arguments; this
         A   B
   is a situation which is strikingly atypical of most modern marriages.
                    C   D
   No error.
     E

2. I'm willing to sell you this refrigerator at ten percent above cost,
                                           A
   being that you are the Chief of Police and might do me a favor
      B   C   D
   someday. No error.
          E

3. The advance of the Mongol army into Italy's outskirts were so
        A   B
   threatening that the Pope met personally with Genghis Khan to
              C   D
   ask him to retreat. No error.
             E

4. The old song "Our Day Will Come" expressed the <u>same</u> hopes and
   A   B
   dreams <u>which</u> occupy <u>we</u> teenagers today. <u>No error.</u>
   C   D   E

5. In opposition <u>to</u> President Carter's foreign policy <u>was the</u>
   A   B
   <u>House</u> Majority Leader and the Chairman of the <u>Ways and Means</u>
   C   D
   <u>Committee.</u> <u>No error.</u>
   D   E

6. In his valedictory address, the scholar insisted that <u>this here</u>
   A
   society remains <u>decent and strong</u> despite the presence of so many
   B
   <u>who</u> are ignorant and <u>avaricious.</u> <u>No error.</u>
   C   D   E

7. Attorneys <u>these days</u> may practice corporate law, <u>environmental law</u>
   A   B
   or <u>choosing from</u> a variety of <u>other</u> alternatives. <u>No error.</u>
   C   D   E

8. <u>There is</u> only a box of cereal and three breadsticks in the
   A
   cupboard, so we <u>better</u> go to the market and <u>stock up</u> <u>on food</u>
   B   C   D
   <u>No error.</u>
   E

9. I'm sure that I can <u>vault</u> higher than <u>him</u> today, because in
   A   B
   yesterday's warm-up my performance <u>was better</u> <u>than his</u> on three
   C   D
   occasions. <u>No error.</u>
   E

10. When I think about <u>the person</u> I'd like to be in ten years, I
    A
    wonder if <u>this kind</u> of people <u>whom</u> I now associate with <u>will change.</u>
    B   C   D
    <u>No error.</u>
    E

11. Neither my uncle nor my brother ever refused to share their leisure
     A   B   C

    time with me, and so I was never short of companions. No error.
            D   E

12. Jeff is always more talkative than any student in his class because
               A   B   C   D

    he is not afraid of the teacher. No error.
                           E

13. Running good has Cindy feeling fit, so she continues to race 10 miles
         A   B   C

    a day, even when it rains. No error.
                D   E

14. Few scientists today expect their discoveries to be compared with
                           A

    Einstein, yet many work hard to advance knowledge by questioning
      B   C   D

    and clarifying the major discoveries of the past. No error.
        D   E

15. Although my grandfather doesn't scarcely read or write English,
                           A

    he has advanced himself in this country by relying on hard work
                  B   C

    and a quick wit. No error.
        D   E

Sentence Correction

DIRECTIONS

Some part of each sentence below is underlined; sometimes the whole sentence is underlined. Five choices for rephrasing the underlined part follow each sentence; the first choice (A) repeats the original, and the other four are different. If choice (A) seems better than the alternatives, choose answer (A); if not, choose one of the others.

For each sentence, consider the requirements of Standard Written English. Your choice should be a correct and effective expression, not awkward or ambiguous. Focus on grammar, word choice, sentence construction, and punctuation. If a choice changes the meaning of the original sentence, do not select it.

16. Most of us <u>have been told for</u> the decision, but are unsure what to do next
    (A) have been told for
    (B) have been told of
    (C) have been told it
    (D) have been told to
    (E) have been told over

17. Long before the American Revolution there were Colonial disputes over <u>unfair taxes, British arrogance, and that many citiziens were unfairly imprisoned.</u>
    (A) unfair taxes, British arrogance, and that many citizens were unfairly imprisoned.
    (B) that unfair taxes, that British arrogance, and that many citizens were unfairly imprisoned.
    (C) unfair taxes, British taxes, and citizen imprisonment.
    (D) unfair taxes, British arrogance, and unfair imprisonment.
    (E) that the taxes were unfair, that the British were arrogant, and that the citizens were imprisoned.

18. The roller coaster at Magic Mountain allows people to forget their everyday cares, <u>and encourage them to laugh</u> and scream their tensions away.
    (A) and encourage them to laugh
    (B) and encourages them to laugh
    (C) and encouraging them to laugh
    (D) and makes them laugh
    (E) and keeps them laughing

19. Several very distinguished friends of mine <u>they always say clever things</u> while I stand silently by.
    (A) they always say clever things
    (B) they often say clever things
    (C) always say clever things
    (D) often say clever things
    (E) act cleverly

20. Although we're <u>not that good of friends</u>, Ron and I often show up at the same parties and have interesting conversations with each other.
    (A) not that good of friends
    (B) not being very good friends
    (C) just acquaintances
    (D) not good friends
    (E) not very good friends

21. Because many of us refused to do the assigned work, others <u>were assigned</u> to do it, much to their dismay.
    (A) were assigned
    (B) was assigned
    (C) found workers
    (D) became assigned
    (E) assigning themselves

22. <u>Having celebrated through the night with casks of wine, beautiful women, and loud disco music that almost burst our eardrums.</u>
    (A) Having celebrated through the night with casks of wine, beautiful women, and loud disco music that almost burst our eardrums.
    (B) Having celebrated through the night with casks of wine, beautiful women, and loud disco music we burst our eardrums.
    (C) We celebrated through the night with casks of wine, beautiful women, and loud disco music that almost burst our eardrums.
    (D) After celebrating through the night we almost burst our eardrums with casks of wine, beautiful women, and loud disco music that almost burst our eardrums.
    (E) Having celebrated through the night casks of wine, beautiful women, and loud disco music almost burst our eardrums.

23. Socrates is a man, and men are mortal; <u>therefore Socrates is mortal.</u>
    (A) therefore Socrates is mortal.
    (B) therefore Socrates is a mortal.
    (C) therefore Socrates became mortal.
    (D) therefore Socrates is a man.
    (E) therefore men are mortal.

24. <u>I have and always will be conscious</u> of my moral obligation as a citizen.
    (A) I have and always will be conscious
    (B) I have to and always will be conscious
    (C) I have been being and always will be conscious
    (D) I have been and always will be conscious
    (E) I am and always will be

25. Looking closely at the intersection, <u>the remains</u> of the accident told a tale of carelessness and death.
    (A) the remains
    (B) remains
    (C) I saw that the remains
    (D) the accident's remaining
    (E) all that remained

26. <u>That all the people</u> gathered here—parents, teachers, students—are interested in upgrading the quality of education in local schools, then we can begin drawing up a plan within the next few days.
    (A) That all the people
    (B) That all these people
    (C) If all the people
    (D) If all these people
    (E) All the people

27. Even when political issues tear at the very fiber of American society, <u>they do not bother to learn</u> about the issues fully or to vote.
    (A) they do not bother to learn
    (B) they do not care to learn
    (C) votives do not bother to learn
    (D) that fiber does not bother to learn
    (E) people do not bother to learn

28. When a local sportswriter said that Joe Namath was <u>the best quarterback when compared to</u> Roman Gabriel, many Southern Californians called him wrong.
    (A) the best quarterback when compared to
    (B) a better quaterback than
    (C) one of the best quarterbacks when compared to
    (D) the best quarterback that compared to
    (E) the best quarterback compared to

29. <u>Hunger plagued the jungle village, which resulted from a lack of fresh meat</u>.
    (A) Hunger plagued the jungle village, which resulted from a lack of fresh meat.
    (B) Hunger as a result of a lack of fresh meat plagued the jungle village.
    (C) Hunger, which had resulted from the lacking of fresh meat, plagued the jungle village.
    (D) Hunger, caused by a lack of fresh meat, plagued the jungle village.
    (E) The jungle village, plagued by a lack of fresh meat, went hungry.

30. <u>Knowing that he ought to of been</u> more careful, the man nevertheless stubbed his toe while turning a corner in the dark.
    (A) Knowing that he ought to of been
    (B) Knowing that he may have been
    (C) Knowing that he should have been
    (D) Knowing that he had better be
    (E) Knowing to be

31. Her Thanksgiving dinner was always more digestible than the neighbors.
    (A) Her Thanksgiving dinner was always more digestible than the neighbors.
    (B) Her Thanksgiving dinner was always more digestible than were the neighbors.
    (C) Her Thanksgiving dinner was always more digestible than that of the neighbors.
    (D) Her Thanksgiving dinner was always more digestible for the neighbors.
    (E) Her Thanksgiving dinner gave the neighbors indigestion.

32. Laying down their arms, the enemy surrendered.
    (A) Laying down their arms, the enemy surrendered.
    (B) Having lain down their arms, the enemy surrendered.
    (C) In laying down their arms, the enemy surrendered.
    (D) Lowering their arms, the enemy surrendered.
    (E) Lying down their arms, the enemy surrendered.

33. More and better workspaces, according to a national labor leader, is going to encourage workers to do more efficient jobs.
    (A) is going to encourage workers to do more efficient jobs.
    (B) are going to encourage workers to do a more efficient job.
    (C) are going to encourage workers to be efficient.
    (D) is going to encourage workers to be efficient.
    (E) makes workers efficient.

34. The top of the letter said, "To whom it may concern."
    (A) The top of the letter said, "To whom it may concern."
    (B) The top of the letter introduced, "To whom it may concern."
    (C) The top of the letter said to whom it may concern.
    (D) The top of the letter was of general concern.
    (E) The top of the letter addressed whoever was concerned.

35. To become rich, to become famous, and having many close friends were his goals when he was eighteen, but by age forty, Harry had attained none of them.
    (A) To become rich, to become famous, and having many close friends
    (B) To become rich, to become famous, and to have many close friends
    (C) Rich, famous, and friendly
    (D) To be rich, famous, and friendly
    (E) Riches, fame, and friends

Usage

DIRECTIONS

Some of the following sentences are correct. Others contain problems in grammar, usage, idiom, or diction (word choice). There is not more than one error in any sentence.

If there is an error, it will be underlined and lettered. Find the one underlined part that must be changed to make the sentence correct, and choose the corresponding letter on your answer sheet. Mark (E) if the sentence contains no error.

36. Henry Kissinger, the former <u>Secretary of State</u>, once called for
                                        A
    <u>bi-partisan</u> agreement <u>among</u> the members of Congress <u>whom</u>, he
        B   C   D
    declared, were slowing his efforts toward peace. <u>No error.</u>
                                                          E

37. Because fuel supplies are <u>finite</u> and many men <u>are</u> wasteful, we
                                   A   B
    <u>will be forced</u> to install some <u>type of a</u> solar heating device in our
         C   D
    home by the middle of the 1980s. <u>No error.</u>
                                          E

38. Although he was <u>nowheres near</u> the finish line, the aging <u>but</u> famous
                         A   B
    runner stopped in <u>exhaustion,</u> smiling and nodding while <u>his</u> young
                           C   D
    friend passed him and raced on to victory. <u>No error.</u>
                                                     E

39. Standing <u>alongside</u> my friend and <u>me</u> in the hallway <u>were</u> Robert
                  A   B   C
    Redford and Dustin Hoffman, but we <u>were</u> too shy to step up and say
                                            D
    hello. <u>No error.</u>
                E

40. <u>Whether</u> the civic leaders can pass a tax reduction bill, the
         A
    citizens <u>will continue</u> to <u>demonstrate</u> their anger at the <u>ever-</u>
                  B   C   D
    <u>rising</u> cost of government. <u>No error.</u>
         D   E

41. There <u>was</u> forecasts and a warning on television about an approach-
   A B

ing <u>hurricane; citizens</u> were advised <u>to stay</u> indoors all evening.
   C   D

<u>No error.</u>
 E

42. Unable to prepare <u>real</u> well for the test, Joan nevertheless
      A

received <u>an "A"</u> because <u>her</u> guesses turned out <u>to be</u> correct.
   B   C   D

<u>No error.</u>
 E

43. Hal was my best friend for <u>some time,</u> and we were such an <u>in-</u>
         A   B

<u>separable pair</u> that <u>no one</u> in the neighborhood was ever surprised
 B   C

to see <u>him and I.</u> <u>No error.</u>
   D   E

44. Both opinions are <u>respectable, but</u> the <u>one which</u> is supported
       A   B

by a specific plan <u>should</u> impress everyone as the <u>most</u> admirable.
      C   D

<u>No error.</u>
 E

45. Only one <u>of the dozen</u> apartment <u>units</u> I inspected <u>show</u> any neglect
    A   B   C

on <u>the part</u> of the manager. <u>No error.</u>
  D   E

46. At six A.M. <u>in the morning</u> we trudged up the hill, <u>groggily</u>
     A   B

<u>looking</u> forward to a <u>fifteen-mile</u> hike. <u>No error.</u>
 C   D   E

47. A flock of <u>pigeons</u> <u>are</u> unexpected this time of year, and <u>it's</u>
    A B   C

especially surprising to see them winging through the city <u>amidst</u>
                    D

a snowstorm. <u>No error.</u>
    E

48. Before the earth had <u>it's</u> land masses, the entire planet was a
                          A
    <u>bubbling, soupy</u> sea of elements which we <u>now</u> call the building
         B   C
    blocks <u>of life.</u> <u>No error.</u>
            D   E

49. <u>Few</u> of us don't realize until <u>too</u> late what we <u>ought to of</u> studied <u>in</u>
    A   B   C   D
    high school. <u>No error.</u>
                  E

50. Music <u>in</u> <u>Beethoven's</u> <u>time</u> may not have sounded as <u>sweetly</u> as
          A   B   C   D
    it does on modern instruments. <u>No error.</u>
                                     E

STOP. IF YOU FINISH BEFORE TIME IS CALLED, CHECK YOUR
WORK ON THIS SECTION ONLY. DO NOT WORK ON ANY
OTHER SECTION IN THE TEST.

SECTION IV: VERBAL ABILITY

Time 30 Minutes
40 Questions

In this section, choose the best answer for each question and blacken the corresponding space on the answer sheet.

Antonyms

DIRECTIONS

Each word in CAPITAL LETTERS is followed by five words or phrases. The correct choice is the word or phrase whose meaning is most nearly *opposite* to the meaning of the word in capitals. You may be required to distinguish fine shades of meaning. Look at all choices before marking your answer.

1. CONCLAVE
   - (A) marriage
   - (B) ritual
   - (C) public assembly
   - (D) display
   - (E) divorce

2. UNISON
   - (A) symmetry
   - (B) discord
   - (C) amity
   - (D) distance
   - (E) consent

3. PRIMEVAL
   - (A) indigenous
   - (B) secondary
   - (C) prime
   - (D) uncreated
   - (E) modern

4. PICTURESQUE
   - (A) impending
   - (B) beauteous
   - (C) grotesque
   - (D) unruly
   - (E) fine

5. DARKSOME
   - (A) clear
   - (B) elliptical
   - (C) turbid
   - (D) criminal
   - (E) white

6. AFFIDAVIT
   (A) forgery
   (B) note
   (C) curse
   (D) opinion
   (E) report

7. LACONICALLY
   (A) compendiously
   (B) obtrusively
   (C) verbosely
   (D) lethargically
   (E) creatively

8. METAMORPHOSE
   (A) conserve
   (B) remain the same
   (C) modify
   (D) keep hold
   (E) commute

9. RESUSCITATE
   (A) succumb
   (B) crush
   (C) flatter
   (D) kill
   (E) succeed

10. ESTHETICISM
    (A) tastelessness
    (B) formlessness
    (C) pragmatism
    (D) resolution
    (E) enthusiasm

Sentence Completion

DIRECTIONS

Each blank in the following sentences indicates that something has been omitted. Consider the lettered words beneath the sentence and choose the word or set of words that best fits the whole sentence.

11. In Angola, where the local currency is all but _____, people use cans of beer or Coca Cola as a means of exchange.
    (A) over
    (B) valued
    (C) worthless
    (D) earned
    (E) paramount

12. In a landscape so calm and beautiful, it was hard to believe that anything _____ could occur.
    (A) untoward
    (B) temperate
    (C) halcyon
    (D) seemly
    (E) refined

13. If both political parties can abandon _____ positions in the face of economic realities, a _____ may be achieved that will permit the government to function.
   (A) sensible . . . compromise
   (B) dogmatic . . . consensus
   (C) incisive . . . schism
   (D) irrational . . . dichotomy
   (E) reasoned . . . division

14. As a young man, he regarded France as _____, but in his malcontent maturity, he considered visiting anyplace outside of Ireland to be _____.
   (A) hostile . . . irritating
   (B) Elysium . . . jocund
   (C) irksome . . . drab
   (D) Eden . . . perplexing
   (E) Arcadia . . . martyrdom

15. In the unsuccessful conference, none of the speakers _____ much response from the audience, but Dr. Schultz's address reached the _____ in tediousness.
   (A) aggrandized . . . pinnacle
   (B) elicted . . . nadir
   (C) attributed . . . record
   (D) raised . . . ebb
   (E) induced . . . medley

Analogies

DIRECTIONS

In each question below, you are given a related pair of words or phrases. Select the lettered pair that best expresses a relationship similar to that in the original pair of words.

16. BOW : VIOLIN : :
   (A) brass : tuba
   (B) pedal : piano
   (C) percussion : cymbal
   (D) stop : clarinet
   (E) drumstick : drum

17. SLOTH : RAIN FOREST : :
   (A) cow : barn
   (B) pride : ocean
   (C) Gila monster : desert
   (D) elephant : zoo
   (E) porpoise : waterpark

18. SKILLET : BACON ::
    (A) palette : paints
    (B) napkin : grease
    (C) grass : lawnmower
    (D) skeptic : doubt
    (E) cocoon : twig

19. CALLOUS : TACT ::
    (A) certain : carelessness
    (B) dark : mourning
    (C) awkward : grace
    (D) cheerful : joy
    (E) mature : growth

20. ARIA : OPERA ::
    (A) song : music
    (B) waltz : dance
    (C) chapter : novel
    (D) artist : painting
    (E) poem : epic

21. QUILL : MANUSCRIPT ::
    (A) scalpel : operation
    (B) monk : prayer
    (C) brush : fresco
    (D) gearshift : automobile
    (E) editor : newspaper

22. VICTIM : MARTYR ::
    (A) trade : barter
    (B) action : crusade
    (C) zealot : fanatic
    (D) intention : purpose
    (E) liberty : freedom

23. DUCHY : DUKE ::
    (A) monarchy : queen
    (B) county : count
    (C) knighthood : knight
    (D) marchioness : marquis
    (E) state : earl

24. PRIDE : PEACOCK ::
    (A) lust : goat
    (B) rapine : dog
    (C) stars : crab
    (D) school : fish
    (E) error : mistake

25. DORSAL : VENTRAL ::
    (A) snowy : windy
    (B) dexterous : ambidextrous
    (C) red : crimson
    (D) retreating : advancing
    (E) oblique : indirect

Reading Comprehension

DIRECTIONS

Questions follow each of the passages below. Using only the stated or implied information in each passage, answer the questions.

Questions 26 through 29 are based on the following passage.

I will now teach, offering my way of life to whomsoever desires to commit suicide by the scheme which has enabled me to beat the doctor and the hangman for seventy years. Some of the details may sound untrue, but they are not. I am not here to deceive; I am here to teach.

I have made it a rule never to smoke more than one cigar at a time. I have no other restriction as regards smoking. I do not know just when I began to smoke, I only know that it was in my father's lifetime, and that I was discreet. He passed from this life early in 1847, when I was a shade past eleven; ever since then I have smoked publicly. As an example to others, and not that I care for moderation myself, it has always been my rule never to smoke when asleep, and never to refrain when awake. It is a good rule. I mean, for me; but some of you know quite well that it wouldn't answer for everybody that's trying to get to be seventy.

I smoke in bed until I have to go to sleep; I wake up in the night, sometimes once, sometimes twice, sometimes three times, and I never waste any of these opportunities to smoke. This habit is so old and dear and precious to me that I would feel as you sir, would feel if you should lose the only moral you've got—meaning the chairman—if you've got one; I am making no charges. I will grant, here, that I have stopped smoking now and then, for a few months at a time, but it was not on principle, it was only to show off; it was to pulverize those critics who said I was a slave to my habits and couldn't break my bonds.

26. The author's primary purpose in this passage is evidently to
    (A) teach
    (B) deceive
    (C) persuade
    (D) satirize
    (E) amuse

27. The tone of this passage is best described as
    (A) solemn
    (B) didactic
    (C) ironic
    (D) hopeful
    (E) urgent

28. The passage was probably written in the
    (A) early nineteenth century
    (B) mid-nineteenth century
    (C) late nineteenth century
    (D) early twentieth century
    (E) mid-twentieth century

29. If the author were to discuss eating habits, he would probably recommend eating foods that are
    (A) hard to digest
    (B) inexpensive
    (C) low in calories
    (D) low in cholesterol
    (E) high in vitamin content

Questions 30 through 33 are based on the following passage.

Laboratory evidence indicates that life originated through chemical reactions in the primordial mixture (water, hydrogen, ammonia, and hydrogen cyanide) which blanketed the earth at its formation. These reactions were brought about by the heat, pressure, and radiation
(5) conditions then prevailing. One suggestion is that nucleosides and amino acids were formed from the primordial mixture, and that nucleosides produced nucleotides which produced the nucleic acids (DNA, the common denominator of all living things, and RNA). The amino acids became polymerized (chemically joined) into proteins, including
(10) enzymes, and lipids were formed from fatty acids and glycerol-like molecules. The final step appears to have been the gradual accumulation of DNA, RNA, proteins, lipids, and enzymes into a vital mass which began to grow, divide, and multiply.

The evolution of the various forms of life from this biochemical mass
(15) must not be considered a linear progression. Rather, the fossil record suggests an analogy between evolution and a bush whose branches go every which way. Like branches, some evolutionary lines simply end, and other branch again. Many biologists believe the pattern to have been as follows: bacteria emerged first and from them branched viruses, red
(20) algae, blue-green algae, from which higher plants evolved, and colorless rhizoflagellates, from which diatoms, molds, sponges, and protozoa evolved. From ciliated protozoa (ciliophora) evolved multinucleate (syncytial) flatworms. These branched into five lines, one of which leads to the echinoderms and chordates. The remaining lines lead to most of
(25) the other phyla of the animal world.

Ostracoderms were the first vertebrates to evolve from the invertebrate stock of the chordate line, and from the ostracoderms, lampreys and placoderms evolved. Cartilagenous fish (sharks, skates, and rays) and bony fish evolved from the placoderms; and the crossopterygians
(30) (lobe-fin), which subsequently branched into the coelacanth and diplovertebron (an early amphibian), evolved from bony fish. The diplovertebron was the forerunner of modern amphibia and reptiles. The first reptiles, the cotylosaurs, branched into the unsuccessful dinosaurs and marine reptiles and into the successful turtles, crocodiles, birds, lizards,
(35) snakes, and mammals.

The line leading to man proceeds from the tree shrews to the early primates which branched into the New World monkeys, Old World monkeys, prongids, and hominids. From the prongids (true apes) came the gorilla, orangutan, and chimpanzee. From the hominids came
(40) contemporary man's immediate ancestor, Cro-Magnon man (Homo sapiens). Fossils of earlier "true men" (hominids that used tools) include East African man (Zinjanthropus) and Java ape man (Pithecanthropus).

30. Which of the following best describes the organization of the passage?
    (A) Paragraph one is about plants; paragraphs two, three, and four are about animals.
    (B) Paragraphs one and two are about plants; paragraphs three and four are about animals.
    (C) Paragraph one is about biochemical components; paragraphs two, three, and four are about life forms.
    (D) Paragraph one is about biochemical components; paragraph two is about plants; paragraphs three and four are about animals.
    (E) Paragraph one is about biochemical components; paragraph two is about invertebrates; paragraphs three and four are about vertebrates.

31. The passage states that all of the following were necessary for the beginning of life *except*
    (A) oxygen
    (B) radiation
    (C) water
    (D) hydrogen
    (E) heat

32. In lines 34–35, the author calls turtles, lizards, and snakes "successful" because
    (A) they are reptiles
    (B) they have not become extinct
    (C) their range is wide
    (D) they can endure extremes of climate
    (E) their populations have steadily increased

33. Which of the following is/are true of both East African man and Java ape man?

    I. They are hominids.
    II. They are the immediate ancestors of modern man.
    III. They used tools.

    (A) III only   (D) II and III
    (B) I and II   (E) I, II, and III
    (C) I and III

Questions 34 through 36 are based on the following passage.

Two separate worlds, that of the West and that of the East, had been established by the fourth century. Because of this split, the Eastern Empire, beginning with the foundation of Constantinople on the site of Byzantium, was called the Byzantine Empire. Still, its Greek-speaking inhabitants called themselves *Romaioi* (Romans) until its fall. The Eastern Empire proved to be stronger than its Western counterpart; there, the papacy filled a vacuum left by the disintegrating secular government. In the East, however, the central government remained powerful, and the emperor appointed the Patriarchs of Constantinople and sometimes even dictated the tenets of Christian dogma. A large bureaucracy inherited from the Roman Empire was supported by intolerable taxes. At periods when there was no ruler (as in the Roman Empire, there were no succession laws), the empire was administered by the bureaucrats.

In trying to reform the government, Justinian succeeded in reducing the number of bureaucrats, but taxes still remained high. Justinian's enduring achievement was his law code, in which irrelevant and illogical laws were eliminated. The Code of Justinian (538) together with other legal documents made up the Body of Civil Law (*Corpus Iuris Civilis*); it was modified in the eighth century according to certain Christian precepts, with fewer crimes made punishable by death. This body of Civil Law is today the foundation for the law codes of many European states.

34. According to the passage, the Eastern Empire was characterized by all of the following *except*
    (A) a powerful secular government
    (B) secular control of the church
    (C) a large bureaucracy
    (D) clear rules of succession
    (E) high taxes

35. The passage suggests that Justinian ruled the Eastern Empire in the
    (A) third century   (D) sixth century
    (B) fourth century   (E) seventh century
    (C) fifth century

36. According to the passage, the greatest influence of the Eastern Empire on the modern world is in the area of
    (A) taxes   (D) art
    (B) religious ritual   (E) bureaucracy
    (C) law

Questions 37 through 40 are based on the following passage.

More students than ever before tell me and my colleagues that they are bad writers and need lots of help with grammar and punctuation. I feel like a doctor; it seems that given the widespread presumption that most students now have ill-literacy, my job is to diagnose the disease and prescribe cures whenever I read student writing. But I suspect my comments on their papers to little more than confirm students' fears about how crippled they are. Faced with a thoroughly corrected paper, the student feels helpless, convinced that only teachers can spot flaws in standard English. Of course, he's wrong.

After all, mechanical errors usually happen because a student is pressed for time, too lazy to check the dictionary or the textbook, not very clear on the subject under discussion, and so forth. Errors do not happen because the student doesn't know what the rules for correctness are, or at least where to look them up. Every student with whom I discuss a corrected essay says something like, "I knew that was wrong," or "I always do that." Many students even anticipate their errors before turning anything in, with a remark like, "My spelling is really bad, so don't be surprised," or "I always get marked down on punctuation." Then they go ahead and spell badly or punctuate poorly, as if they are only responsible for a passive knowledge of where their writing is flawed. I wonder whether students so convinced about what is wrong with them aren't quite capable of making things right without much interference from me. I suspect that students are self-corrective when allowed to be, and the more time and money we spend showing them errors, the more they'll look to us to keep doing it.

37. The speaker in the passage is probably a(n)
    (A) editor
    (B) doctor
    (C) graduate student
    (D) English teacher
    (E) journalist

38. According to the passage, students make mechanical errors for all of the following reasons *except*
    (A) laziness
    (B) the complexity of English grammar rules
    (C) uncertainty about the subject under discussion
    (D) shortness of time
    (E) overdependence on a teacher's corrections

39. Of the following, which would the author be most likely to use to improve student writing?
    (A) class instruction on mechanical errors
    (B) providing dictionaries and texts for students
    (C) longer writing assignments
    (D) students' correcting each other's papers
    (E) more complex writing assignments

40. Which of the following sentences would be the best conclusion for the passage?
    (A) The less student papers are corrected, the fewer errors they will eventually make.
    (B) The more carefully a paper is corrected, the better its revised form is likely to be.
    (C) We should spend more time and less money on showing students their mechanical errors.
    (D) We should spend less time and more money on showing students their mechanical errors
    (E) Mechanical errors are the least important part of student writing.

STOP. IF YOU FINISH BEFORE TIME IS CALLED, CHECK YOUR WORK ON THIS SECTION ONLY. DO NOT WORK ON ANY OTHER SECTION IN THE TEST.

SECTION V: MATHEMATICAL ABILITY

Time: 30 Minutes
35 Questions

DIRECTIONS

Solve each problem in this section by using the information given and your own mathematical calculations. Then select the *one* correct answer of the five choices given. Use the available space on the page for scratchwork.

Data That May Be Used as Reference for This Section

The area formula for a circle of radius r is: $A = \pi r^2$
The circumference formula is: $C = 2\pi r$
A circle is composed of 360°.
A straight angle measures 180°.

Triangle: The sum of the angles of a triangle is 180°.
If angle ADB is a right angle, then

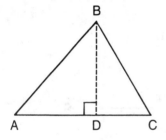

(1) The area of triangle ABC is $\dfrac{AC \times BD}{2}$

(2) $AD^2 + BD^2 = AB^2$

Symbol References:
= is equal to   ≥ is greater than or equal to
≠ not equal to   ≤ is less than or equal to
> is greater than   ∥ is parallel to
< is less than   ⊥ is perpendicular to

NOTE: Some problems may be accompanied by figures or diagrams. These figures are drawn as accurately as possible, EXCEPT when it is stated in a specific problem that the figure is not drawn to scale. The figures are meant to provide information useful in solving the problem or problems but are not meant to be measured.

Unless otherwise stated or indicated, all figures lie in a plane.

All numbers used are real numbers.

1. If $\dfrac{3}{x} = 6$, then $x - 1 =$

   (A) 1   (B) ½   (C) −½   (D) −⅔   (E) −1½

2. A suit that originally sold for $120.00 was on sale for $90.00. What was the rate of discount?
   (A) 75%   (B) 33⅓%   (C) 30%   (D) 25%   (E) 20%

3. Find x if the average of 93, 82, 79, and x is 87.
   (A) 87   (B) 90   (C) 93   (D) 94   (E) 348

4. How many combinations are possible if a person has 4 sport jackets, 5 shirts, and 3 pairs of slacks?
   (A) 4   (B) 5   (C) 12   (D) 60   (E) 120

5. If $x = \dfrac{3}{4}$ and $y = \dfrac{4}{7}$ then $\dfrac{y - x}{y + x} =$

   (A) −1   (B) −⁵/₃₇   (C) ⁵/₃₇   (D) ½   (E) ¹¹/₂₁

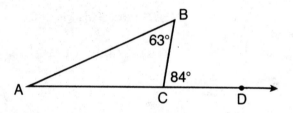

6. Given △ABC with ∠BCD = 84° and ∠B = 63°. Find the measure of ∠A in degrees.

   (A) 21   (B) 27   (C) 84   (D) 96   (E) 116

7. How many inches are there in m yards and n feet?
   (A) m + n   (B) 36m + 12n   (C) 36(m + n)   (D) 3m + n
   (E) 12(m + n)

Quantitative Comparison

DIRECTIONS

In this section you will be given two quantities, one in column A and one in column B. You are to determine a relationship between the two quantities and mark—

(A) if the quantity in column A is greater than the quantity in column B.
(B) if the quantity in column B is greater than the quantity in column A.
(C) if the quantities are equal.
(D) if the comparison cannot be determined from the information that is given.

	Column A	Column B
8.	$\dfrac{.89 \times 57}{.919}$	58
9.	$(x^2y^3)^8$	$(x^4y^6)^4$

$$2x + 5y > 4$$

10.	x	y

11.	$\dfrac{\sqrt{3}}{3}$	$\dfrac{1}{\sqrt{3}}$

12.	$ac + bc + a + b$	$(a + b)(c + 1)$

$$x \text{ is } 30\% \text{ of } 60$$
$$20\% \text{ of } y \text{ is } 4$$

13.	x	y

$$x < 0$$

14.	$x^3 - 1$	0

15.	Number of inches in one mile	Number of minutes in one year

$$a = 3b$$
$$b = -2$$

16.	$\dfrac{a^2 + b}{ab}$	$\dfrac{a + b^2}{ab}$

	Column A	**Column B**

Questions 17–19 refer to the diagram.

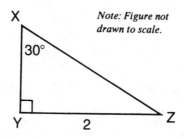

Note: Figure not drawn to scale.

17.	$\angle X + \angle Z$	$\angle Y$
18.	XY	YZ
19.	XY	$3\sqrt{2}$

a, b, and c are positive integers
$(b + c)^a = 81$
$a \neq b \neq c$

20.	a	$b + c$

Questions 21–22 refer to the diagram.

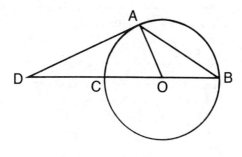

O is the center

	Column A	Column B
21.	$\overset{\frown}{AC}$	$2(\angle B)$
22.	$\angle AOB$	$\angle ADB$
23.	$\sqrt{3^{18}}$	$(\sqrt{27^3})^2$

$$x < y$$

24.	$(x - y)^2$	$x^2 - y^2$

Note: Figure not drawn to scale.

Each dimension of the rectangular solid above is an even number.
The area of face TUWY is 20 and the area of face WXZY is 8.

25.	Total surface area of the rectangular solid	Volume of the rectangular solid

Solve each of the remaining problems in this section and blacken the corresponding space on the answer sheet.

26. There are 36 students in a certain geometry class. If two-thirds of the students are boys and three-fourths of the boys are under six feet tall, how many boys in the class are under six feet tall?
(A) 6   (B) 12   (C) 18   (D) 24   (E) 27

27. If $-4x + 12 > -16$ then
(A) $x < 7$ (B) $x > 7$ (C) $x < 1$ (D) $x > 1$
(E) $x > -7$

28. What is the area of a square inscribed in a circle whose circumference is 16π?
(A) 512   (B) 256   (C) 128   (D) 64   (E) 32

29. A bag contains 20 gumballs. If there are 8 red, 7 white, and 5 green, what is the minimum number of gumballs one must pick from the bag and be assured of one of each color?

    (A) 16   (B) 9   (C) 8   (D) 6   (E) 3

30. If $m * n = \dfrac{m + n - 1}{n^2}$ Then $2 * 3 =$

    (A) $\frac{4}{9}$ (B) $\frac{2}{3}$ (C) 1   (D) $1\frac{1}{3}$ (E) 2

31. $(4\sqrt{3})(2\sqrt{6}) =$

    (A) 24   (B) $11\sqrt{2}$ (C) $24\sqrt{2}$ (D) $16\sqrt{3}$ (E) 32

32. If the volume and the total surface area of a cube are equal, how long must the edge of the cube be?

    (A) 2 units   (B) 3 units   (C) 4 units   (D) 5 units
    (E) 6 units

33. $\dfrac{6^4 + 6^5}{6^4} =$

    (A) 36   (B) 31   (C) 30   (D) 7   (E) 6

34. Find the area in square yards of an equilateral triangle if the length of one of its sides is 12 yards.

    (A) $18\sqrt{3}$ (B) 72   (C) $36\sqrt{3}$ (D) $72\sqrt{3}$
    (E) cannot be determined

35. The midpoint of xy is B. The coordinates of x are $(-4,3)$ and the coordinates of B are $(5,-2)$. What are the coordinates of y?

    (A) $(\frac{1}{2},\frac{1}{2})$ (B) $(1,1)$ (C) $(6,-7)$ (D) $(14,-3)$
    (E) $(14,-7)$

STOP. IF YOU FINISH BEFORE TIME IS CALLED, CHECK YOUR WORK ON THIS SECTION ONLY. DO NOT WORK ON ANY OTHER SECTION IN THE TEST.

SECTION VI: VERBAL ABILITY

Time: 30 Minutes
40 Questions

In this section, choose the best answer for each question and blacken the corresponding space on the answer sheet.

Antonyms

DIRECTIONS

Each word in CAPITAL LETTERS is followed by five words or phrases. The correct choice is the word or phrase whose meaning is most nearly *opposite* to the meaning of the word in capitals. You may be required to distinguish fine shades of meaning. Look at all choices before marking your answer.

1. SKEPTIC
    (A) cynic
    (B) agnostic
    (C) infidel
    (D) orator
    (E) believer

2. PRECARIOUS
    (A) carnivorous
    (B) caring
    (C) equivocal
    (D) soluble
    (E) certain

3. ASTUTE
    (A) artful
    (B) perspicacious
    (C) imbecilic
    (D) subtle
    (E) crazed

4. SAGE
    (A) public
    (B) unconscious
    (C) stupefying
    (D) stupid
    (E) studious

5. ABDICATE
    (A) abjure
    (B) take
    (C) vindicate
    (D) favor
    (E) prefer

6. MITIGATED
   (A) repeated
   (B) aggravated
   (C) terminated
   (D) raised
   (E) risen

7. FERAL:
   (A) golden
   (B) easy
   (C) malleable
   (D) ferocious
   (E) tame

8. ARGOT
   (A) vernacular
   (B) colloquialism
   (C) vulgar words
   (D) extremism
   (E) standard language

9. PARSIMONIOUSNESS
   (A) extravagance
   (B) thrift
   (C) miserliness
   (D) sensitivity
   (E) playfulness

10. INGENUOUS
    (A) not clever
    (B) unimaginative
    (C) dishonest
    (D) good
    (E) uptight

Sentence Completion

DIRECTIONS

Each blank in the following sentences indicates that something has been omitted. Consider the lettered words beneath the sentence and choose the word or set of words that best fits the whole sentence.

11. The land lying at even a slight distance from the river is not _____, so the farming tribes _____ only the fields near its banks.
    (A) arable . . . cultivated
    (B) barren . . . settled
    (C) fallow . . . colonized
    (D) fertile . . . shunned
    (E) fertilizable . . . eschewed

12. The local conversation was nothing if not _____, for no sentence was ever more than four words long.
    (A) ambiguous
    (B) timely
    (C) vague
    (D) terse
    (E) cordial

13. Since my grandmother thinks museums are a very _____ entertainment, she believes my grandfather is a _____ for refusing to accompany her.
    (A) fashionable . . . dandy
    (B) civilized . . . Philistine
    (C) rowdy . . . boor
    (D) gracious . . . gentleman
    (E) snobbish . . . prig

14. The universal Victorian preference of the more conventional morality of Charlotte Brontë to that of her sister is _____ of the nineteenth-century reader's genteel _____.
    (A) symptomatic . . . informality
    (B) disproof . . . ideas
    (C) evidence . . . idiosyncrasy
    (D) refutation . . . principles
    (E) indicative . . . conformity

15. The explorers were astonished by the contrast of the _____ of the rain forest and the barren waste of the desert.
    (A) desiccation   (D) verdure
    (B) flotilla   (E) greengage
    (C) miscreancy

Analogies

DIRECTIONS

In each question below, you are given a related pair of words or phrases. Select the lettered pair that *best* expresses a relationship similar to that in the original pair of words.

16. STALL : EXPEDITE ::
    (A) realize : materialize   (D) expunge : loll
    (B) defuse : detonate   (E) percolate : regulate
    (C) require : rely

17. ACADEMICIAN : STUDIES ::
    (A) teacher : students   (D) safari : hunter
    (B) musician : orchestra   (E) doctor : medicine
    (C) sportscaster : leisure

18. JOVIAL : PRANKSTER ::
    (A) prolific : teacher   (D) pessimistic : doctor
    (B) prosaic : painter   (E) perspicacious : gardener
    (C) perceptive : detective

19. QUARANTINE : DISEASE ::
    (A) incarceration : lawlessness
    (B) domicile : student
    (C) hibernation : honey
    (D) infection : bacteria
    (E) quartz : silicon

20. TANDEM : DISCRETE ::
    (A) plural : singular
    (B) cyclical : quiet
    (C) arboreal : fruitful
    (D) shaded : pristine
    (E) immediate : reflective

21. AZURE : INDIGO ::
    (A) mulatto : servile
    (B) maroon : purple
    (C) lavender : blue
    (D) grassy : chartreuse
    (E) light : dark

22. VARIEGATED : DAPPLED ::
    (A) pettish : testy
    (B) recalcitrant : profligate
    (C) reclined : vertical
    (D) turgid : flat
    (E) obese : pother

23. GARRULOUS : PITHY ::
    (A) abundant : sparse
    (B) rancor : noisy
    (C) angry : solemn
    (D) deciduous : furry
    (E) hardy : inquisitive

24. JABBERWOCKY : SPEECH ::
    (A) poem : humor
    (B) rapidity : movement
    (C) argument : debate
    (D) irrationality : behavior
    (E) rancidity : storage

25. ZEAL : INTEREST ::
    (A) calf : mutton
    (B) demolition : damage
    (C) requirement : allowance
    (D) bungling : mangling
    (E) erosion : salvation

Reading Comprehension

DIRECTIONS

Questions follow each of the passages below. Using only the stated or implied information in each passage, answer the questions.

Questions 26 through 29 refer to the following passage.

The question might be asked: how can we know what is "really" real? Defined phenomenologically, "reality" becomes purely a hypothetical

concept which accounts for the totality of all conditions imposed by the external world upon an individual. But since other individuals are
(5) included in each of our fields of experience, it does become possible as we make identification of similarly perceived phenomena to form consensus groups. In fact, we often tend to ignore and even push out of awareness those persons and their assumptions regarding what is real which do not correspond to our own. However, such a lack of consensus also affords us
(10) the opportunity of checking our hypothesis about reality. We may change our concepts about reality and thus in doing so facilitate changes in our phenomenal world of experience. Scientists, for instance, deliberately set out to get a consensus of both their procedures and their conclusions. If they are successful in this quest, their conclusions are
(15) considered by the consensus group as constituting an addition to a factual body of sharable knowledge. This process is somewhat in contrast, for example, to those religious experiences considered to be mystical. By their nature they are not always available for communication to others. However, even the scientific researcher must finally
(20) evaluate the consequences of his research in his own, personal phenomenological field. To use a cliche: truth as beauty exists in the eyes of the beholder.

26. Which of the following is a specific example supporting the point of the passage?
    (A) Certain established scientific facts have not changed for hundreds of years.
    (B) Part of the phrase in the last sentence is from a poem by Keats.
    (C) Reality is a given, unique experience in an individual's phenomenal world.
    (D) We think of our enemies in war as cruel and regard our own soldiers as virtuous.
    (E) The fans at baseball games often see things exactly as the umpire sees them.

27. Applying the argument of the passage, we might define a political party as
    (A) a political group to which few scientists belong
    (B) a consensus group whose individuals share a similar view of political reality
    (C) a consensus group whose members are deluded about what is really "real" politically
    (D) in touch with reality if it is a majority party and out of touch with reality if it is a minority party
    (E) a collection of individuals who are each fundamentally unsure about what political reality is

28. When the author says that "reality" is a "hypothetical concept," he or she means that
    (A) as for reality, there is none
    (B) we can think about reality but never really experience it
    (C) "reality" is not objective
    (D) "reality" is a figment of your imagination
    (E) "reality" is known only by scientists

29. According to the passage, one difference between a scientist and a mystic is that
    (A) the scientist sees truth as facts, the mystic sees truth as beauty
    (B) scientists are unwilling and unable to lend importance to religious experiences
    (C) the work of the mystic does not have consequences that affect individuals
    (D) the scientist is concerned with sharable knowledge and the mystic may not be
    (E) the scientists cannot believe in anything mystical

Questions 30 through 32 refer to the following passage.

No matter what we think of Warren Beatty or his film *Reds,* we cheer his victory for artistic purity in preventing ABC-TV from editing his movie for television. An arbitrator ruled that Mr. Beatty's contractual right of "final-cut" authority, which forbids editing he doesn't approve, prevented Paramount Pictures from granting that authority to ABC-TV. The network planned to cut six minutes from *Reds,* a 196-minute film, and air the truncated version next week.

Most theatrical films (movies made for theaters) ultimately appear on network television, usually preceded by the brief message "Edited for Television." The popular perception, argues Mr. Beatty, is that this editing removes obscenity. Often it does. Yet, some editing is done purely in the interests of commercial and local programming. Advertisements traditionally hover near hourly and half-hourly intervals. And local affiliate stations zealously protect their 11 p.m. time slot because it is commercially lucrative.

Mr. Beatty's case illustrates why studios contracting with directors for films rarely grant the coveted right of final cut. Televised theatrical movies receive wide exposure and are lucrative; Paramount had a $6.5 million contract with ABC-TV for *Reds.* True artistic control in filmmaking will come only when all directors receive final-cut guarantees, a right the Directors Guild of America hopes to obtain in future talks with movie producers. Mr. Beatty's victory is a step in the direction of protection for film.

30. Which of the following best supports the argument presented in the passage?
   (A) It would be artistically impermissible to delete 64 bars from a Beethoven symphony or to skip Act II from *Hamlet*.
   (B) Warren Beatty would be well served if he planned his theatrical features with television commercials in mind.
   (C) The Directors Guild of America will have a difficult time acquiring artistic control for film directors.
   (D) "Edited for Television" refers only to the removal of obscenities.
   (E) The best time to run commercials for television stations is 11 p.m.

31. Which of the following is implied by the passage?
   (A) Artists should not yield to the pressures of a commercial industry.
   (B) The enormous amount of money involved in commercial television should temper an artist's ideals.
   (C) Film editing should be performed with commercial as well as artistic goals in mind.
   (D) Lucrative contracts demand compromise by all film collaborators.
   (E) Film studios should never allow artists to control final-cut rights on feature films.

32. Which of the following is the best title for the passage?
   (A) Warren Beatty and *Reds*
   (B) The Final Cut: Beatty vs. ABC
   (C) Edited for TV: Removing Obscenity
   (D) How Films Get Cut for Television
   (E) Directors Guild of America: A New Battle

Questions 33 through 36 refer to the following passage.

The Constitution actually makes specific provision for only one court—the Supreme Court of the United States. It authorizes Congress to create such other courts as Congress might consider necessary. Fulfilling this mandate, the first Congress enacted the Judiciary Act of 1789, which created two levels of inferior constitutional courts—the United States District Courts, or so-called trial courts, and the United States Circuit Courts of Appeals, so called because the judges traveled from place to place to hear appeals from the trial courts. All federal court judges are appointed; judges of the constitutional courts— Supreme Court, Courts of Appeals, and District Courts—are appointed to serve a lifetime tenure. Judges of legislative courts are appointed to serve terms fixed by Congress. Since 1803, the Supreme Court has exercised the power of judicial review, the power to declare an act of Congress void because it conflicts with the Court's interpretation of the Constitution.

Does this extreme power vested in the judiciary pose a threat to democratic values and institutions? Some critics declare emphatically that it does. Such power in the hands of people separated from the electoral process and protected by lifetime tenure is sometimes said to be a negation of the basic concept of democracy. If the electoral process is taken as the basic feature of democracy, then this is undoubtedly true. But if the concept of due process of law is seen as the basic democratic feature, then few would fault the federal courts for their respectful adherence to this concept of the essence of justice.

33. The passage is primarily concerned with the
    (A) courts and the Constitution
    (B) power of the courts versus the power of the Congress
    (C) federal courts and their power
    (D) courts and the nature of the democratic process
    (E) Supreme Court, the District Courts, and the Circuit Courts

34. Of the kinds of courts referred to in the passage, which of the following was/were probably the latest to be created?
    (A) constitutional courts   (D) District Courts
    (B) legislative courts   (E) Circuit Courts
    (C) Supreme Court

35. According to the passage, the power of the Supreme Court is often questioned because
    (A) its judges are appointed
    (B) its judges are often old
    (C) its judges may have no prior experience in criminal law
    (D) the Court's interpretation of the Constitution changes in time
    (E) the Court could declare void a law passed by Congress limiting the Court's power

36. The author refers to the idea of due process of law in order to
    I. cite a basic feature of democracy other than the electoral process
    II. call into question the criticism of the power of the judiciary as undemocratic
    III. argue in favor of judicial power as democratic

    (A) I only   (D) II and III
    (B) II only   (E) I, II, and III
    (C) I and II

Questions 37 through 40 refer to the following passage.

Ostensibly, punishment is used to reduce tendencies to behave in certain ways. We spank and scold children for misbehavior; we fine, lock up, or assign to hard labor adults who break laws; we threaten, censure, disapprove, ostracize, and coerce in our efforts to control social behaviors. Does punishment, in fact do what it is supposed to do?

The effects of punishment, it has been found, are not the opposite of reward. It does not subtract responses where reinforcement adds them. Rather it appears to temporarily suppress a behavior, and when punishment is discontinued, eventually responses will reappear. But this is only one aspect of the topic. Let us look at it in further detail.

Skinner defines punishment in two ways, first as the withdrawal of a positive reinforcer and, second, as the presentation of a negative reinforcer or aversive stimulus. We take candy away from a child or we spank him. Note that the arrangement in punishment is the opposite of that in reinforcement, where a positive reinforcer is presented and a negative reinforcer is removed.

Since we remove positive reinforcers to extinguish a response and also to punish it, a distinction must be made. When a response is made and no reinforcement follows, i.e., *nothing* happens, the response gradually extinguishes. However, if we *withdraw* a reinforcer and the withdrawal of a reinforcer is contingent on a response, responding is suppressed more rapidly. The latter is punishment. Sometimes we withdraw a privilege from a child to control his behavior. A teacher might keep a child in the classroom during recess or cancel a field trip as a result of misbehavior. Turning off television when a child puts his thumb in his mouth may effectively suppress thumbsucking. Most punishments of this sort utilize conditioned or generalized reinforcers. Quite frequently one sees adults withdraw attention or affection as punishment for misbehavior, sometimes in subtle ways.

37. The passage equates taking candy away from a child with
    (A) only one of many categories of punishment
    (B) the presentation of a negative reinforcer
    (C) the presentation of an aversion stimulus
    (D) withdrawal of negative reinforcement
    (E) withdrawal of positive reinforcement

38. Which of the following may be concluded from the last paragraph of the passage?
    (A) Most children regard the classroom as a prison.
    (B) It is usually best to ignore whatever bothers us.
    (C) The author considers recess and field trips to be privileges.
    (D) The withdrawal of affection is an unconscious form of punishment.
    (E) Children who do not like television are harder to punish.

39. The passage does not do which of the following?
    (A) give us a definite answer to the question posed in the first paragraph
    (B) discuss generally some of the effects of punishment
    (C) provide examples of some common forms of punishment
    (D) distinguish punishment from reinforcement
    (E) mention the temporary suppression of behavior

40. Which of the following facts, if true, supports one of the author's contentions about punishment?
    (A) Those who were spanked as children may not praise the benefits of such discipline.
    (B) Imposing longer jail terms on criminals does not necessarily permanently reduce their tendency to return to crime.
    (C) Any species or race which is consistently punished will eventually become extinct.
    (D) The temporary suppression of a negative behavior is a fine accomplishment.
    (E) People who are consistently rewarded are incapable of punishing others.

STOP. IF YOU FINISH BEFORE TIME IS CALLED, CHECK YOUR WORK ON THIS SECTION ONLY. DO NOT WORK ON ANY OTHER SECTION IN THE TEST.

ANSWER KEY FOR PRACTICE TEST NO. 2

Mathematics sections II and V in this Answer Key are coded so that you can quickly determine the math area on which you may need to concentrate your study time. AR = arithmetic, AL = algebra, and G = geometry.

Section I		Section II	Section III	
1. B	41. A	1. D (AL)	1. A	41. B
2. B	42. C	2. D (AR)	2. B	42. A
3. D	43. D	3. B (AL)	3. B	43. D
4. C	44. D	4. D (AR)	4. D	44. D
5. E	45. B	5. B (AL)	5. B	45. C
6. B		6. B (AR)	6. A	46. A
7. D		7. B (AL)	7. C	47. B
8. A		8. B (AR)	8. A	48. A
9. C		9. C (G)	9. B	49. C
10. A		10. C (G)	10. B	50. D
11. C		11. D (AL)	11. C	
12. D		12. E (AL)	12. B	
13. A		13. C (G)	13. A	
14. A		14. B (AR)	14. B	
15. A		15. A (AL)	15. A	
16. B		16. E (G)	16. B	
17. E		17. C (AL)	17. D	
18. A		18. D (G)	18. B	
19. E		19. B (G)	19. C	
20. D		20. A (AL)	20. E	
21. E		21. A (G)	21. A	
22. A		22. D (AL)	22. C	
23. D		23. C (G)	23. A	
24. D		24. A (AL)	24. D	
25. C		25. C (AL)	25. C	
26. D			26. C	
27. E			27. E	
28. A			28. B	
29. C			29. D	
30. C			30. C	
31. D			31. C	
32. C			32. A	
33. C			33. B	
34. B			34. A	
35. A			35. B	
36. C			36. D	
37. E			37. D	
38. E			38. A	
39. B			39. E	
40. A			40. A	

ANSWER KEY FOR PRACTICE TEST NO. 2 (continued)

Section IV	Section V	Section VI
1. C	1. C (AL)	1. E
2. B	2. D (AR)	2. E
3. E	3. D (AL)	3. C
4. C	4. D (AR)	4. D
5. A	5. B (AL)	5. B
6. A	6. A (G)	6. B
7. C	7. B (AL)	7. E
8. B	8. B (AR)	8. E
9. D	9. C (AL)	9. A
10. A	10. D (AL)	10. C
11. C	11. C (AL)	11. A
12. A	12. C (AL)	12. D
13. B	13. B (AL)	13. B
14. E	14. B (AL)	14. E
15. B	15. B (AR)	15. D
16. E	16. A (AL)	16. B
17. C	17. C (G)	17. E
18. A	18. A (G)	18. C
19. C	19. B (G)	19. A
20. C	20. D (AL)	20. A
21. C	21. C (G)	21. E
22. B	22. A (G)	22. A
23. A	23. C (AL)	23. A
24. A	24. D (AL)	24. D
25. D	25. A (G)	25. B
26. E	26. C (AL)	26. D
27. C	27. A (AL)	27. B
28. D	28. C (G)	28. C
29. A	29. A (AR)	29. D
30. E	30. A (AL)	30. A
31. A	31. C (AL)	31. A
32. B	32. E (G)	32. B
33. C	33. D (AR)	33. C
34. D	34. C (G)	34. B
35. D	35. E (G)	35. A
36. C		36. E
37. C		37. E
38. B		38. C
39. D		39. A
40. A		40. B

HOW TO SCORE YOUR EXAM

1. Add the total number of correct responses for each Verbal Section.
2. Add the total number of incorrect responses (only those attempted or marked in) for each Verbal Section.
3. The total number of incorrect responses should be divided by 4, giving the adjustment factor.
4. Subtract this adjustment factor from the total number of correct responses to obtain a raw score in the Verbal Section.
5. This score is then scaled from 200 to 800.
6. Repeat this process for the Mathematical Section, but remember to divide the total of the incorrect QUANTITATIVE COMPARISON responses by 3, instead of 4.
7. The Mathematical Ability Raw Score is then scaled from 200 to 800.

Example:
A. If the total number of correct answers was 40 out of a possible 85.
B. And 20 problems were attempted but missed.
C. Dividing the 20 by 4 gives an adjustment factor of 5.
D. Subtracting this adjustment factor of 5 from the original 40 correct gives a raw score of 35.
E. This raw score is then scaled to range of 200 to 800.

ANALYZING YOUR TEST RESULTS

The charts on the following pages should be used to carefully analyze your results and spot your strengths and weaknesses. The complete process of analyzing each subject area and each individual problem should be completed for each Practice Test. These results should then be reexamined for trends in types of errors (repeated errors) or poor results in specific subject areas. THIS REEXAMINATION AND ANALYSIS IS OF TREMENDOUS IMPORTANCE TO YOU IN ASSURING MAXIMUM TEST PREPARATION BENEFIT.

PRACTICE TEST NO. 2: VERBAL ABILITY ANALYSIS SHEET

SECTION I: VERBAL ABILITY

	Possible	Completed	Right	Wrong
Antonyms	15			
Sentence Completion	5			
Reading Comprehension	10			
Sentence Completion	5			
Analogies	10			
SUBTOTAL	45			

SECTION IV: VERBAL ABILITY

	Possible	Completed	Right	Wrong
Antonyms	10			
Sentence Completion	5			
Analogies	10			
Reading Comprehension	15			
SUBTOTAL	40			

SECTION VI: VERBAL ABILITY

	Possible	Completed	Right	Wrong
Antonyms	10			
Sentence Completion	5			
Analogies	10			
Reading Comprehension	15			
SUBTOTAL	40			
OVERALL VERBAL ABILITY TOTALS	125			

RAW SCORE = NUMBER RIGHT MINUS ONE-FOURTH POINT FOR EACH ONE ATTEMPTED BUT MISSED. (NO POINTS SUBTRACTED FOR BLANK ANSWERS.)

PRACTICE TEST NO. 2: MATHEMATICAL ABILITY ANALYSIS SHEET

SECTION II: MATHEMATICAL ABILITY

	Possible	Completed	Right	Wrong
Math Ability	25			
Arithmetic	(5)			
Algebra	(12)			
Geometry	(8)			
SUBTOTAL	25			

SECTION V: MATHEMATICAL ABILITY

	Possible	Completed	Right	Wrong
Math Ability	17			
Arithmetic	(4)			
Algebra	(8)			
Geometry	(5)			
Quantitative Comparison	18			
Arithmetic	(2)			
Algebra	(10)			
Geometry	(6)			
SUBTOTAL	35			
OVERALL MATHEMATICAL ABILITY TOTALS	60			

RAW SCORE = NUMBER RIGHT MINUS ONE-FOURTH POINT FOR EACH ONE ATTEMPTED BUT MISSED. (NO POINTS SUBTRACTED FOR BLANK ANSWERS.)

PRACTICE TEST NO. 2: TEST OF STANDARD WRITTEN ENGLISH ANALYSIS SHEET

SECTION III: TSWE

	Possible	Completed	Right	Wrong
Usage	30			
Sentence Correction	20			
OVERALL TSWE TOTALS	50			

WHY???????????????????????????????

ANALYSIS: TALLY SHEET FOR PROBLEMS MISSED

One of the most important parts of test preparation is analyzing WHY! you
missed a problem so that you can reduce the number of mistakes. Now that
you have taken the practice test and corrected your answers, carefully tally
your mistakes by marking them in the proper column.

REASON FOR MISTAKE

	Total Missed	Simple Mistake	Misread Problem	Lack of Knowledge
SECTION I: VERBAL ABILITY				
SECTION IV: VERBAL ABILITY				
SECTION VI: VERBAL ABILITY				
SUBTOTAL				
SECTION II: MATH ABILITY				
SECTION V: MATH ABILITY				
SUBTOTAL				
TOTAL MATH AND VERBAL				

Reviewing the above data should help you determine WHY you are missing
certain problems. Now that you have pinpointed the type of error, compare it
to the first practice test analysis to spot other common mistakes.

COMPLETE ANSWERS AND EXPLANATIONS FOR
PRACTICE TEST NO. 2

SECTION I: VERBAL ABILITY

Antonyms

1. (B) A *fantasy* is a *creation of the imagination unrestrained by reality.* Since fantasies are unreal, the opposite word is *reality. Substance* is not the correct choice because it may refer to any material, real or unreal.

2. (B) To *mope* is to be *gloomy, dull,* or *in low spirits.* Its opposite is *rollick,* to be *gay* or *carefree.*

3. (D) *Forthwith* means *immediately;* therefore, its opposite is *after a while.*

4. (C) The opposite of *praise* is *vilification* (*vile* = *base, evil*), which refers to the act of *blaming with abusive language.*

5. (E) *Frenzy* is *wild excitement* or *delirium.* Its opposite is *calm.*

6. (B) To *pardon* is to release *someone from punishment.* Its opposite, then, is *punish.*

7. (D) *Conciliatory* means *reconciling, tending to conciliate, placating.* The opposite is *divisive.*

8. (A) One of the meanings of *ambiguous* is *unclear.* The opposite is *clear.*

9. (C) *Dispassionate* means *free from passion,* hence, *impartial, calm.* The opposite is *partial.*

10. (A) *Prim* means *formal, proper, demure.* Its opposite is *pert,* which means *bold* or *saucy.*

11. (C) One of the meanings of *dogmatic* is *positive.* The opposite is *doubtful.*

12. (D) *Transient* means *temporary* or *passing.* The opposite is *permanent.*

13. (A) *Contumacious* refers to *defiance of authority.* Its opposite is *compliant,* which refers to *agreeing* or *giving in.*

14. (A) To *cloy* is to *oversatisfy* or *surfeit.* Its opposite is to *starve.*

15. (A) *Veracity* (*verus* = *true*) means *truthfulness.* So its opposite is *falseness.*

Sentence Completion

16. (B), *exceeded*. *Additional spending would be impossible* because past *expenditures had already* exceeded *the budget*. None of the other choices indicates that monies are no longer available in the budget.

17. (E), *fauna ... valueless*. The missing noun must refer to African *animals*. The missing adjective must mean *useless*.

18. (A), *deduced*. We need a verb here that means something like *inferred* or *reasonably concluded*. Only *deduced* fits clearly.

19. (E), *hustle-bustle ... exhilarating*. The sentence opposes the *city* and *smoke* to the *mountains* and *peace*. The first noun must accord with the city and differ from peace (A, B, or E would fit), and the adjective modifying *air* must have favorable associations, eliminating choices (A) and (B).

20. (D), *premise ... subtlety*. The missing noun must be something upon which a novel may be developed. The idiom to *develop ... upon* could be used with either *theory* or *premise*. The missing noun must go with *intelligence*, so we can eliminate choice (A).

Reading Comprehension

21. (E) The passage specifically contradicts all of the first four choices. The first, third, and fourth sentences of the first paragraph support choice (E).

22. (A) Though glaciation occurs at rare intervals, the passage insists that the principles of cause and effect have been dependable.

23. (D) Raindrop impressions are one of the features which show which side of a bedded rock was turned up, according to the fourth paragraph.

24. (D) Only option (D) is supported by the passage. The other answers are irrelevant and untrue.

25. (C) This is stated in the fifth paragraph.

26. (D) This is stated in the last sentence of the first paragraph.

27. (E) Rhyme is characteristic of poetry, and the third paragraph states that the body of science fiction poetry is quite small.

28. (A) The first sentence says that *many people* seem to define science fiction by pulp-magazine standards. Something which is popular is something accepted by many people.

29. (C) The first paragraph leads up to the central question—*What is science fiction?* All of the passage is an attempt to answer that question. Choices (A) and (D) are too specific, (B) is too general, and (E) does not fit the tone of the passage.

30. (C) The second paragraph says that *science fiction . . . postulates a change (for human beings) from conditions as we know them.* In other words, science fiction treats the unknown, unfamiliar, unusual.

Sentence Completion

31. (D) With *insignificant* and *surprising,* we need a final adjective contrary to *insignificant.*

32. (C) The first adjective should mean *well known.* Of the choices, *notorious* is the best choice, since *notorious* means *well known for some unfavorably regarded trait or action.* Of the verbs, *verified* is also the best choice.

33. (C) The first adverb must mean *enthusiastically,* but the verb must express some doubts or reservations. Choices (A), (C), or (D) would satisfy the adverb requirement, but only choice (C) has a verb that follows logically after *but.*

34. (B) The adjective that refers to representing something as existing at other than its proper time is *anachronistic.*

35. (A) The missing noun must be a quality attributable to traveling or not traveling and to narrow-mindedness. All of the nouns except (E) would fit. Given the narrowness of the noun described, we can infer his dislike of travel rather than an interest in other lands or people. *Parochialism* means *narrowness of interest or thought, provincialism.*

Analogies

36. (C) A *senator* is a member of the larger organization of people that makes up the *Congress.* A *spectator* is a member of a *crowd.*

37. (E) A *choreographer* designs the movements of a *dance* as a *playwright* is responsible for the contents of a *play.* In both, the relationship is between the inventor and the work of art created.

38. (E) A *constellation* is made up of more than one *star* as the *solar system* is made up of more than one *planet.*

39. (B) *Lamb* is *meat from a young sheep; mutton* is *meat from a mature sheep.* Similarly, *veal* is *meat from a young cow; beef* is *meat from a mature cow.*

40. (A) To *earn* is to *receive as the result of service or merit,* but to *filch* is to *steal* or *pilfer.* The parallel is to *plagiarize,* which is to *take ideas or words from someone else and pass them off as one's own,* a form of theft.

41. (A) To *loathe* is to *dislike intensely* as to *extol* is to *praise intensely.*

42. (C) The adjective *credulous* means *easily convinced* or *gullible,* and thus would describe a person who is unlikely to harbor *doubt.* Similarly a *complacent* person, that is, *smug* or *self-satisfied,* is unlikely to be *modest.*

43. (D) *Slander* is a *spoken false statement,* while *libel* is *written.* The parallel here is *speech* and *essay.*

44. (D) The *gladiolus* is susceptible to infestation by *aphids* as the *apple tree* is by *scale.*

45. (B) A *surfeit* is an *oversupply;* a *dearth* is a *lack* or *scarcity.* The best analogy here is *flood* and *drought.*

SECTION II: MATHEMATICAL ABILITY

1. (D) $.0039y = \dfrac{39}{10,000}$ $y = 39$

$$y = \dfrac{(10,000)}{39} \times (39)$$

$$y = 10,000$$

2. (D) $\dfrac{.25 \times \dfrac{2}{3}}{0.6 \times 15} = \dfrac{\dfrac{25}{100} \times \dfrac{2}{3}}{\dfrac{6}{100} \times \dfrac{15}{1}}$

$$= \dfrac{\dfrac{1}{4} \times \dfrac{2}{3}}{\dfrac{3}{50} \times \dfrac{15}{1}}$$

$$= \dfrac{\dfrac{1}{6}}{\dfrac{9}{10}}$$

$$= \dfrac{1}{6} \times \dfrac{10}{9}$$

$$= \dfrac{5}{27}$$

Hence the reciprocal of $\dfrac{.25 \times \dfrac{2}{2}}{.06 \times 15}$ is the reciprocal of $\dfrac{5}{27}$, or $\dfrac{27}{5}$.

3. (B) If $\frac{2}{3}$ of the container is full, there remains $\frac{1}{3}$ of the container to fill. The time to fill $\frac{1}{3}$ of the container will be half as long as the time needed to fill $\frac{2}{3}$ of the container. Hence $\frac{1}{2}$ (18 minutes) = 9 minutes

4. (D) The 4 pounds of steak would cost

   $4 \times \$3.89 = \$15.56$

   The change from a twenty-dollar bill would be
   $$\begin{array}{r} \$20.00 \\ -15.56 \\ \hline \$\ 4.44 \end{array}$$

5. **(B)** Since the square of a positive number is a positive number, choice **(B)** is the correct answer.

6. **(B)** Since $16\frac{1}{2}$ feet = 1 rod, in 4 rods there are $(4)(16\frac{1}{2}) = 66$ feet.

   Since 1 foot = 12 inches, in 66 feet there are $(12)(66) = 792$ inches.

   Hence in 4 rods there are 792 inches.

7. **(B)** Since a = p + prt

$$a - p = p + prt - p$$

$$a - p = prt$$

$$\frac{a - p}{pt} = \frac{prt}{pt}$$

$$\frac{a - p}{pt} = r$$

   Hence $r = \dfrac{a - p}{pt}$

8. **(B)** $\dfrac{\text{percent}}{100} = \dfrac{\text{is Number}}{\text{of Number}}$

$$\frac{30}{100} = \frac{x}{\dfrac{25}{18}}$$

   Cross multiplying we have

$$100x = \frac{\overset{5}{\cancel{30}}}{1} \times \frac{25}{\underset{3}{\cancel{18}}}$$

$$100x = \frac{125}{3}$$

$$x = \frac{\overset{5}{\cancel{125}}}{3} \times \frac{1}{\underset{4}{\cancel{100}}}$$

$$x = \frac{5}{12}$$

9. (C) On a clock, 60 minutes = 360°

Hence $\dfrac{12 \text{ minutes}}{60 \text{ minutes}} = \dfrac{x°}{360°}$

$$\frac{1}{5} = \frac{x}{360}$$

$$5x = 360$$

$$\frac{5x}{5} = \frac{360}{5}$$

$$x = 72$$

Hence the minute hand has moved 72°.

10. (C) Using the Pythagorem theorem $a^2 + b^2 = c^2$

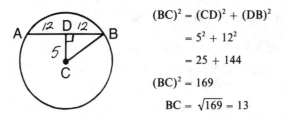

$$(BC)^2 = (CD)^2 + (DB)^2$$
$$= 5^2 + 12^2$$
$$= 25 + 144$$
$$(BC)^2 = 169$$
$$BC = \sqrt{169} = 13$$

Hence the radius of the circle is 13.

11. (D) Since the ten's digit (r) must be multiplied by 10 and the unit's digit (s) must be multiplied by 1, and the number is the sum of these, we represent the number by 10r + s.

12. (E) In the ordered pair (0,2), a = 0 and b = 2.
For 2a − 3b we have

$$2(0) - 3(2) = 0 - 6 = -6 \neq 6.$$

Hence the ordered pair (0,2) is not a member of the solution set of 2a − 3b = 6.

13. (C) Since the area of a trapezoid = ½ · h · (b_1 + b_2), we need to find the altitude, h.

Draw altitudes in the figure as follows:

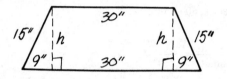

Since the triangles formed are right triangles, we use the Pythagorean theorem, which says

$c^2 = a^2 + b^2$

$15^2 = 9^2 + h^2$

$225 = 81 + h^2$

$h^2 = 225 - 81$

$h^2 = 144$

$h = \sqrt{144} = 12$ inches

Hence the area of the trapezoid will be

$$\frac{1}{2} \cdot h \cdot (b_1 + b_2) = \frac{1}{2} \cdot 12 \cdot (30 + 48)$$

$$= (6)(78)$$

$$= 468 \text{ square inches}$$

14. (B) (A) $\frac{1}{8} = .125$

(B) $(.3)^2 = .09$

(C) $\dfrac{1}{.3} = \dfrac{1}{\frac{3}{10}} = \dfrac{10}{3} = 3.\overline{33}$

(D) $\sqrt{.36} = .6$

(E) $\dfrac{11}{100} = .11$

Hence $(.3)^2 = .09$ is the smallest number.

15. (A) Adding the two equations, we have

$x - y = 15$

$\dfrac{3x + y = 13}{4x \qquad = 28}$

$\dfrac{4x}{4} = \dfrac{28}{4}$

$x = 7$

Since x = 7	or	Since x = 7

Since x = 7   or   Since x = 7

and x − y = 15   and 3x + y = 13

7 − y = 15   3(7) + y = 13

7 − 7 − y = 15 − 7   21 + y = 13

−y = 8   21 − 21 + y = 13 − 21

y = −8   y = −8

Hence x = 7 and y = −8

16. (E) Since there are many different rectangles with a diagonal of 16, we cannot determine the lengths of the sides and hence we cannot determine the area of the rectangle (see figures).

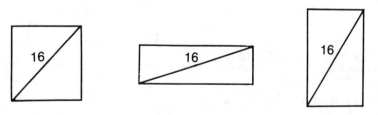

17. (C) Let x = first number

2x + 1 = second number

3x − 4 = third number

Since the average of the three numbers is 55, we have

$$\frac{x + (2x + 1) + (3x - 4)}{3} = 55$$

Multiplying both sides of our equation by 3, we have

$$x + (2x + 1) + (3x - 4) = 165$$
$$6x - 3 = 165$$
$$6x - 3 + 3 = 165 + 3$$
$$6x = 168$$

$$\frac{6x}{6} = \frac{168}{6}$$

$$x = \frac{168}{6}$$

$$x = 28 = \text{first number}$$
$$2x + 1 = 57 = \text{second number}$$
$$3x - 4 = 80 = \text{third number}$$

Hence the largest number is 80.

18. (D) A rectangular solid consists of six rectangular faces. This one is particular has two 7 x 6, two 6 x 3, and two 7 x 3 rectangles with areas of 42, 18, and 21, respectively. Hence the total surface area will be

$$2(42) + 2(18) + 2(21) = 84 + 36 + 42 = 162 \text{ square meters.}$$

19. (B) Area of larger circle $= 144\pi$

Since area $= \pi r^2$, then

$$\pi r^2 = 144\pi$$

$$r^2 = 144$$

$$r = 12$$

Radius of larger circle $= 12$

Diameter of smaller circle $= 12$

Radius of smaller circle $= 6$

$$\begin{aligned}
\text{Area of smaller circle} &= \pi r^2 \\
&= \pi(6)^2 \\
&= 36\pi
\end{aligned}$$

20. (A) b = Bob's age
         c = Jane's age
         d = Jim's age

Since Bob is older than Jane, we have c < b.
Since Bob is younger than Jim, we have b < d.
Hence, c < b and b < d, or c < b < d.

21. (A) Let

5x = first angle
2x = second angle
5x − 2x = 3x = third angle

Since the sum of the angles in any triangle is 180°, we have

$$5x + 2x + 3x = 180°$$

$$10x = 180°$$

$$\frac{10x}{10} = \frac{180°}{10}$$

$$x = 18°$$

Hence   5x = 90°
          2x = 36°
          3x = 54°

The smallest angle will have a measure of 36°.

22. (D)

If $\frac{a}{b} = \frac{c}{d}$ then, by cross multiplying, we get ad = bc.

If $\frac{d}{b} = \frac{c}{a}$ then we get the same result by cross multiplying,

ad = bc.

Hence if $\frac{a}{b} = \frac{c}{d}$, then $\frac{d}{b} = \frac{c}{a}$

23. (C) Let

x = length of equal sides in feet
x + 8 = length of base in feet

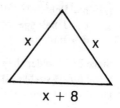

Since the perimeter is 89 feet, we have

$$x + x + x + 8 = 89$$
$$3x + 8 = 89$$
$$3x + 8 - 8 = 89 - 8$$
$$3x = 81$$
$$\frac{3x}{3} = \frac{81}{3}$$
$$x = 27$$

Hence the length of the base is x + 8, or 35 feet.

24. (A) $(-2,3) \oplus (4,-1) = [(-2)(4) - (3)(-1), (-2)(-1)]$
$$= [(-8) - (-3), (2)]$$
$$= (-5,2)$$

25. (C) Since $\sqrt{mn} = 10$, mn = 100 and the possible values for m and n would be:

> 1 and 100
> 2 and 50
> 4 and 25
> 5 and 20
> 10 and 10

Since none of these combinations yield m + n = 50, choice (C) is correct.

SECTION III: TEST OF STANDARD WRITTEN ENGLISH

Usage

1. **(A)** *Between he* should be replaced with *between him.*

2. **(B)** *Being that* is nonstandard usage; *because* would be correct.

3. **(B)** The subject of the sentence is singular, *advance,* so the verb must also be singular—*was* instead of *were.*

4. **(D)** *Occupy we* should be changed to *occupy us.*

5. **(B)** In this sentence the subject (*House Majority Leader* and *the Chairman of the Ways and Means Committee,* follows the verb, *was.* Since the subject is plural, the verb must be plural—*were* instead of *was.*

6. **(A)** *This here,* used for *this,* is nonstandard usage.

7. **(C)** *Choosing from* disrupts the parallelism in this sentence; it should be eliminated.

8. **(A)** In this sentence, the subject (*a box of cereal and three bread-sticks*) follows the verb (*is*). Since the subject is plural, the verb must be plural—*are* instead of *is.*

9. **(B)** *Him* should be changed to *he* (which stands for *he can* in this case).

10. **(B)** *People* is plural, so *this kind* must be made plural—*the kind.*

11. **(C)** *Neither my uncle nor my brother* is a *singular* subject; a plural compound subject uses *and* instead of *or* or *nor.* Since the subject is singular, the pronoun which refers to it must be singular—*his* instead of *their.*

12. **(B)** *Any student* must be changed to *any other student* to specify that Jeff is not more talkative than *himself.*

13. **(A)** *Good* is an adjective. Since it describes an action word (*running*), it must be changed to an adverb—*well.*

14. **(B)** You cannot compare *discoveries* (things) with *Einstein* (a person), but you can logically compare *discoveries* with *Einstein's discoveries* or with *Einstein's.*

15. **(A)** *Doesn't scarcely* is nonstandard usage. *Scarcely reads or writes* would be correct.

Sentence Correction

16. **(B)** *Told for the decision* is an unidiomatic expression; that is, it doesn't sound right to most native English speakers. *Told of the decision* is idiomatically correct.

17. **(D)** *And, that many citizens* disrupts the parallelism of this sentence; choice (D) restores it.

18. **(B)** The subject of the sentence is singular, *roller coaster,* so the verb must also be singular—*encourages* instead of *encourage.* Note that the first verb, *allows,* signals you to add an *s* to *encourage.*

19. **(C)** *They* unnecessarily repeats the meaning of *several very distinguished friends;* it may be eliminated. (D) and (E) change the meaning of the sentence.

20. **(E)** *That good of friends* is nonstandard usage; (E) is correct and retains the meaning of the original.

21. **(A)** This sentence contains no error.

22. **(C)** This is a fragment sentence; (C) clears up the mistake by providing a complete subject and a complete verb—*we have.*

23. **(A)** This sentence is fine as it stands.

24. **(D)** Both *have* and *will be* are meant to connect with *conscious. I have . . . conscious* is ungrammatical, but *have been conscious* is both a complete and grammatical phrase.

25. **(C)** This sentence contains a dangling modifier. It seems to say that the *remains* are doing the looking! (C) clearly indicates that a person (*I*) is doing the looking.

26. **(C)** The *then* following the comma indicates that this is an *if . . . then* sentence.

27. **(E)** This is a pronoun error. *They* doesn't clearly refer to any other word in the sentence, although it seems to mean *people.* (C) and (D) provide meaningless alternatives (a *votive* is done in fulfillment of a vow).

28. **(B)** Clearly, the original is not the most efficient, effective way of stating a comparison. (B) is more direct and economical, and *better* is necessary for the comparative degree.

29. **(D)** This sentence contains a dangling modifier. It seems to say that the village resulted from a lack of fresh meat. This meaning is illogical. (D)

tells us clearly that a lack of fresh meat caused hunger, and also uses a more direct verb—*caused*—without changing the meaning of the sentence.

30. (C) *Ought to of been* is nonstandard usage. *Should have been* standardizes the sentence without changing its meaning.

31. (C) This is an incomplete comparison. The sentence seems to say that the neighbors are less digestible than the dinner! Including *that of* in (C) makes it clear that the sentence is comparing dinners with dinners.

32. (A) This sentence is fine. *Laying,* meaning *to put in place,* is used correctly.

33. (B) The subject of the sentence is plural—*workspaces*—so the verb must be plural—*are* instead of *is*. (C) unnecessarily changes the meaning of the sentence.

34. (A) This sentence is fine. It is punctuated properly, and *whom* is used correctly.

35. (B) *Having many close friends* disrupts the parallelism of this sentence; *to have many close friends* is parallel in form to the other goals listed.

Usage

36. (D) This is a pronoun error. *Whom* should be changed to *who.*

37. (D) *Type of a* is nonstandard usage; *type of* is correct.

38. (A) *Nowheres near* is nonstandard usage; *not near* is correct.

39. (E) This sentence contains no error.

40. (A) *Whether* makes no sense; *whether or not* or *unless* does.

41. (B) In this sentence, the subject (*forecasts and a warning*) follows the verb (*was*). Since the subject is plural, the verb must be plural—*were* instead of *was*.

42. (A) *Real* is an adjective. Since it refers to an action (*prepare*), it should be changed to an adverb—*really.*

43. (D) This is a pronoun error. *Him and I* should be changed to *him and me.*

44. (D) Since only two opinions are being compared, *most admirable* (which correctly refers to more than two things) should be changed to *more admirable.*

45. (C) Since the subject of the sentence is singular, *one,* the verb must be singular—*shows* instead of *show.*

46. (A) *In the morning* is an unnecessary repetition of the meaning of A.M.

47. (B) The subject of the sentence is singular, *flock,* so the verb must be singular—*is* instead of *are.*

48. (A) *It's* means *it is;* the correct spelling here is without the apostrophe—*its.*

49. (C) *Ought to of* is nonstandard usage.

50. (D) *Sweetly* is an adverb. Since it refers to a *thing* (*music*), it must be changed to an adjective—*sweet.*

SECTION IV: VERBAL ABILITY

Antonyms

1. (C) A *conclave* (*con* = *with, together*) is a *secret gathering*. The most nearly opposite choice is *public assembly*.

2. (B) *Unison* (*uni* = *one*) refers to a *harmony* of parts or parties. Its opposite is *discord* (*dis* = *a part*), which refers to *disharmony* and *disagreement*.

3. (E) *Primeval* (*prime* = *first*) means *earliest in time;* therefore its opposite must be *modern*.

4. (C) *Picturesque* refers to something which would make a *striking picture*. Its opposite is *grotesque*, which means *horribly ugly*.

5. (A) *Darksome* means *mysterious, hard to understand*. Its opposite is *clear*.

6. (A) An *affidavit* is a *sworn statement in writing, witnessed by an official*. The most nearly opposite word is *forgery*, meaning a *false piece of writing or printing*.

7. (C) *Laconically* refers to a *response which is very short*. Its opposite is *verbosely*, which refers to *using many words*. *Compendiously* refers to *saying much in few words*.

8. (B) To *metamorphose* (*meta* = *over; morphe* = *shape*) is to *change in structure*, as a caterpillar metamorphoses into a butterfly. The opposite, then, is to *remain the same*.

9. (D) *Resuscitate* (*re* = *again; cit* = *to put into motion*) means to *revive, bring back to life*. Its opposite is *kill*. To *succumb* may mean to *die*, but could be an opposite only if *resuscitate* meant to *live*.

10. (A) *Estheticism* is a *strong liking for art, beauty, and good taste*. Its opposite is *tastelessness*.

Sentence Completion

11. (C), *worthless*. If the people must use other tokens for exchange, the currency must be *worthless*.

12. (A), *untoward*. Here we need an adjective opposed to our normal associations of *calm* and *beautiful*. Only *untoward* (*perverse, unseemly*) will fit.

13. (B), *dogmatic . . . consensus.* The missing first adjective is evidently opposed to *realities,* eliminating options (A), (C), and (E). *Consensus* makes good sense, while *dichotomy* in this context makes no sense at all, as it denotes a *division.*

14. (E) *Arcadia . . . martyrdom.* The adjective *malcontent* tells us the second blank requires a noun suggesting something disliked; the *but* tells us that the missing first word should have pleasant associations. Only choice (E) fits both requirements.

15. (B), *elicited . . . nadir.* If the conference was unsuccessful, we can infer that the audience response was indifferent and that the noun needed refers to a low point, not a success.

Analogies

16. (E) A *bow* (noun) is the slender stick drawn across the strings of the *violin* to produce sound. The *drumstick* is also a separate piece used to produce sound from a *drum.*

17. (C) A *sloth* is an animal whose natural habitat is the *rain forest* as the natural habitat of the *Gila monster* is the *desert.*

18. (A) A *skillet* is a frying pan, the utensil on which *bacon* is prepared as a *palette* is a utensil on which *paint* is prepared.

19. (C) The adjective *callous* means *unfeeling* or *insensitive.* A callous person would almost certainly lack *tact.* Similarly an *awkward* person would be likely to be deficient in *grace.*

20. (C) An *aria* is a melody or song in an *opera,* a smaller part of the whole, as a *chapter* is a smaller part of a *novel.*

21. (C) A *quill* was at one time the instrument with which a writer produced a *manuscript.* The best parallel is *brush* and *fresco;* a fresco is a painting on a plaster surface.

22. (B) A *victim* is someone or something killed or injured while a *martyr* is a victim who suffers for principles or beliefs. A *crusade* is an *action* undertaken on behalf of some cause or idea.

23. (A) A *duke* rules a *duchy;* a *queen* rules a *monarchy.*

24. (A) The *peacock* is the common symbol for *pride* as the *goat* is the conventional symbol for *lust.*

25. (D) *Dorsal* and *ventral* are adjectives referring to the *back* and *front* of a human or animal. The relationship is closest here to that of *retreating* and *advancing.*

Reading Comprehension

26. (E) The passage depends upon the frequent use of surprise, of saying just the opposite of what we expect, and the effect is comic.

27. (C) Someone is ironic when he says one thing and means another. But we cannot believe that the author really is attempting to *teach* or that he believes smoking is the best way to assure a long life.

28. (D) If the author was eleven in 1847 and is now seventy, the time of writing would be 59 years than 1847, or 1906, in the early twentieth century.

29. (A) Since the technique of the passage is irony and the recommendations are unconventional and contrary to medical authority, *foods hard to digest* is the best answer.

30. (E) Though choice (C) describes the passage, the summary in choice (E) is accurate and more detailed.

31. (A) The passage explicitly mentions all of the other options.

32. (B) The meaning of *successful* in this sentence is made clear by the use of *unsuccessful* to describe the extinct dinosaurs.

33. (C) Cro-Magnon man is called the *immediate ancestor.* I and III are correct.

34. (D) The last sentence of the first paragraph says *there were no succession laws.*

35. (D) The only specific date given is 538, the Code of Justinian. We can assume that Justinian's reign was at this time, in the sixth century.

36. (C) The last sentence of the passage asserts the importance of Justinian law in the codes of modern Europe.

37. (C) Since the passage speaks of *students,* reading student writing, and correcting mechanical errors on papers, it is very likely that the writer is an English teacher.

38. (B) The passage does not complain of the complexity of English grammar. Its point is that too many writers are needlessly afraid.

39. (D) Since the author believes students are capable of self-correction but lack confidence, he would be likely to favor this device. None of the others answer the objections raised in the second paragraph of the passage.

40. (A) The passage is arguing that students are too dependent on instructors, and if there were fewer errors corrected by the teachers, the students would be self-correcting and independent.

SECTION V: MATHEMATICAL ABILITY

SECTION V: MATHEMATICAL ABILITY

1. (C) Since $\dfrac{3}{x} = \dfrac{6}{1}$

   Cross multiplying gives $6 \cdot x = 3$
   and $\qquad\qquad\qquad\quad x = \frac{1}{2}$
   Therefore $\qquad\qquad x - 1 = (\frac{1}{2}) - 1 = -\frac{1}{2}$

2. (D) The amount of discount was \$120.00 $-$ \$90.00 = \$30.00
   The rate of discount is a percent so

   $$\frac{percent}{100} = \frac{is\ number}{of\ number}$$

   $$\frac{x}{100} = \frac{30}{120} \qquad \text{Cross multiplying}$$

   $$120x = 3000$$

   $$\frac{120x}{120} = \frac{3000}{120}$$

   $$x = 25$$

   Hence the rate of discount was 25%

3. (D) Average $= \dfrac{93 + 82 + 79 + x}{4} = 87$

   $$93 + 82 + 79 + x = 87 \cdot 4$$

   $$254 + x = 348$$

   $$x = 94$$

4. (D) Since each of the 4 sport jackets may be worn with 5 different
   shirts, we have 20 possible combinations. These may be worn with each
   of the 3 pairs of slacks for a total of 60 possible combinations. Stated
   simply, $5 \cdot 4 \cdot 3 = 60$ possible combinations.

5. (B) $\dfrac{y - x}{y + x} = \dfrac{\dfrac{4}{7} - \dfrac{3}{4}}{\dfrac{4}{7} + \dfrac{3}{4}}$

   $$= \frac{28\left(\dfrac{4}{7} - \dfrac{3}{4}\right)}{28\left(\dfrac{4}{7} + \dfrac{3}{4}\right)} \quad \begin{array}{l}\text{Multiplying by the}\\ \text{Lowest Common Denominator,}\\ \text{which is 28}\end{array}$$

$$= \frac{16 - 21}{16 + 21}$$

$$= \frac{-5}{37}$$

6. **(A)** $\angle BCD = \angle A + \angle B$ (Exterior angle of a triangle equals the sum of the opposite two.)

   Then $84 = \angle A + 63$
   and $\angle A = 21$

7. **(B)** Since m yards = 36m inches
   and n feet = 12n inches
   m yards and n feet = (36m + 12n) inches.

Quantitative Comparison—Answers 8-25

8. **(B)** By inspection, if you multiply $(.89/.919) \times 57$, this must be less than 57 (as you are multiplying 57 by a fraction less than 1). Therefore it must be less than 58. The correct answer is (B).

9. **(C)** Simplifying columns A and B leaves $x^{16}y^{24} = x^{16}y^{24}$
   Note that when you have a number with an exponent to a power, you simply multiply the exponents together.

10. **(D)** This problem is best solved by inspection or insight. Since there are two variables in this single inequality, there are many possible values for x and y; therefore a comparison cannot be made.

11. **(C)** Cross multiplying the values in each column gives

    $$\frac{\sqrt{3}}{3} \qquad\qquad \frac{1}{\sqrt{3}}$$

    $$\sqrt{3} \cdot \sqrt{3} \qquad\qquad 3 \cdot 1$$

    therefore $3 = \qquad 3$

12. **(C)** Solve by factoring column A into $c(a + b) + 1(a + b)$. Using the distributive property gives $(c + 1)(a + b)$, which is the same as column B. Or substitute in numbers and you will notice that both columns consistently come out equal. Let's try a = 0, b = 1, and c = 2.

$$\frac{0\,(2) + 1\,(2) + \;0 + 1}{\underset{3}{2\;+\;\;\;\;\;1}} \;\;=\;\; \frac{(0 + 1)\,(2 + 1)}{\underset{3}{1(3)}}$$

13. (B) Solve the first problem as follows:

x is 30% of 60

Replacing "=" for "is" and "·" for "of" (30% = 3/10)

$$x = (3/10) \cdot 60$$
then $x = 18$

Solve the second problem as follows:

20% of y is 4
(20% = 1/5)
(1/5) · y = 4
(1/5)y = 4

Multiplying by 5/1 gives (5/1) · (1/5)y = 4 · (5/1)
then y = 20

14. (B) Substituting -1 for x gives $(-1)^3 - 1 = -1 - 1 = -2$. Now trying -2 for x gives $(-2)^3 - 1 = -8 - 1 = -9$. It is evident that this phrase will always generate negative values if $x < 0$. Therefore, the correct answer is (B). The cube of a negative is negative. One less than a negative is negative. Any negative is less than 0.

15. (B) First set up the numbers for each side:

Number of inches in 1 mile	Number of minutes in 1 year
(12 inches in 1 ft) × (5280 ft in 1 mile)	(60 minutes in 1 hr) × (24 hrs in 1 day) × (365 days in 1 yr)
12 × 5280	60 × 24 × 365

Now dividing out, a 10 and 12 leaves

1 × 528	6 × 2 × 365
or 528	12 × 365

Column B is obviously greater

16. **(A)** Since $a = 3b$ and $b = -2$, then $a = 3(-2) = -6$, substituting into the numerator of each expression (since the denominators are positive and alike, they can be eliminated)

$$\frac{a^2 + b}{\cancel{ab}} \qquad \frac{a + b^2}{\cancel{ab}}$$

$$(-6)^2 + -2 \qquad -6 + (-2)^2$$
$$36 + -2 \qquad -6 + 4$$

therefore $34 \qquad > \qquad -2$

17. **(C)** Since a triangle has 180° in the interior angles, if one angle is 90°, then the other two must total 90°.

18. **(A)** In the triangle $\angle Z$ must be 60° and $\angle X$ is given as 30°. Since the side across from the larger angle in a triangle is the longer side, then $XY > YZ$.

19. **(B)** The ratio of the sides of a 30-60-90 triangle is 1, 2, $\sqrt{3}$, and since the side across from 30° is 2, the side across from 90° is $2\sqrt{3}$. Compare each column by squaring the number outside and multiply by the numbers under the radical.

$$2\sqrt{3} \qquad 3\sqrt{2}$$
$$\sqrt{3 \cdot 4} \qquad \sqrt{2 \cdot 9}$$
$$\sqrt{12} \quad < \quad \sqrt{18}$$

20. **(D)** There are only two ways for a positive integer to a positive power to equal 81: 9^2 or 3^4. Thus $(b + c)^a$ could be, say, $(3 + 6)^2$. Or it could be $(1 + 2)^4$. In the first case $b + c$ is greater than a. But in the second instance $b + c$ is less than a. Therefore the answer is (D).

21. **(C)** $\overset{\frown}{AC} = 2(\angle B)$, since an inscribed angle is half of the arc it subtends (connects to).

22. **(A)** Since $\angle AOB$ is a central angle, it equals the measure of $\overset{\frown}{AB}$ and since $\angle ADC$ is outside the circle, but connects to $\overset{\frown}{AB}$, it is less than half of $\overset{\frown}{AB}$ therefore

$\angle AOB \quad > \quad \angle ADC$

Alternate Method: The external angle AOB must be larger than either of the remote interior angles.

23. (C) Simplifying columns A and B gives

$\sqrt{3^{18}}$ $(\sqrt{27^3})^2$
        27^3
        $(3 \cdot 3 \cdot 3)^3$
3^9 = $(3^3)^3$

The correct answer is (C).

24. (D) Substituting x = 0 and y = 1

        $(x - y)^2$ $x^2 - y^2$
        $(0 - 1)^2$ $(0)^2 - (1)^2$
then   1   > -1

now substituting   x = -1 and y = 0
gives $(-1 - 0)^2$ $(-1)^2 - (0)^2$
                  $(-1)^2$ $(-1)^2$
then   1   =   1

Since different values give different comparisons then no comparison can be made.

25. (A) Since the area of face TUWY is 20, the dimensions must be 2 × 10. Remember each dimension must be an even number. The dimensions of face WXZY must therefore be 2 × 4. Since edge WY is in common to both faces, the dimensions of face UVXW is 10 × 4.

The surface area of the rectangular solid is

2 × 10 = 20 (doubled) =   40
2 × 4 = 8 (doubled) =   16
10 × 4 = 40 (doubled) =   80
                        ———
                        136

Volume equals 2 × 10 × 4 = 80
Therefore the surface area is greater.

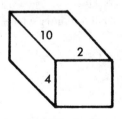

26. (C) Since two-thirds of the students are boys we have ⅔ (36) = 24 boys in the class.

Out of the 24 boys in the class, three-fourths of them are under six feet tall or

¾ (24) = 18 boys under six feet tall

27. (A) $-4x + 12 > -16$

$-4x + 12 + (-12) > (-16) + (-12)$

$-4x > -28$

$(-\frac{1}{4}) \times (-4x) < (-\frac{1}{4}) \times (-28)$ (Note: The inequality is reversed.)

$x < 7$

28. (C) Circumference $= \pi d$

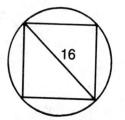

$16\pi = \pi d$

$d = 16$

diameter of circle = diagonal of square

area of square = $\frac{1}{2}$ (product of diagonals)

$= \frac{1}{2} d_1 \times d_2$

$= \frac{1}{2} (16)(16) = 128$

Hence the area of the square is 128.

Alternate Method: Using the Pythagorean theorem for isosceles right triangles, gives $x^2 + x^2 = 16^2$, $2x^2 = 256$, and $x^2 = 128$, which is the area of the square.

29. (A) If 15 gumballs were picked from the bag it is possible that 8 of them are red and 7 are green. On the next pick however (the 16th), one is assured of having one gumball of each color.

30. (A) Substituting 2 for m and 3 for n gives

$2 * 3 = \dfrac{2 + 3 - 1}{3^2}$

$= \dfrac{5 - 1}{9}$

$= 4/9$

31. (C)

Multiply $(4\sqrt{3})(2\sqrt{6}) = 8\sqrt{18}$

Now Simplifying $= 8(\sqrt{9 \cdot 2})$

$= 8(3\sqrt{2})$

$= 24\sqrt{2}$

32. (E) Let x equal the length of a side of the cube. The volume $V = x^3$ and the surface area $S = 6x^2$.

Since $V = S$
$x^3 = 6x^2$
Hence $x = 6$

33. (D) $\dfrac{6^4 + 6^5}{6^4} = \dfrac{6^4}{6^4} + \dfrac{6^5}{6^4}$

$\qquad\qquad = 1 + 6$
$\qquad\qquad = 7$

34. (C) Area $= \frac{1}{2} \times$ base $\times$ altitude

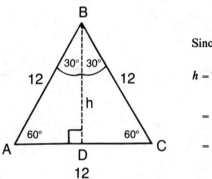

Since $\triangle BCD$ is a 30-60-90 triangle,

$$h = \frac{\sqrt{3}}{2}(BC)$$

$$= \frac{\sqrt{3}}{2}(12)$$

$$= 6\sqrt{3}$$

Hence area of $\triangle ABC = \frac{1}{2}(AC)(BD)$
$\qquad\qquad\qquad\quad = \frac{1}{2}(12)(6\sqrt{3})$
$\qquad\qquad\qquad\quad = (6)(6\sqrt{3})$
$\qquad\qquad\qquad\quad = 36\sqrt{3}$ square yards

35. (E) If the coordinates of two points x and y are (x_1, y_1) and (x_2, y_2), respectively, then the coordinates of the midpoint B (m_1, m_2) of xy are

$$\left(\frac{x_1 + x_2}{2}, \frac{y_1 + y_2}{2}\right) = (m_1, m_2)$$

Hence

$$m_1 = \frac{x_1 + x_2}{2} \quad \text{and} \quad m_2 = \frac{y_1 + y_2}{2}$$

$$5 = \frac{-4 + x_2}{2} \quad \text{and} \quad -2 = \frac{3 + y_2}{2}$$

$$(2)(5) = (2)\frac{(-4 + x_2)}{2} \quad \text{and} \quad (2)(-2) = (2)\frac{(3 + y_2)}{2}$$

$$10 = -4 + x_2 \qquad\qquad -4 = 3 + y_2$$
$$10 + 4 = -4 + x_2 + 4 \qquad -4 - 3 = 3 + y_2 - 3$$
$$14 = x_2 \qquad\qquad\qquad -7 = y_2$$

Hence the coordinates of y are $(x_2, y_2) = (14, -7)$.

SECTION VI: VERBAL ABILITY

Antonyms

1. (E) A *skeptic* is *one who doubts;* the opposite is *believer.*

2. (E) *Precarious* describes an *uncertain, often dangerous, situation.* The most nearly opposite choice is *certain.*

3. (C) Something done *astutely* is something done *with extreme shrewdness.* The opposite of *extremely shrewd* is *imbecilic (imbecile = mentally deficient).*

4. (D) *Sage* means *wise* or *showing wisdom.* Its opposite is *stupid.*

5. (B) *Abdicate (ab = away from; dicere = to say)* refers to *renouncing authority or power,* saying it is no longer yours. The opposite of *abdicating* power is *taking* power.

6. (B) Something *mitigated* has become *less severe or painful.* Something *aggravated* has become *worse. Raised* merely indicates direction of movement, but not whether the movement is for better or worse.

7. (E) The adjective *feral* means *wild, untamed,* or *savage.* The opposite here is *tame.*

8. (E) *Argot* is a *type of slang;* the opposite of *slang language* is *standard language.*

9. (A) *Parsimoniousness* is *excessive saving or thrift.* Its opposite is *extravagance,* or *wastefulness.*

10. (C) *Ingenuous* means *honest* and *straightforward.* Its opposite is *dishonest.*

Sentence Completion

11. (A), *arable . . . cultivated.* The negative describing lands not used by farming tribes calls for an adjective like *arable (capable of being plowed)* or *fertile.* The verb needed must refer to *planting* or *farming; cultivated* is clearly the best choice.

12. (D), *terse.* The right choice here must define a very short sentence. Only *terse* is suitable.

13. (B), *civilized . . . Philistine.* The sense of the sentence requires that the missing adjective and missing noun be opposite. If museums are viewed favorably, the grandfather is criticized or vice versa. In the correct answer, the museums are appropriately praised and the grandfather is called a *Philistine,* that is, *someone lacking in culture.*

14. (E), *indicative . . . conformity*. The tie between *genteel* and *conventional* indicates that the sentence is asserting, not denying, a quality. The first blank might be filled with choice (A), (C), or (E), but only *conformity* fits the context for the second blank.

15. (D), *verdure*. The correct choice here must be opposite to *barren waste*. *Verdure* is *greenery, flourishing vegetation*.

Analogies

16. (B) *Stall*, to *slow* or *stop*, is the opposite of *expedite*, to *speed up the process*, in the same way as *defuse*, to *make less harmful*, is the opposite of *detonate*, to *explode*.

17. (E) *Academician, scholar*, is to *studies*, the *scholar's pursuit or calling*, in the same way as *physician* is to *medicine*, the *physician's calling*.

18. (C) *Jovial, good humored*, is a quality of a *prankster* in the same way as *perceptive* is a quality of a *detective*.

19. (A) *Quarantine* restrains sick persons and helps to control the spread of *disease* in the same way as *incarceration* restrains criminals and helps to control the spread of *lawlessness*.

20. (A) *Tandem*, indicating *two or more*, is to *discrete*, one meaning of which is *by itself*, in the same way as *plural, two or more*, is to *singular, by itself*.

21. (E) *Azure*, a *light shade of blue*, is to *indigo*, a *deep, dark shade of blue*, in the same way as *light* is to *dark*.

22. (A) *Variegated* is to *dappled* (synonyms, both meaning *varied in appearance*) in the same way as *pettish* is to *testy* (both meaning *ill-humored*).

23. (A) *Garrulous, long-winded*, is to *pithy, succinct* or *using few words*, in the same way as *abundant, plentiful*, is to *sparse, scarce*.

24. (D) *Jabberwocky, meaningless speech*, is to *speech* in the same way as *irrationality, behavior without rhyme or reason*, is to *behavior*.

25. (B) *Zeal, ardent enthusiasm* or *extreme interest*, is to *interest* in the same way as *demolition, complete demolishing* or *destroying*, is to *damage*.

Reading Comprehension

26. (D) The point of the passage is that *reality* varies according to who experiences it and what *consensus group* he or she is a member of. Along this line, a war is a conflict between two different consensus groups, and so the example given by (D) is appropriate.

27. (B) Both choices (B) and (C) mention *consensus group,* but (C) says that the members of the group are deluded about reality, which contradicts the author's argument that no view of reality is, strictly speaking, a delusion.

28. (C) Once again, the point of the passage is that different people or groups acquire different versions of reality based on their differing experiences. Reality is, therefore, subjective, but not a mere figment of imagination.

29. (D) This choice is validated by lines 12–18 of the passage.

30. (A) Beatty argues that cutting even six minutes from his film destroys its artistic integrity. A similar and supporting line or argument would say that deleting parts of Beethoven's music or Shakespeare's plays would do the same.

31. (A) The final sentence of the passage indicates that the author supports Beatty's demands. Only choice (A) reflects this point of view.

32. (B) The thrust of the passage is the battle between Beatty and ABC for the final cut of the film *Reds.*

33. (C) Of the five choices, (C) is the best. It specifies the *federal courts* (Choices A, B, and D do not), the subject of the first paragraph; their power is the issue in the second paragraph.

34. (B) We know that the Supreme Court was established in the Constitution and that the first Congress established the Circuit and District Courts in 1789. Thus, the constitutional courts were almost certainly established before the legislative courts.

35. (A) Though some of the statements here are true, only choice (A) is a correct answer, mentioned by the passage. Some feel the court cannot be a truly democratic institution if its members have not been elected.

36. (E) All three are reasons for the author's reference to due process.

37. (E) According to the third paragraph, taking candy away is the withdrawal of a positive reinforcer, and spanking is the presentation of a negative reinforcer.

38. (C) The mention of *recess* and *field trips* follows this sentence: *Sometimes we withdraw a privilege from a child to control his behavior.* Therefore, we can conclude that the author is using recess and field trips as *examples* of such privileges.

39. (A) The question posed in the first paragraph—*Does punishment, in fact, do what it is supposed to do?*—is not answered in a definite way. The first sentence of the passage says that *punishment is used to reduce tendencies to behave in certain ways.* The second paragraph goes on to state that punishment *seems to temporarily suppress a behavior.* This is a less than definite answer to the question.

40. (B) Each of the other choices draws conclusions beyond the scope of the passage. The author suggests in the third paragraph that imposing punishment does not seem to have any *permanent* effect.

FINAL PREPARATION: "The Final Touches"

1. Make sure that you are familiar with the testing center location and nearby parking facilities.
2. The last week of preparation should be spent primarily on reviewing strategies, techniques, and directions for each area.
3. Don't *cram* the night before the exam. It's a waste of time!
4. Remember to bring the proper materials to the test—identification, admission ticket, three or four sharpened Number 2 pencils, a watch, and a good eraser.
5. Start off crisply, working the ones you know first, and then coming back and trying the others.
6. If you can eliminate one or more of the choices, make an educated guess.
7. Mark in reading passages, underline key words, write out information, make notations on diagrams, take advantage of being permitted to write in the test booklet.
8. Make sure that you are answering "what is being asked" and that your answer is reasonable.
9. Using the TWO SUCCESSFUL OVERALL APPROACHES (p. 7) is the key to getting the ones right that you should get right—resulting in a good score on the SAT.

Cliffs
Math Review
for
Standardized
Tests

FOR ANYONE TAKING A STANDARDIZED TEST WITH MATH SECTIONS

GMAT — SAT — NTE — GRE — State Teacher Credential Tests — PSAT — CBEST — ACT — PPST — GED
and many more!

Use your time efficiently with exactly the review material you need for standardized tests.

Provides insights and strategies for specific problem types, plus intensive review in the most needed basic skills in arithmetic, algebra, geometry, and word problems.

Includes hundreds of practice problems to reinforce learning at each step in a unique easy-to-use format.

Available at your local bookseller, or send in check or money order with the coupon below.

Cliffs Notes, Inc., P.O. Box 80728, Lincoln, NE 68501
